FLYING KITES

A STORY OF THE 2013 CALIFORNIA PRISON HUNGER STRIKE

By the 2018–2019 Stanford Graphic Novel Project

Flying Kites is dedicated to the faculty of the Stanford Creative Writing Program: Elizabeth Tallent, Patrick Phillips, Chang-rae Lee, Adam Johnson, and--most especially--the late Eavan Boland. Their support and inspiration constantly remind us not just of the power of story, but of its absolute essentialness.

We would also like to dedicate this work to everyone who participated in the California Prisoner Hunger Strike in 2013. The ripple-effects of your brave action are still being seen today in a younger generation that refuses to accept the status quo of dehumanization and unjust punishment.

Also, to the 80,000-100,000 individuals suffering in solitary confinement across the country today: Don't give up. We are out here, fighting for you, slowly but surely giving birth to a better world.

This book is a composite story with significant fictional elements, inspired by the events of the historic 2013 California prison hunger strike. The statistics, dates, numbers, and names of the Short Corridor Collective leaders and Prisoner Hunger Strike Solidarity Coalition are historical, but the characters (prisoners, family members, activists, guards, warden) and dialogue are invented. Any resemblance to real-life people is coincidental.

Researched, written, and illustrated by the members of the 2019 Stanford University Graphic Novel Project: Bae, Peter DiCampo, Elena Kamas, Candice Kim, Katherine Liu, Lily Nilipour, Danial Shadmany, Sarah Shourd, Luke Soon-Shiong, Sharon Tran, Nik Wesson, Serena Zhang, Lucy Zhu
EDITORS: Scott Hutchins and Shimon Tanaka
ART DIRECTOR: Andy Warner

All royalties from this book will go to Solitary Watch, a nonprofit national watchdog group that investigates, documents, and disseminates information on the widespread use of solitary confinement in U.S. prisons and jails.

Published in 2021 by Haymarket Books in Chicago
Haymarket Books
P.O. Box 180165
Chicago, IL 60618
773-583-7884
www.haymarketbooks.org
info@haymarketbooks.org

ISBN: 978-1-64259-513-0

Distributed to the trade in the US through Consortium Book Sales and Distribution (www.cbsd.com) and internationally through Ingram Publisher Services International (www.ingramcontent.com).

This book was published with the generous support of Lannan Foundation and Wallace Action Fund.

Special discounts are available for bulk purchases by organizations and institutions. Please call 773-583-7884 or email info@haymarketbooks.org for more information.

Library of Congress Cataloging-in-Publication data is available.

Printed in Canada by union labor

2 4 6 8 10 9 7 5 3 1

MIX
Paper from responsible sources
FSC® C103567
FSC www.fsc.org

GCC/IBT

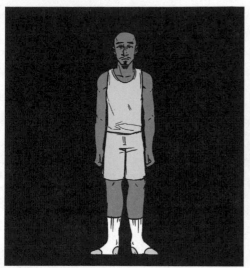

This is how they break you.

They call this the SHU. Secure Housing Unit. We call it the hole or the box. Most people know it as solitary confinement.

My cell is six by nine feet, the size of a handicapped bathroom stall.

It's where I eat, sleep, and shit 23 hours a day, 365 days a year.

It feels smaller every day.

And that 24th hour? Spent in a slightly larger box we call the dog run, just so they can say we get some fresh air and exercise.

I haven't seen a blade of grass in ten years.

3

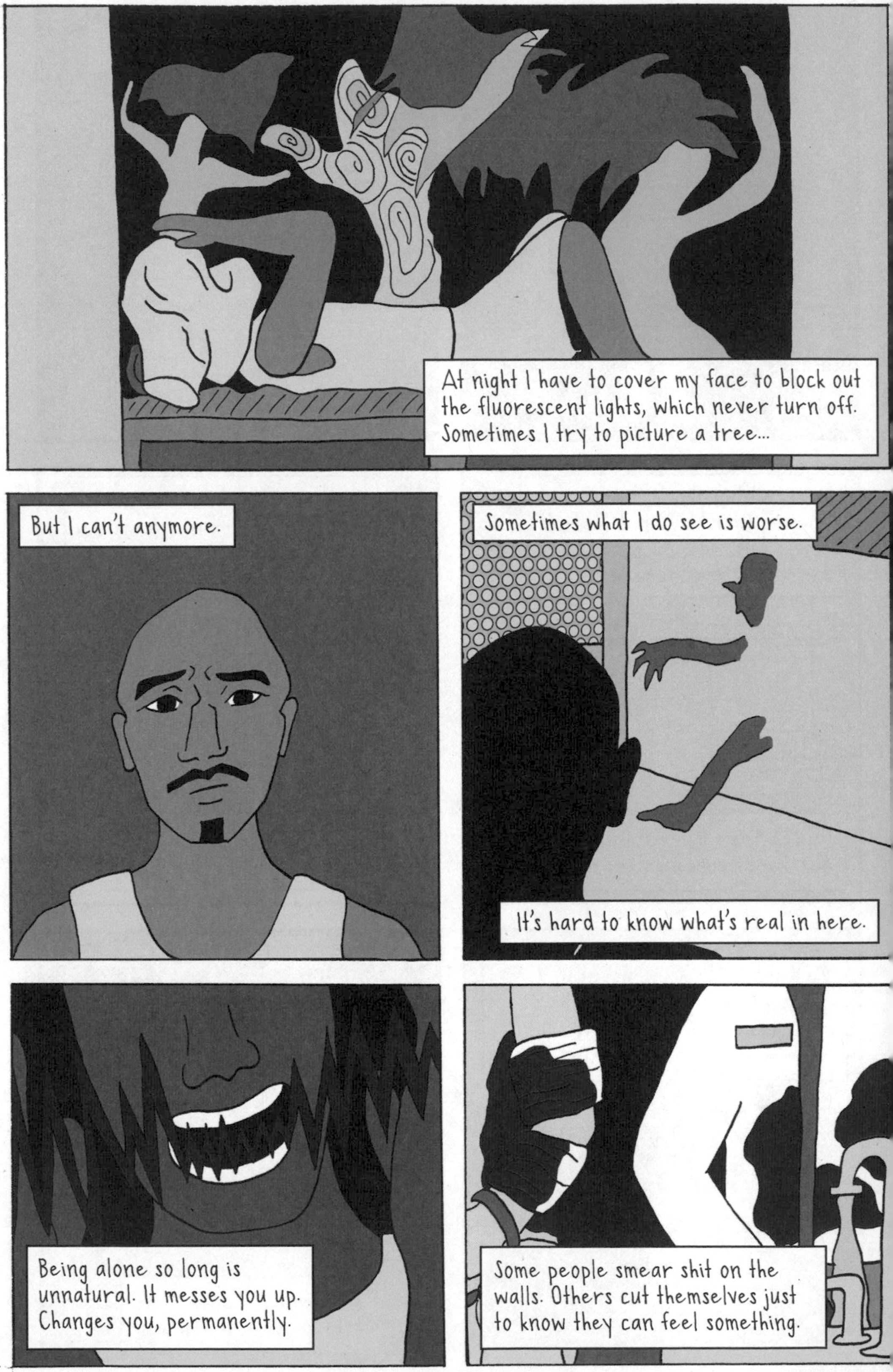
At night I have to cover my face to block out the fluorescent lights, which never turn off. Sometimes I try to picture a tree...
But I can't anymore.
Sometimes what I do see is worse.
It's hard to know what's real in here.
Being alone so long is unnatural. It messes you up. Changes you, permanently.
Some people smear shit on the walls. Others cut themselves just to know they can feel something.

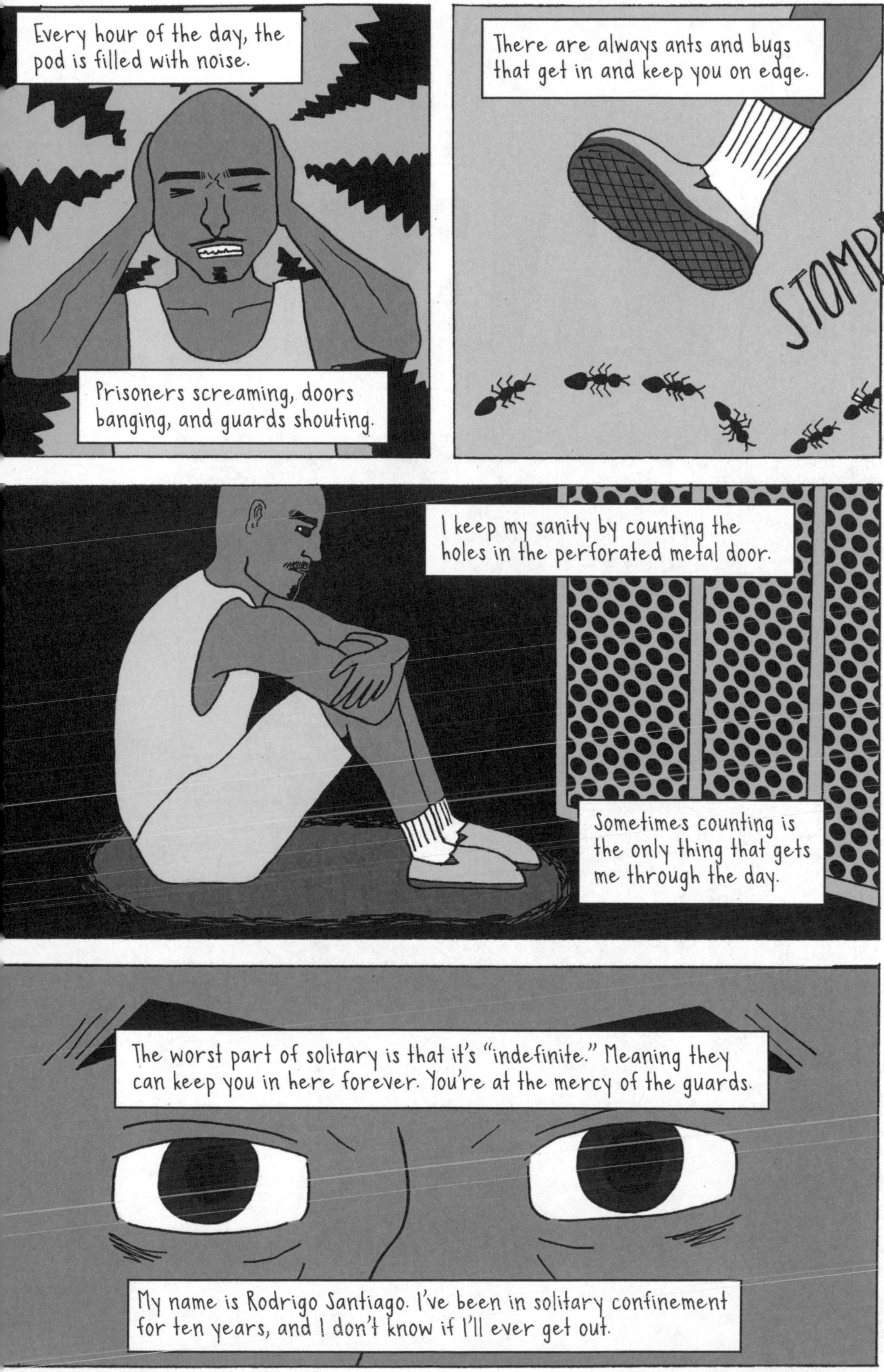
Every hour of the day, the pod is filled with noise.
Prisoners screaming, doors banging, and guards shouting.
There are always ants and bugs that get in and keep you on edge.
STOMP!
I keep my sanity by counting the holes in the perforated metal door.
Sometimes counting is the only thing that gets me through the day.
The worst part of solitary is that it's "indefinite." Meaning they can keep you in here forever. You're at the mercy of the guards.
My name is Rodrigo Santiago. I've been in solitary confinement for ten years, and I don't know if I'll ever get out.

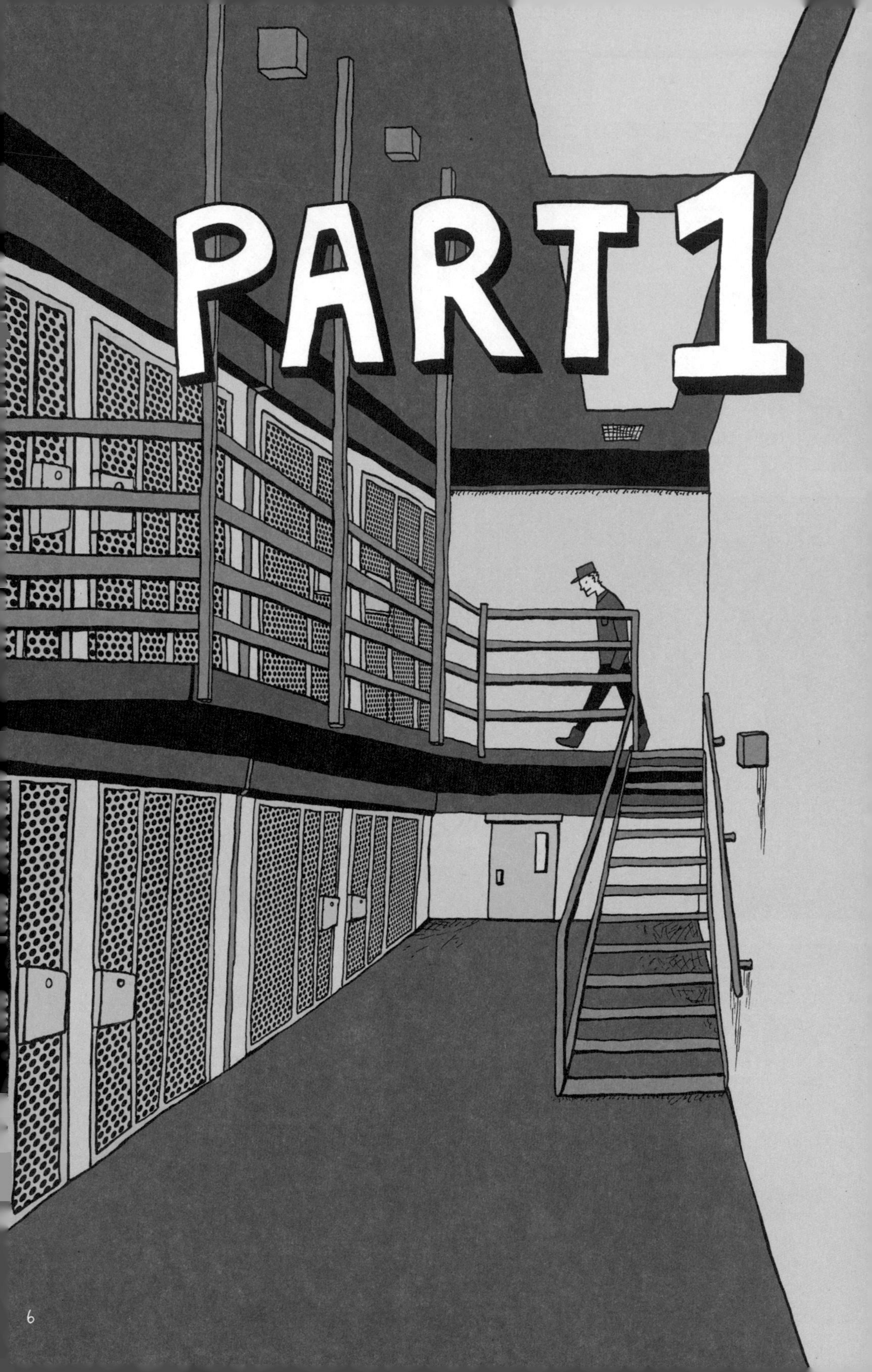
PART 1

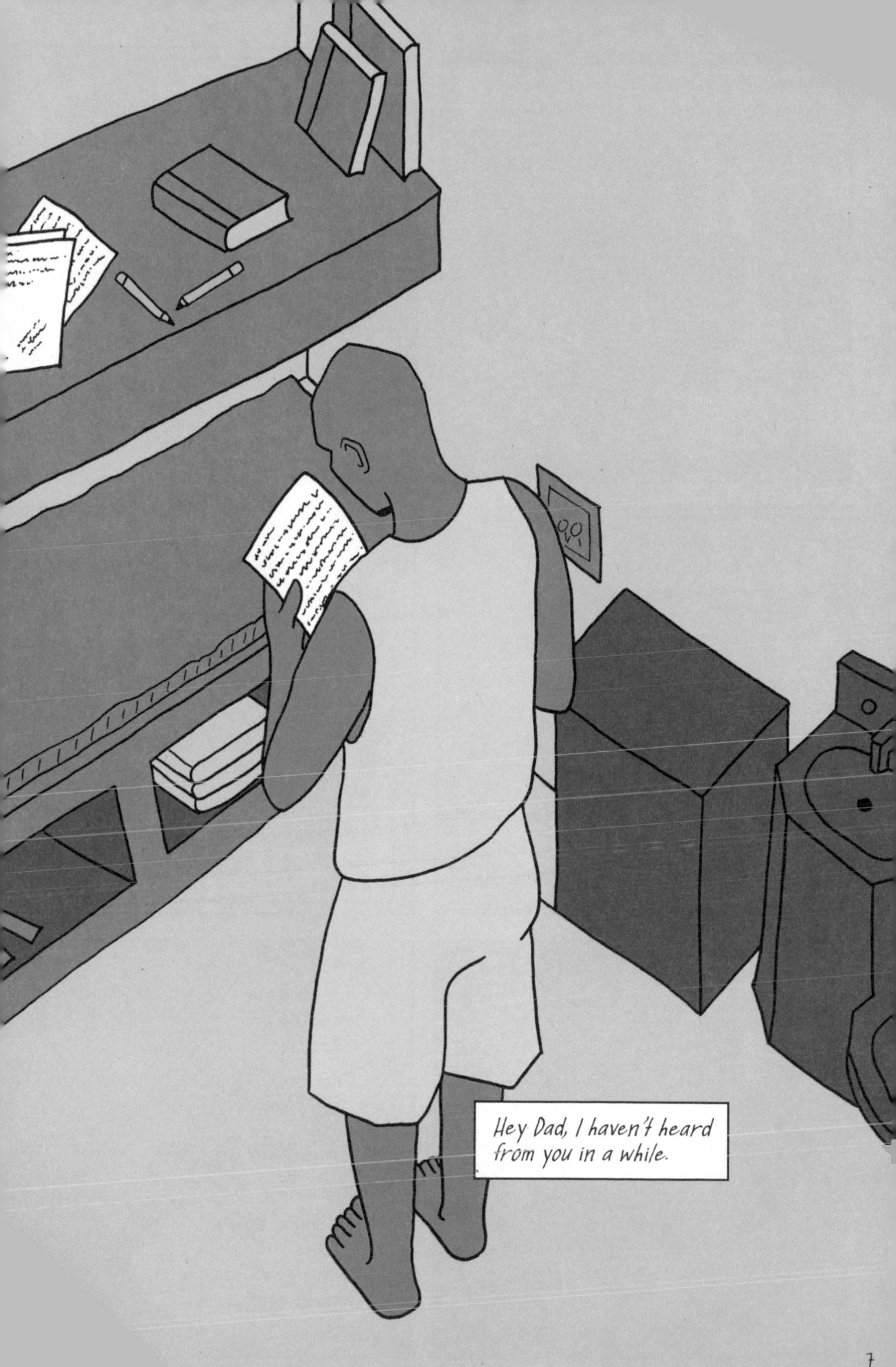
Hey Dad, I haven't heard from you in a while.

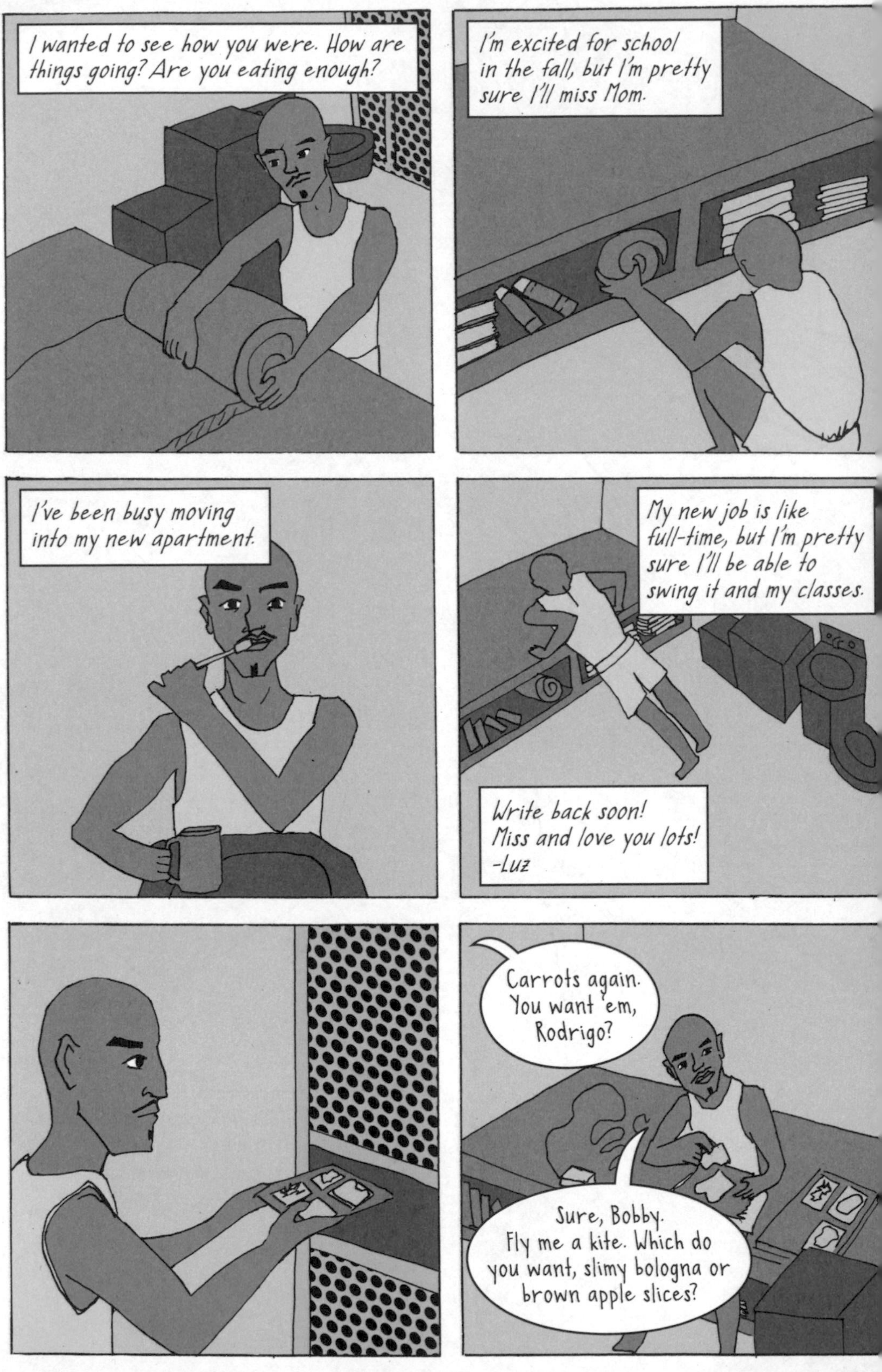
I wanted to see how you were. How are things going? Are you eating enough?
I'm excited for school in the fall, but I'm pretty sure I'll miss Mom.
I've been busy moving into my new apartment.
My new job is like full-time, but I'm pretty sure I'll be able to swing it and my classes.
Write back soon! Miss and love you lots! -Luz
Carrots again. You want 'em, Rodrigo?
Sure, Bobby. Fly me a kite. Which do you want, slimy bologna or brown apple slices?

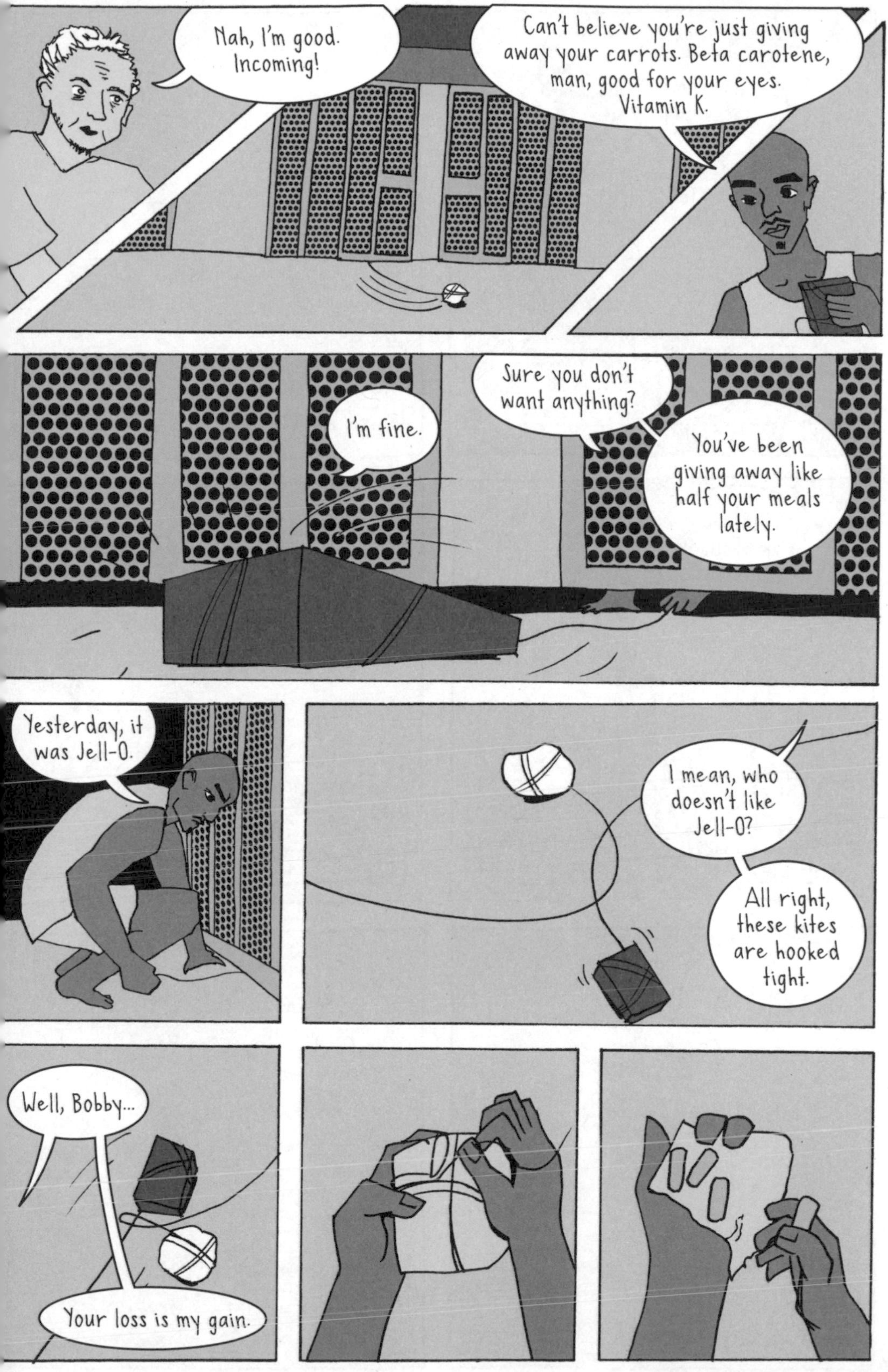
Nah, I'm good. Incoming!
Can't believe you're just giving away your carrots. Beta carotene, man, good for your eyes. Vitamin K.
I'm fine.
Sure you don't want anything?
You've been giving away like half your meals lately.
Yesterday, it was Jell-O.
I mean, who doesn't like Jell-O?
All right, these kites are hooked tight.
Well, Bobby...
Your loss is my gain.

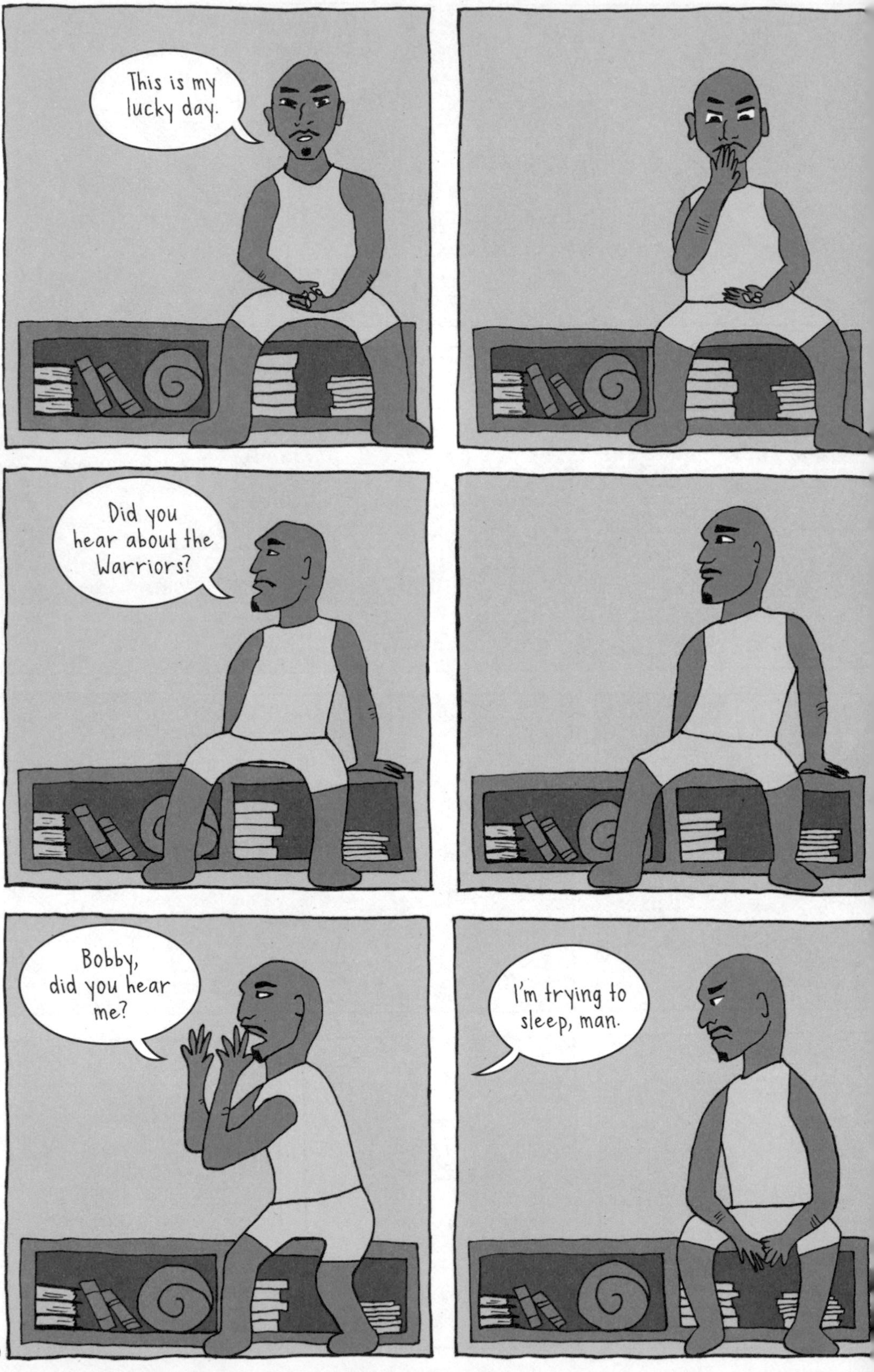
This is my lucky day.
Did you hear about the Warriors?
Bobby, did you hear me?
I'm trying to sleep, man.

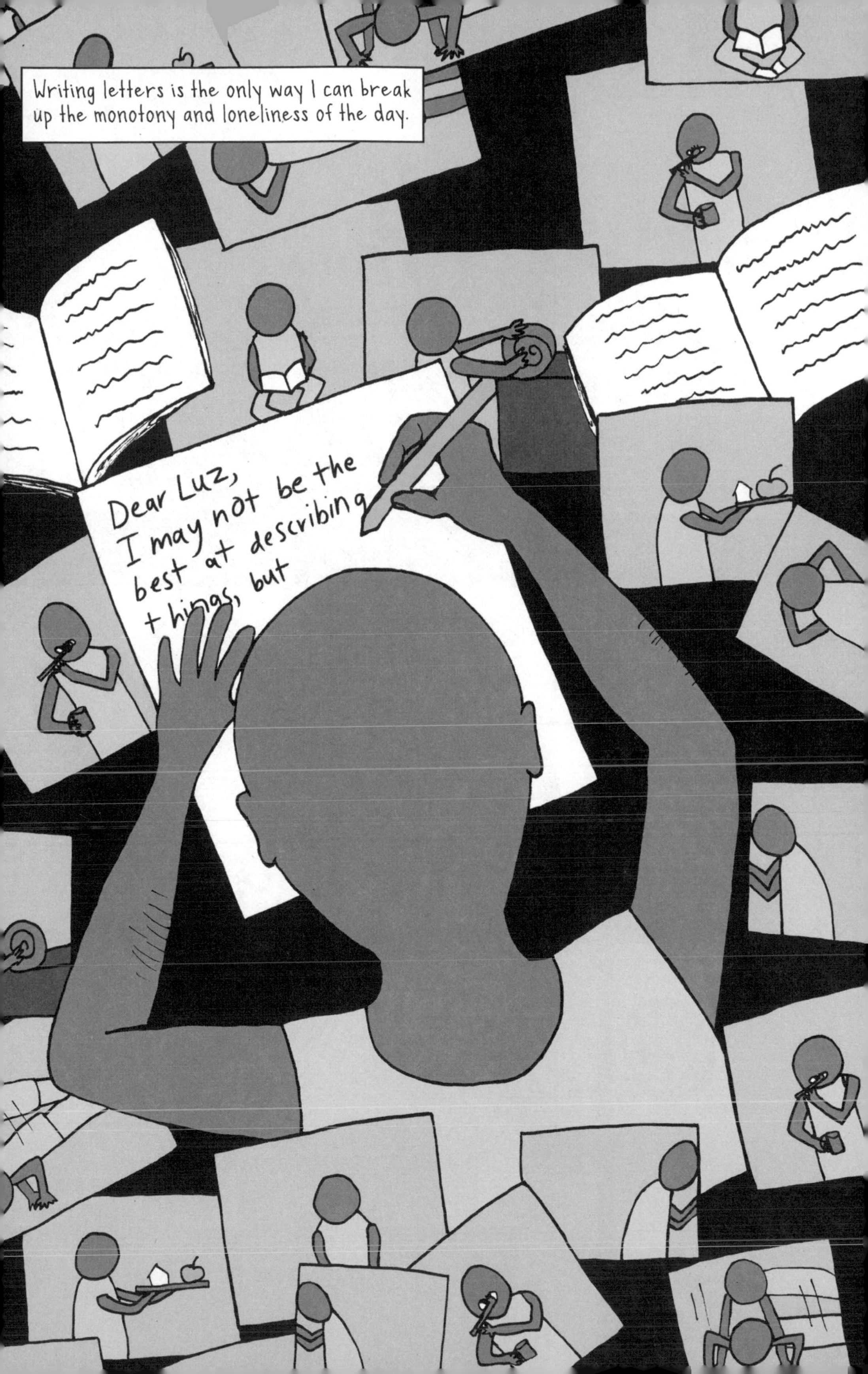
Writing letters is the only way I can break up the monotony and loneliness of the day.
Dear Luz,
I may not be the best at describing things, but

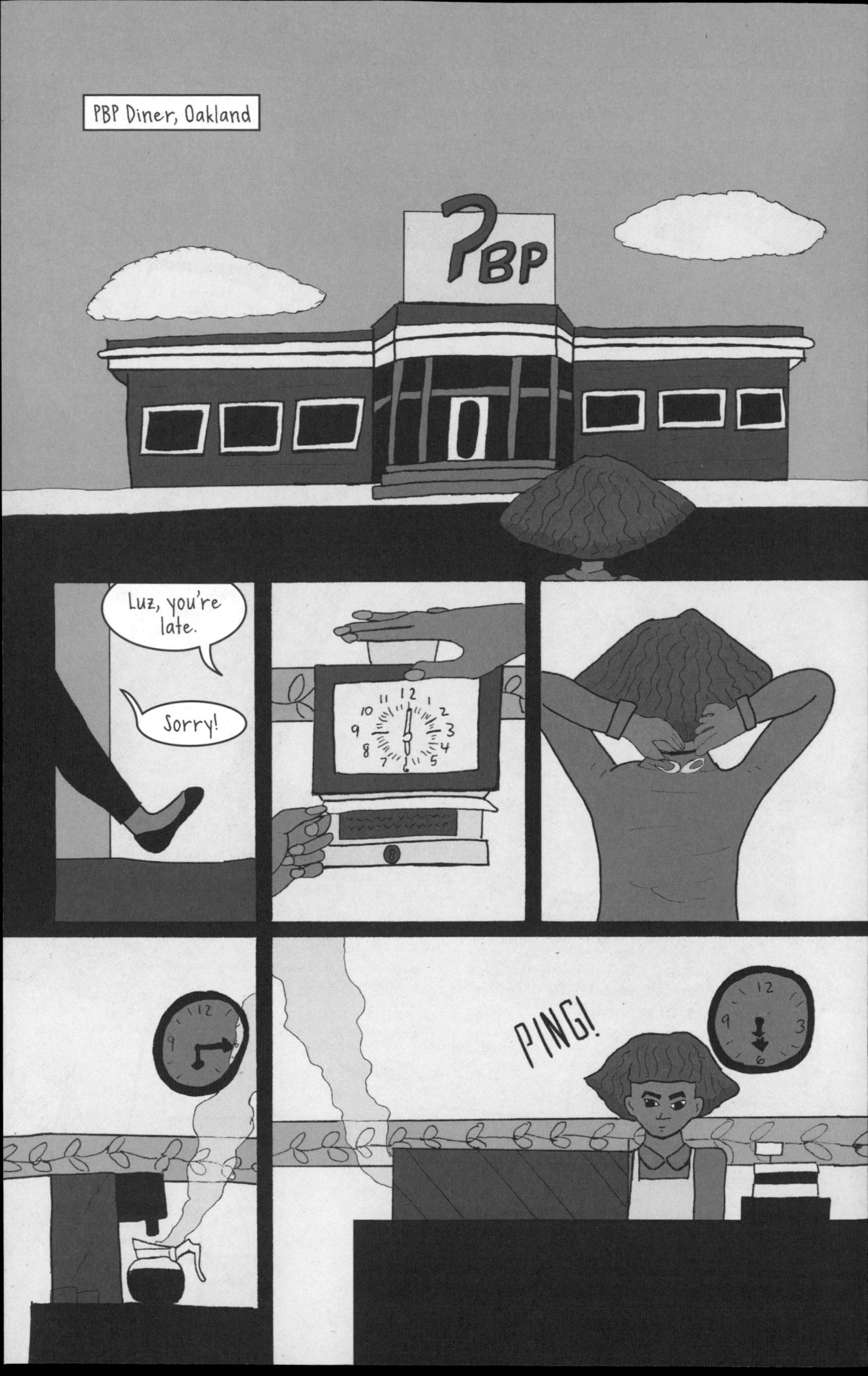
PBP Diner, Oakland
PBP
Luz, you're late.
Sorry!
PING!

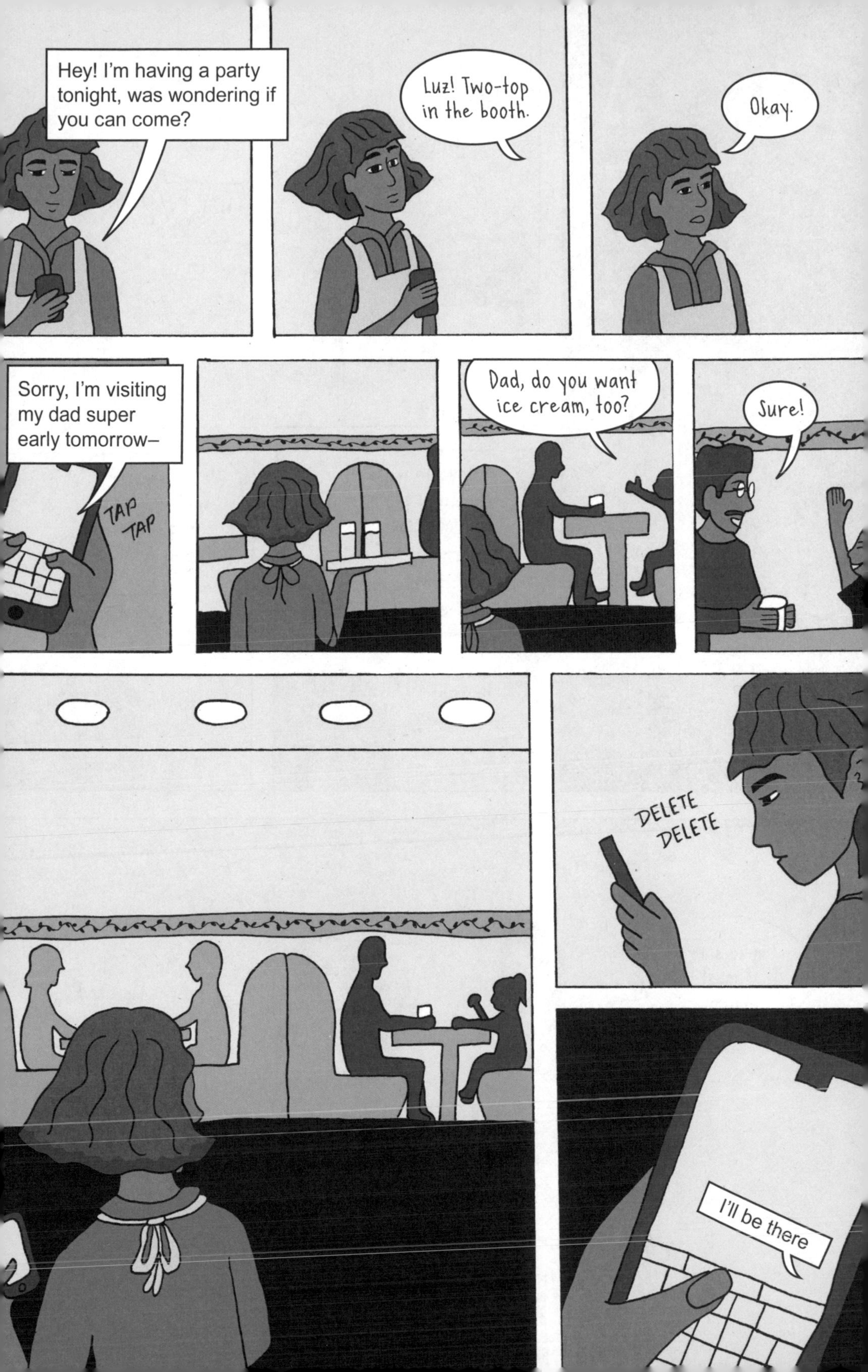
Hey! I'm having a party tonight, was wondering if you can come?
Luz! Two-top in the booth.
Okay.
Sorry, I'm visiting my dad super early tomorrow–
TAP TAP
Dad, do you want ice cream, too?
Sure!
DELETE DELETE
I'll be there

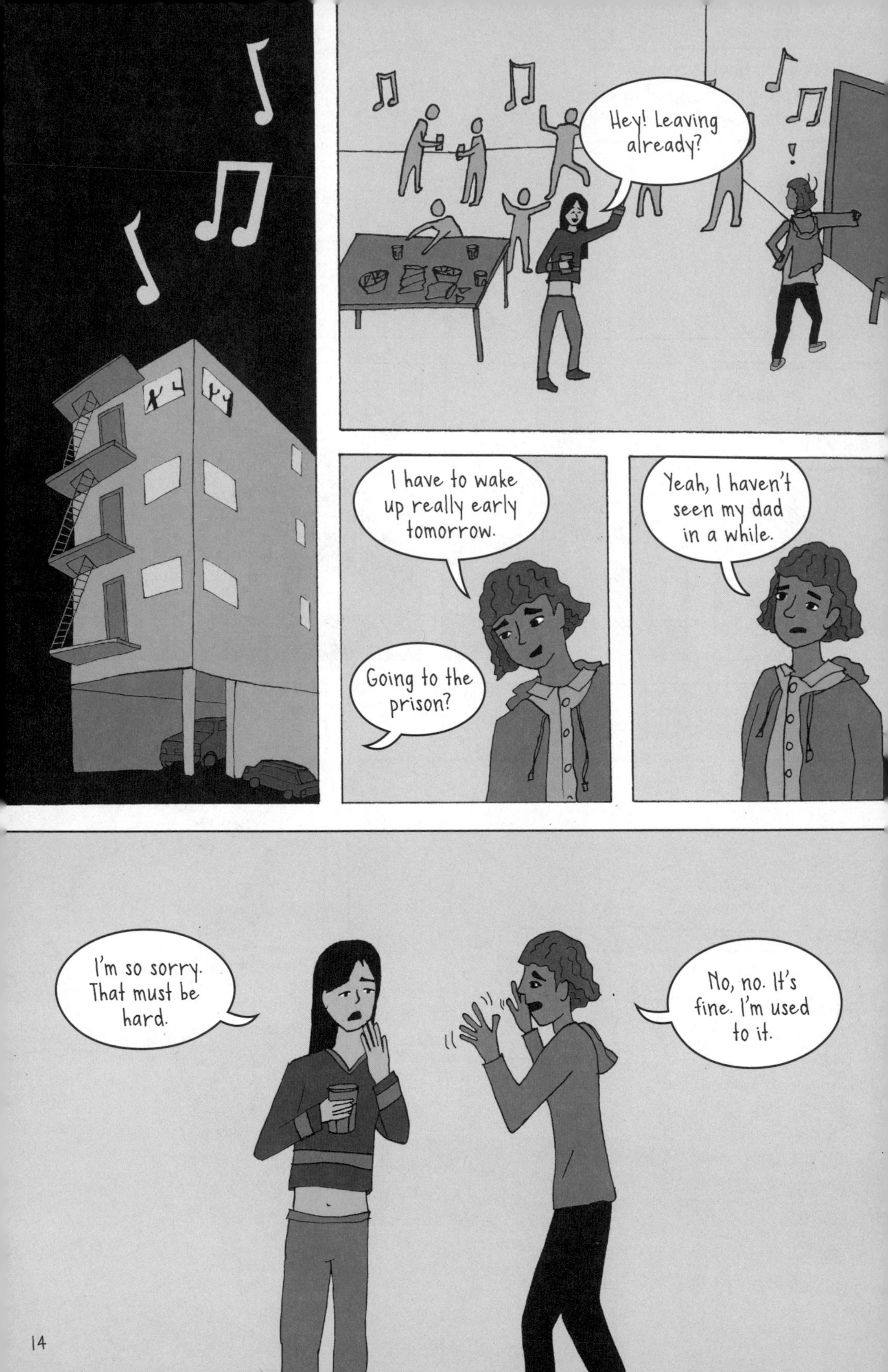

Hey! Leaving already?
I have to wake up really early tomorrow.
Going to the prison?
Yeah, I haven't seen my dad in a while.
I'm so sorry. That must be hard.
No, no. It's fine. I'm used to it.

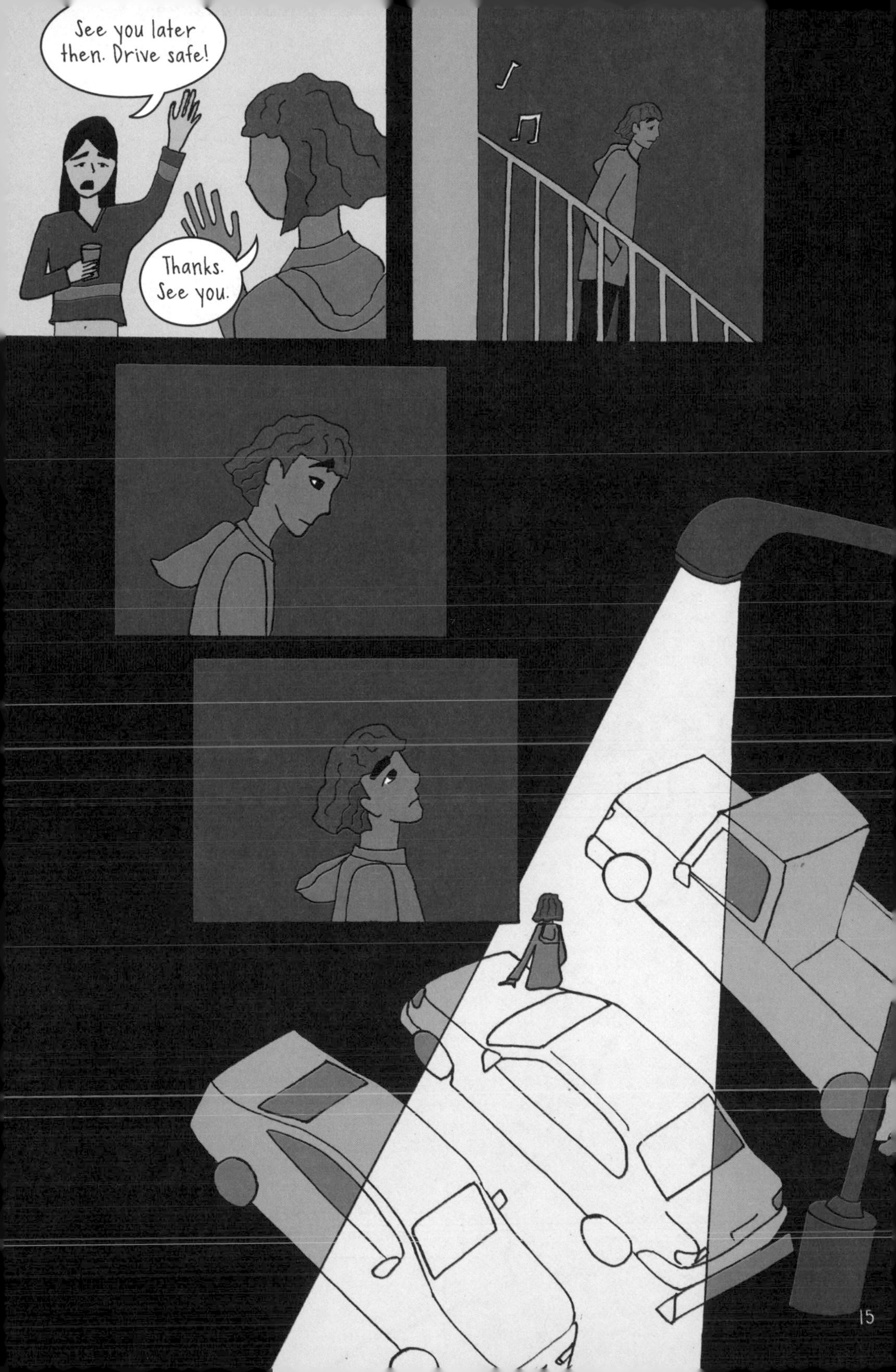
See you later then. Drive safe!
Thanks. See you.

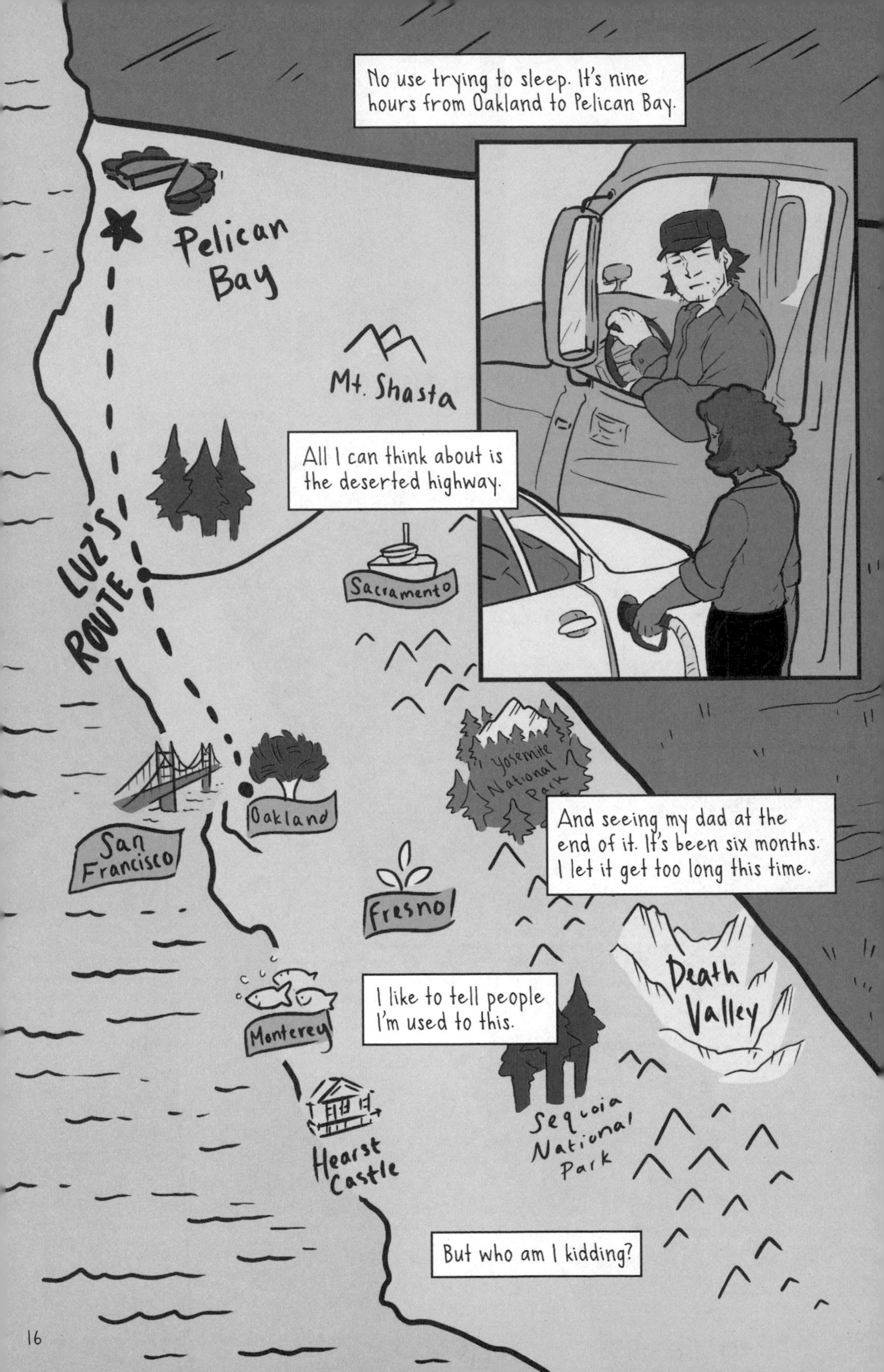
No use trying to sleep. It's nine hours from Oakland to Pelican Bay.
Pelican Bay
Mt. Shasta
All I can think about is the deserted highway.
LUZ'S ROUTE
Sacramento
Yosemite National Park
Oakland
San Francisco
And seeing my dad at the end of it. It's been six months. I let it get too long this time.
Fresno
Death Valley
I like to tell people I'm used to this.
Monterey
Hearst Castle
Sequoia National Park
But who am I kidding?

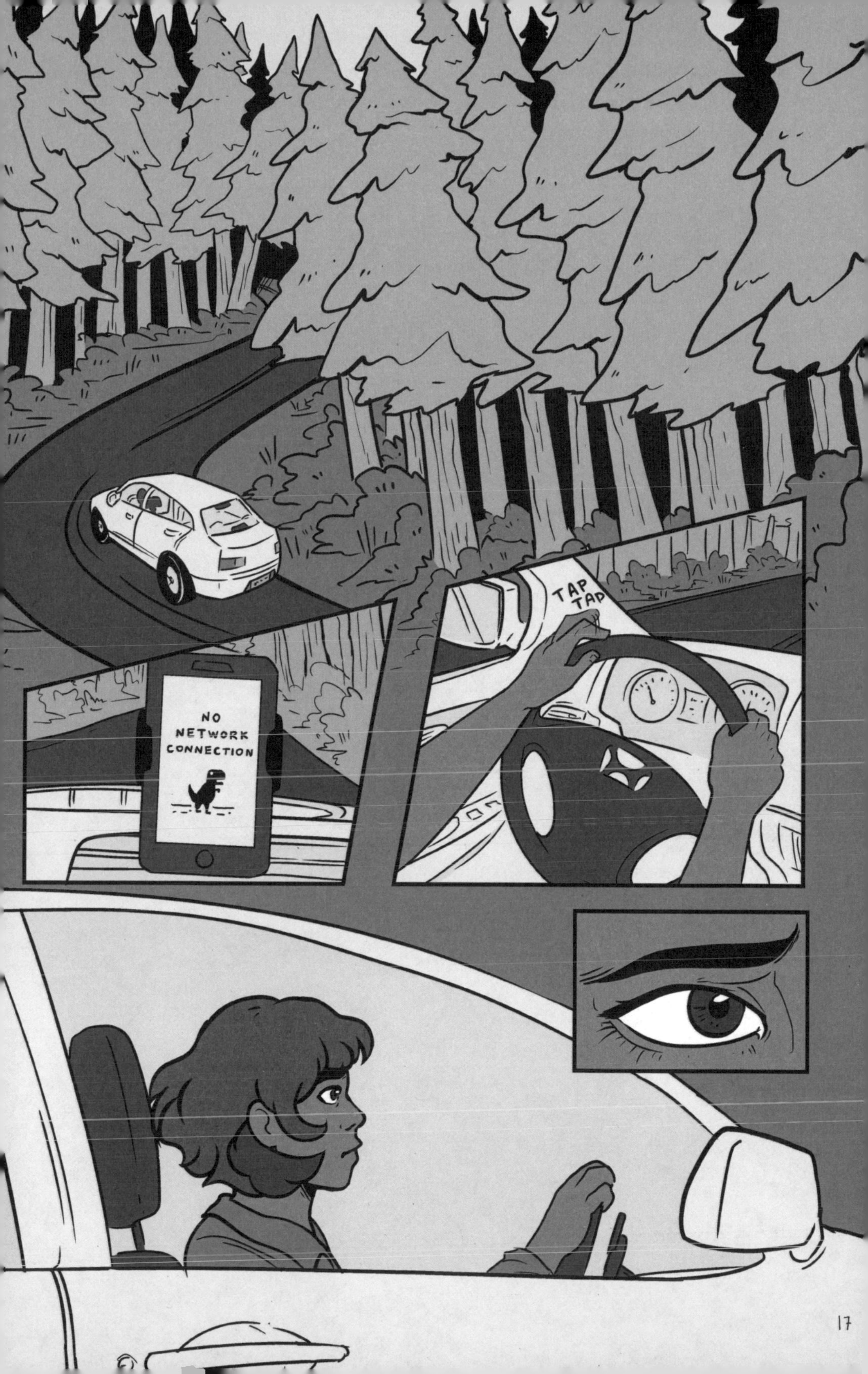
TAP
TAP
NO NETWORK CONNECTION

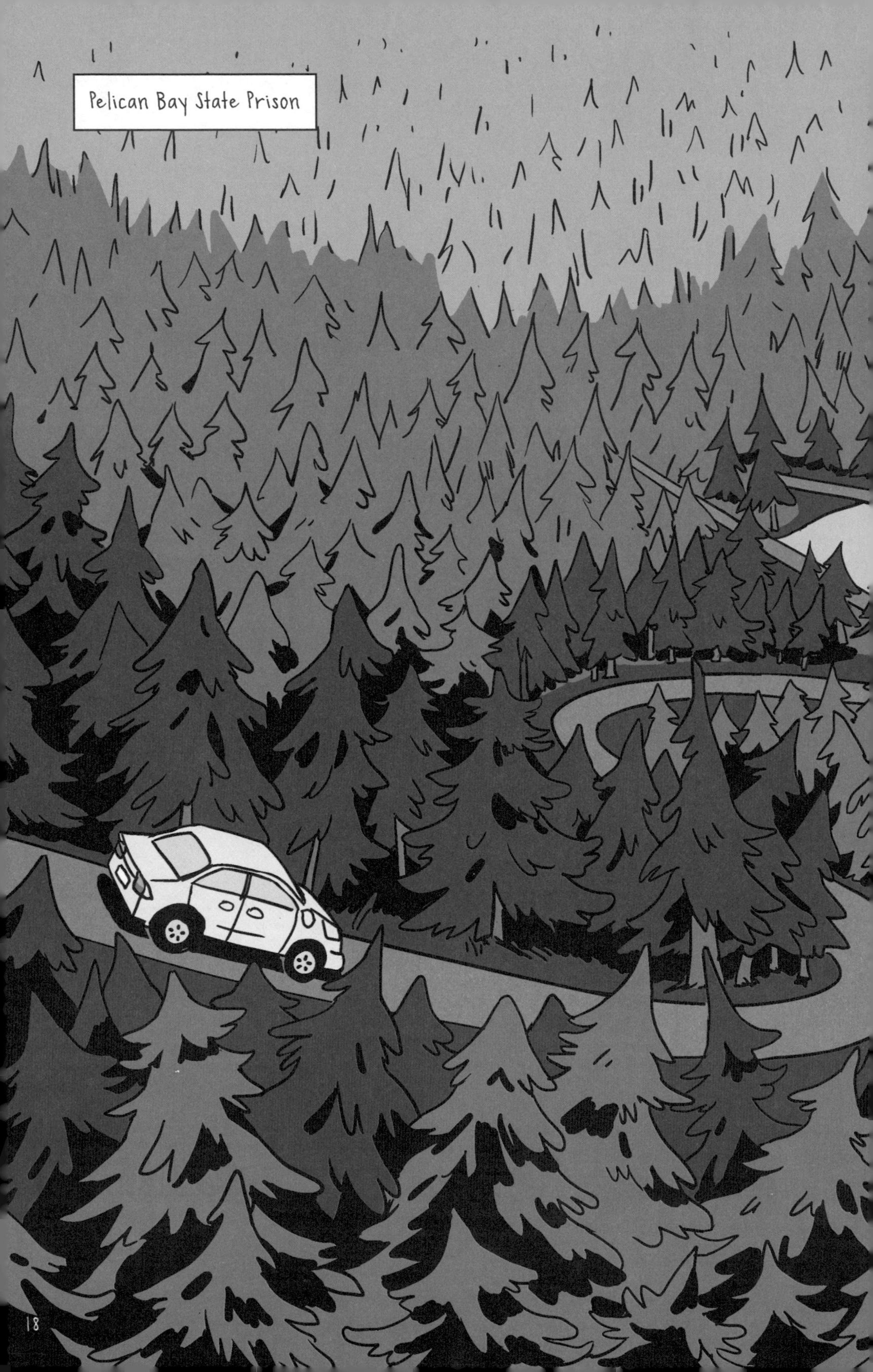
Pelican Bay State Prison

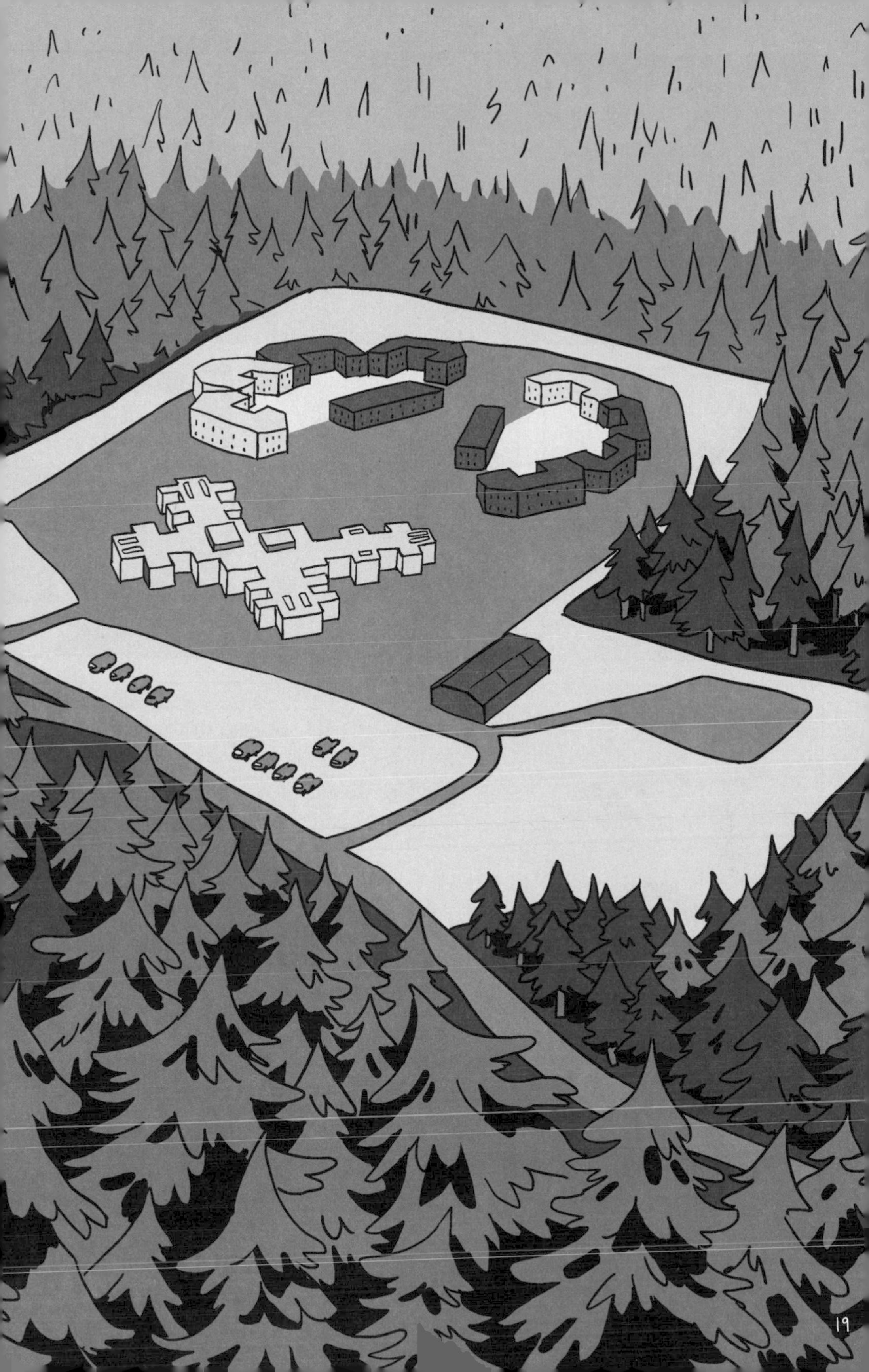

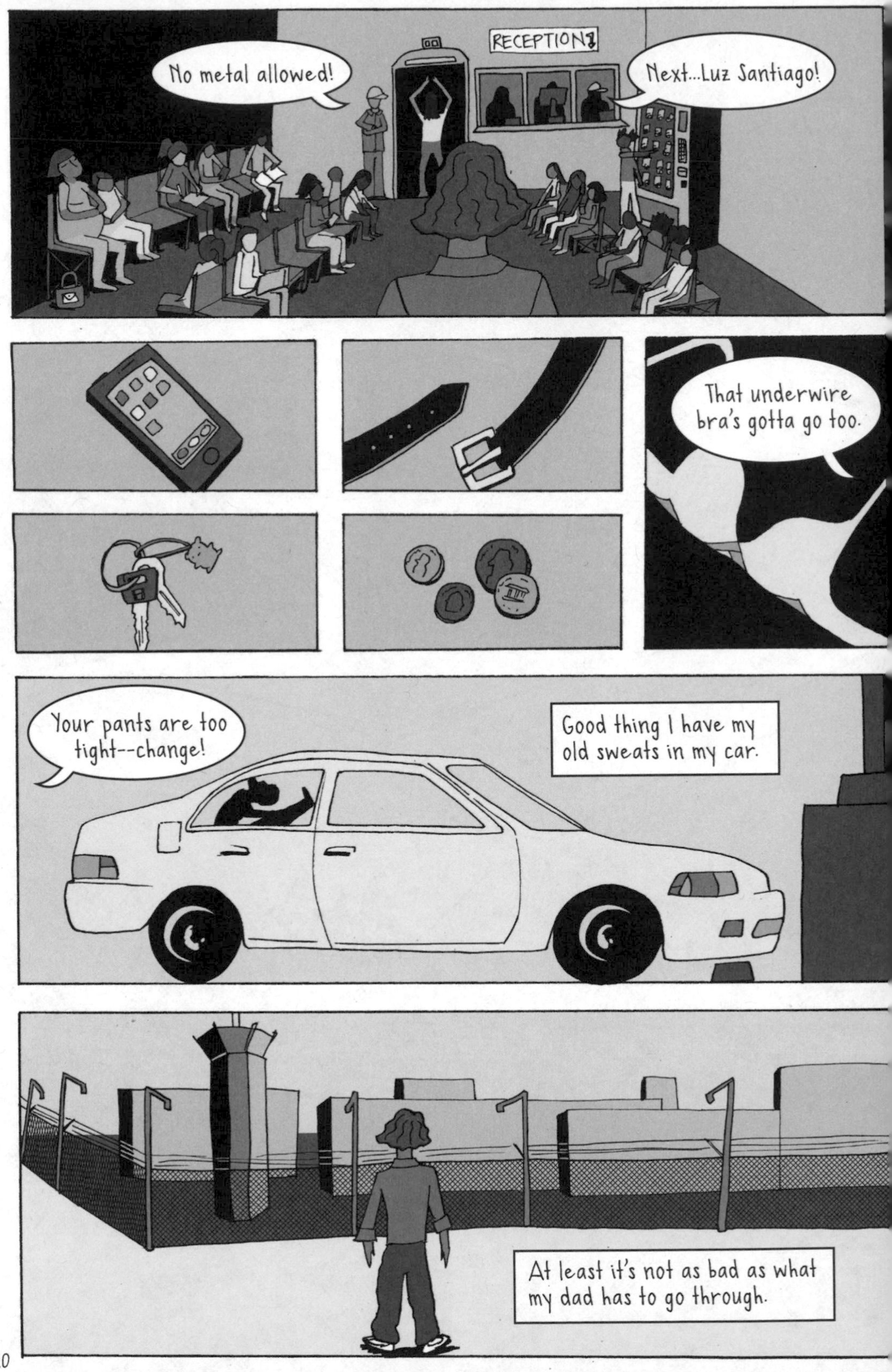
RECEPTION
No metal allowed!
Next...Luz Santiago!
That underwire bra's gotta go too.
Your pants are too tight--change!
Good thing I have my old sweats in my car.
At least it's not as bad as what my dad has to go through.

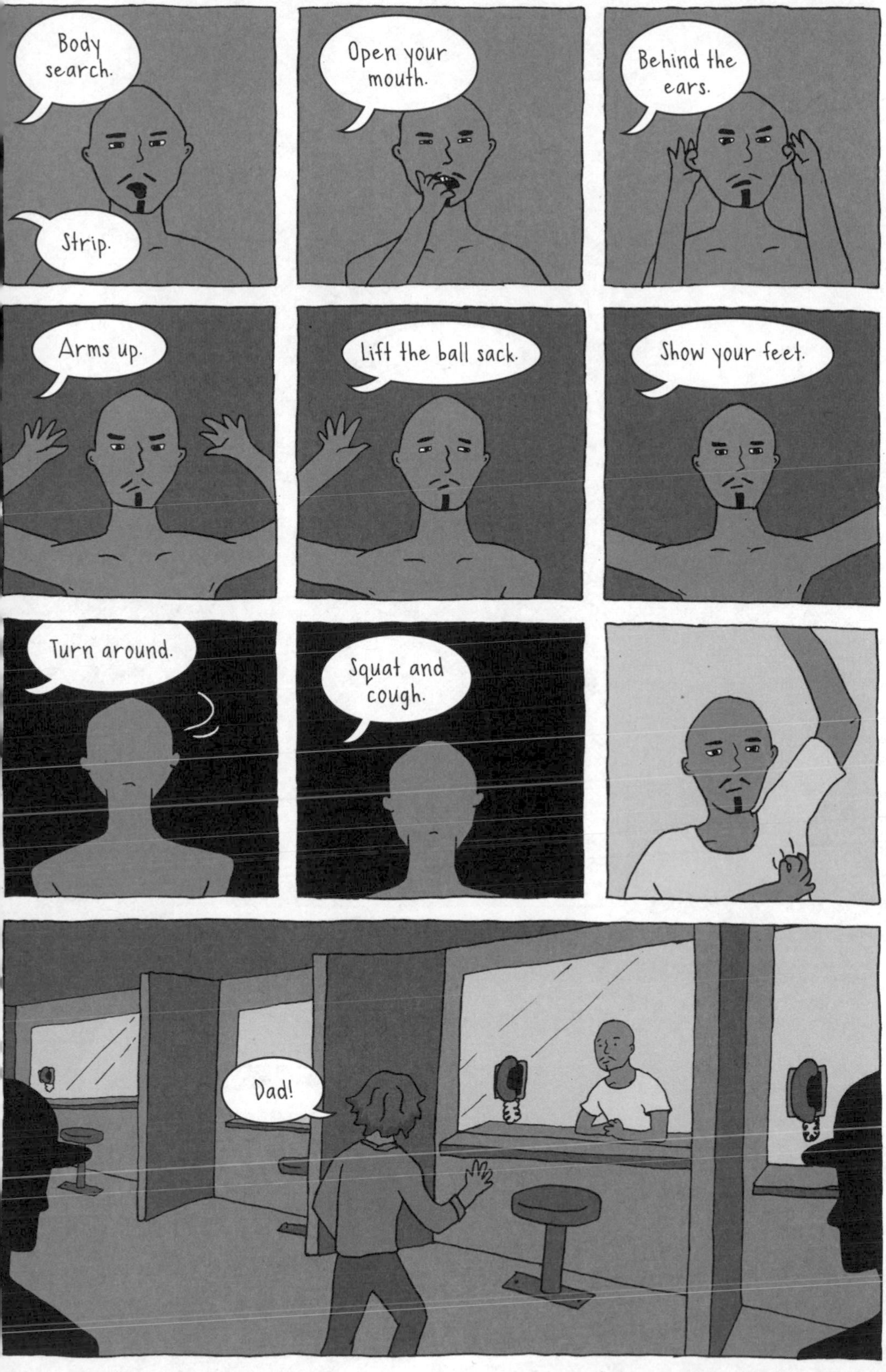
Body search.
Strip.
Open your mouth.
Behind the ears.
Arms up.
Lift the ball sack.
Show your feet.
Turn around.
Squat and cough.
Dad!

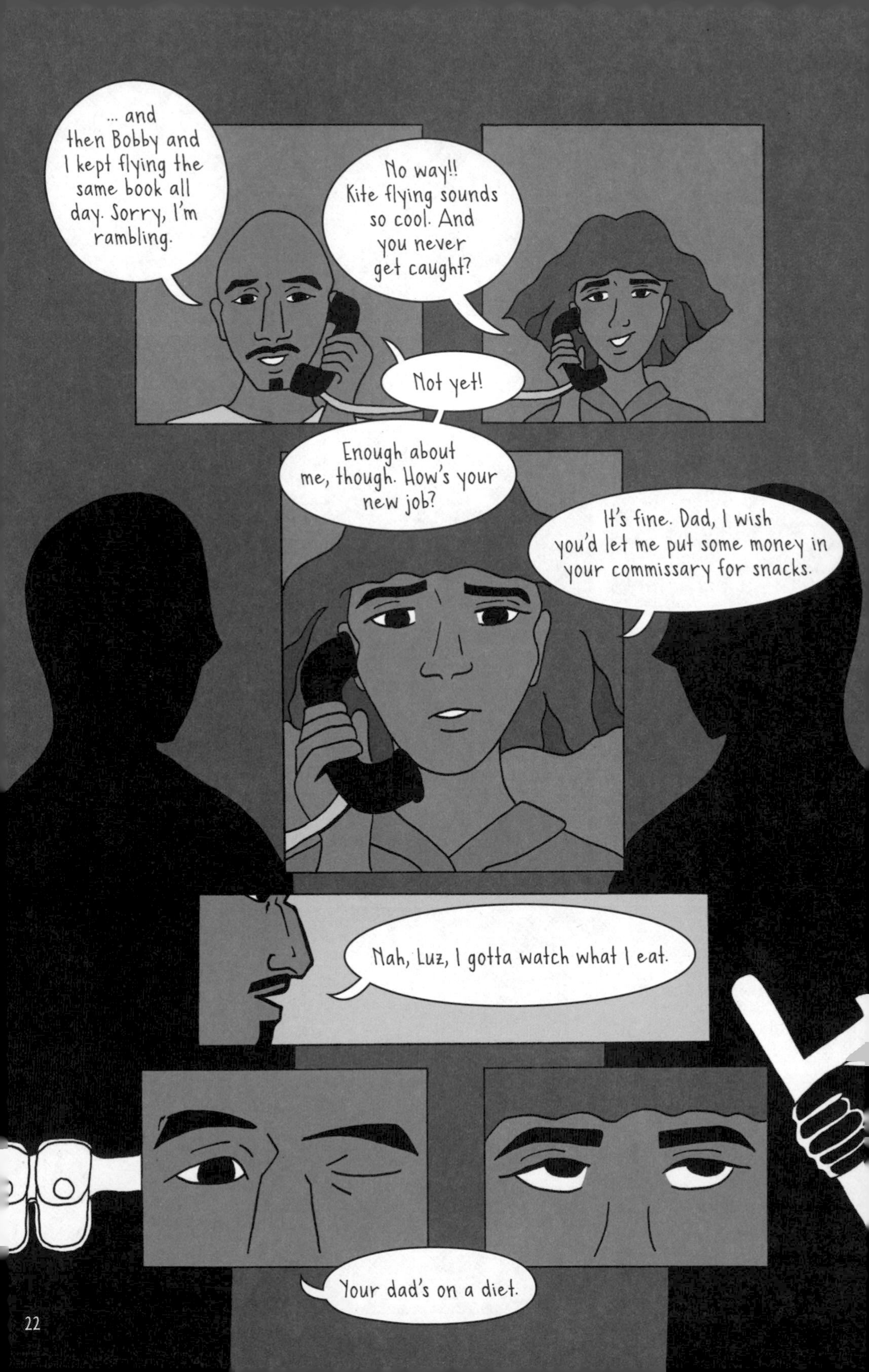
... and then Bobby and I kept flying the same book all day. Sorry, I'm rambling.
No way!! Kite flying sounds so cool. And you never get caught?
Not yet!
Enough about me, though. How's your new job?
It's fine. Dad, I wish you'd let me put some money in your commissary for snacks.
Nah, Luz, I gotta watch what I eat.
Your dad's on a diet.

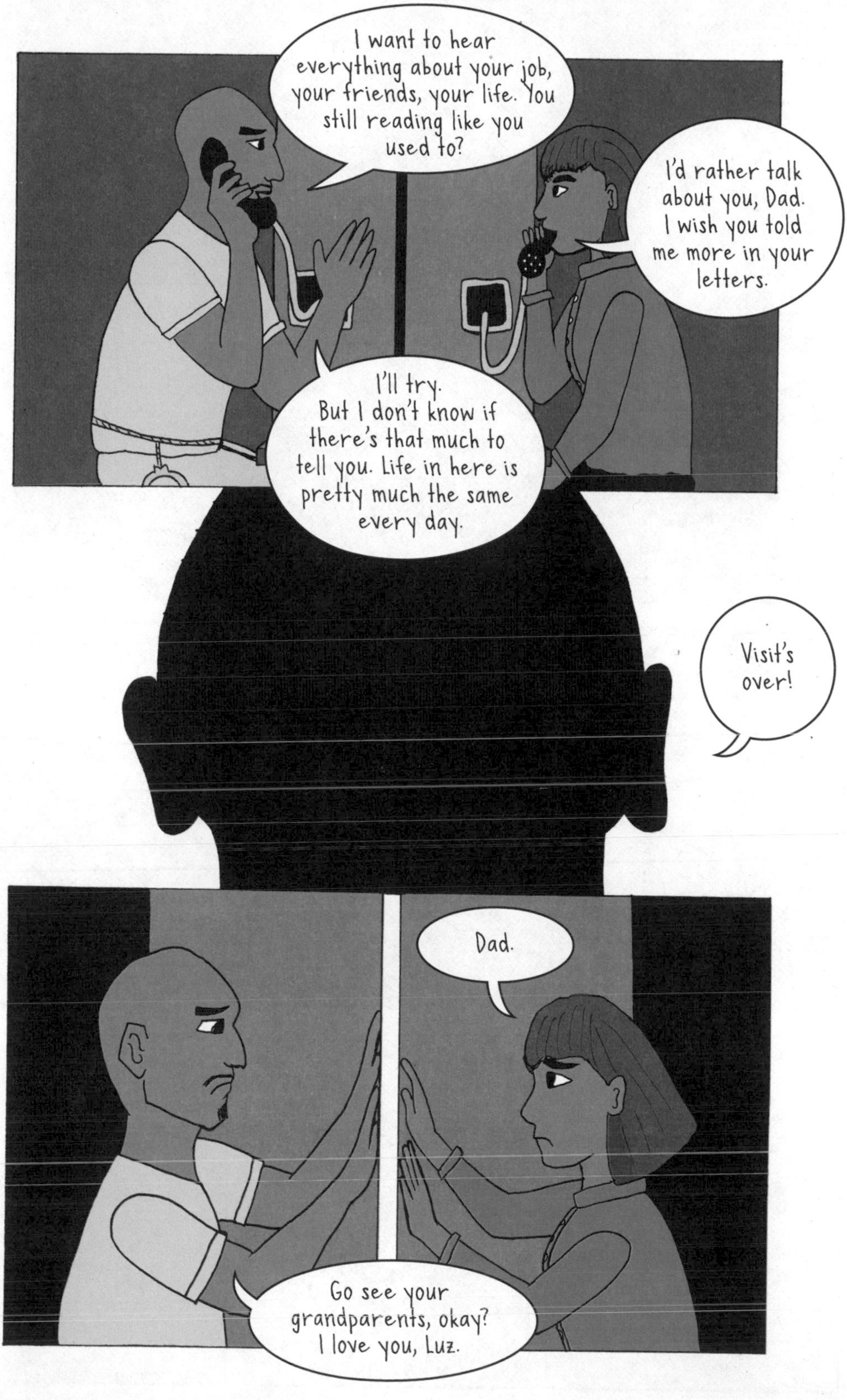
I want to hear everything about your job, your friends, your life. You still reading like you used to?
I'd rather talk about you, Dad. I wish you told me more in your letters.
I'll try. But I don't know if there's that much to tell you. Life in here is pretty much the same every day.
Visit's over!
Dad.
Go see your grandparents, okay? I love you, Luz.

Dear Luz,
It was so good to see you today. It always is.
Dear Luz,
Dear Luz,
At the same time, it always reminds me of how much of your life I've missed.
crumple
crumple

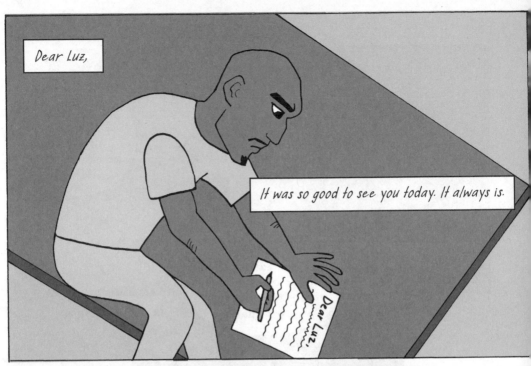

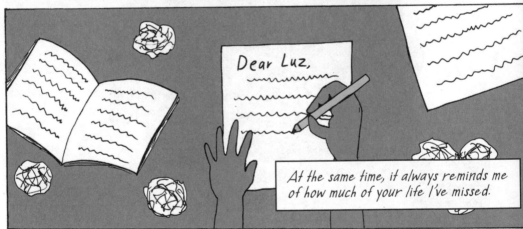

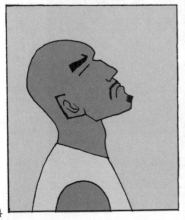

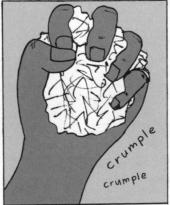

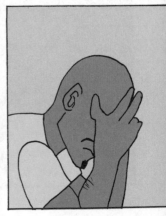

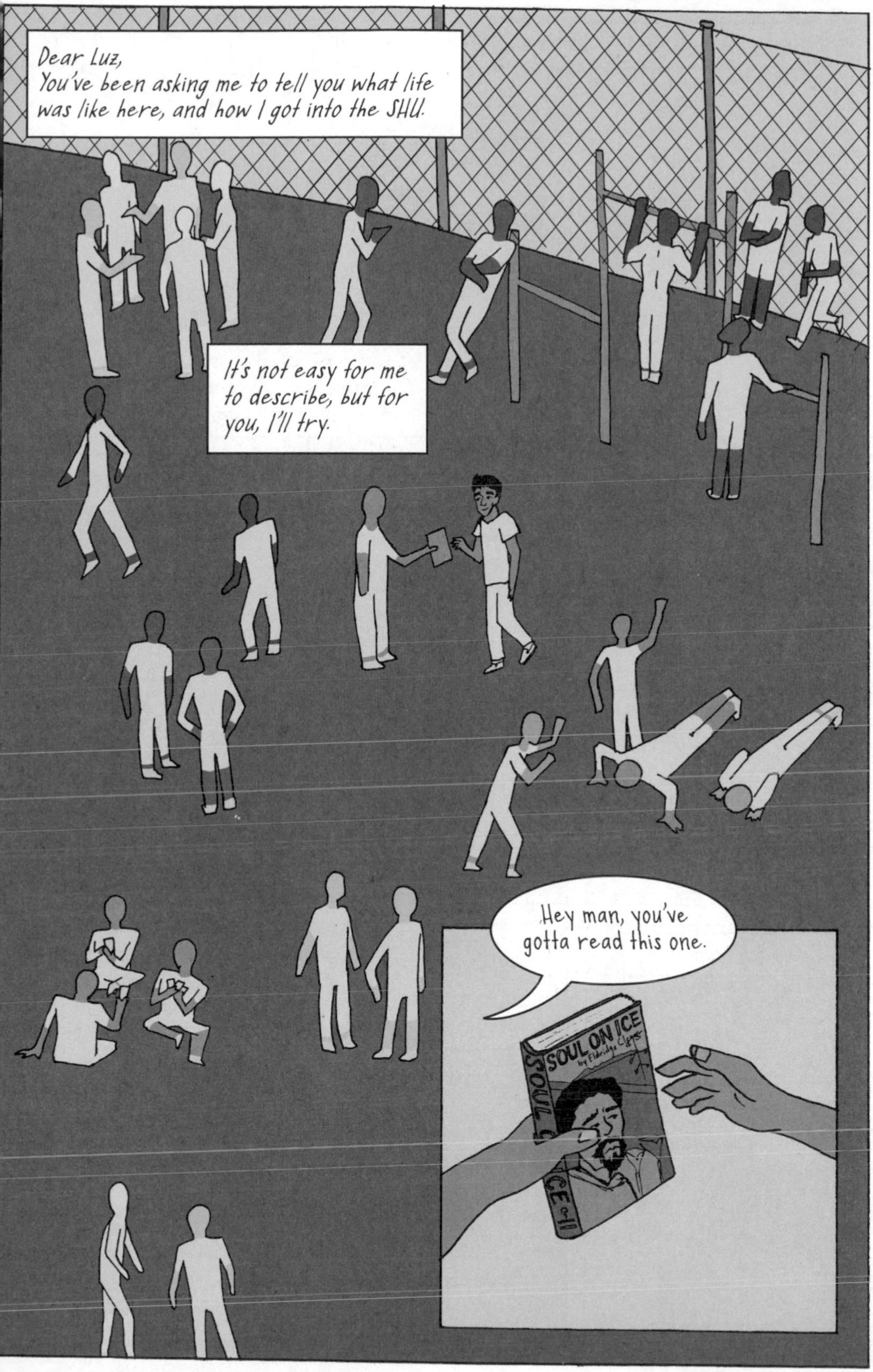

Dear Luz,
You've been asking me to tell you what life was like here, and how I got into the SHU.
It's not easy for me to describe, but for you, I'll try.
Hey man, you've gotta read this one.
SOUL ON ICE

I hardly even got the chance to open that book.

The guards sometimes shake down rooms for no reason. Someone has a bad day, and the prisoners get it.

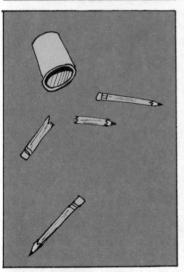

They tear up your letters and photos.

I came back from lunch.

Clean your messy room.

But I'll be keeping this book here.

The book had Carlos Aguirre's name written in it. He was considered a gang member.

A name and a book. That's all it took to throw me in solitary and put me under investigation.

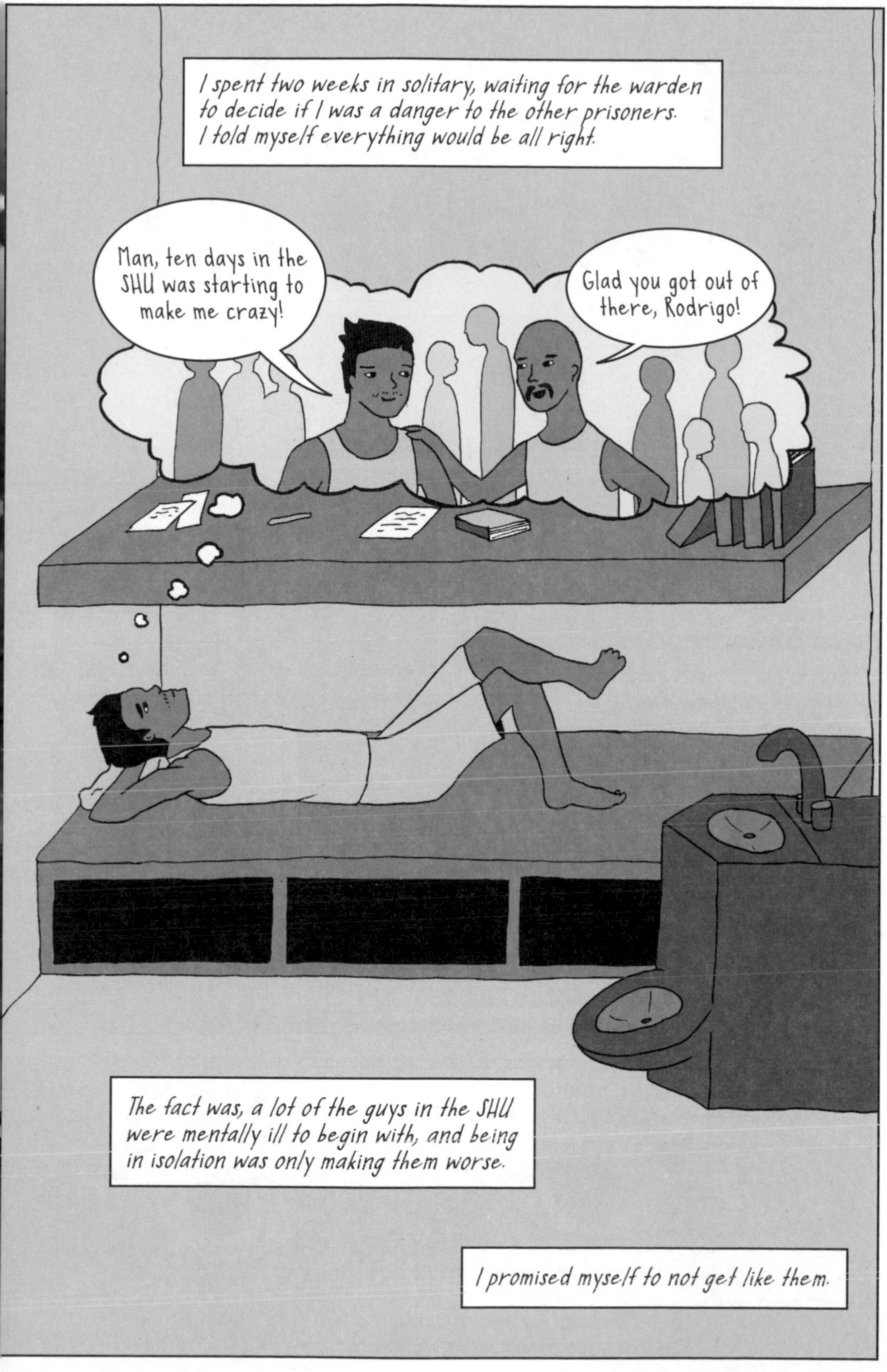
I spent two weeks in solitary, waiting for the warden to decide if I was a danger to the other prisoners. I told myself everything would be all right.
Man, ten days in the SHU was starting to make me crazy!
Glad you got out of there, Rodrigo!
The fact was, a lot of the guys in the SHU were mentally ill to begin with, and being in isolation was only making them worse.
I promised myself to not get like them.

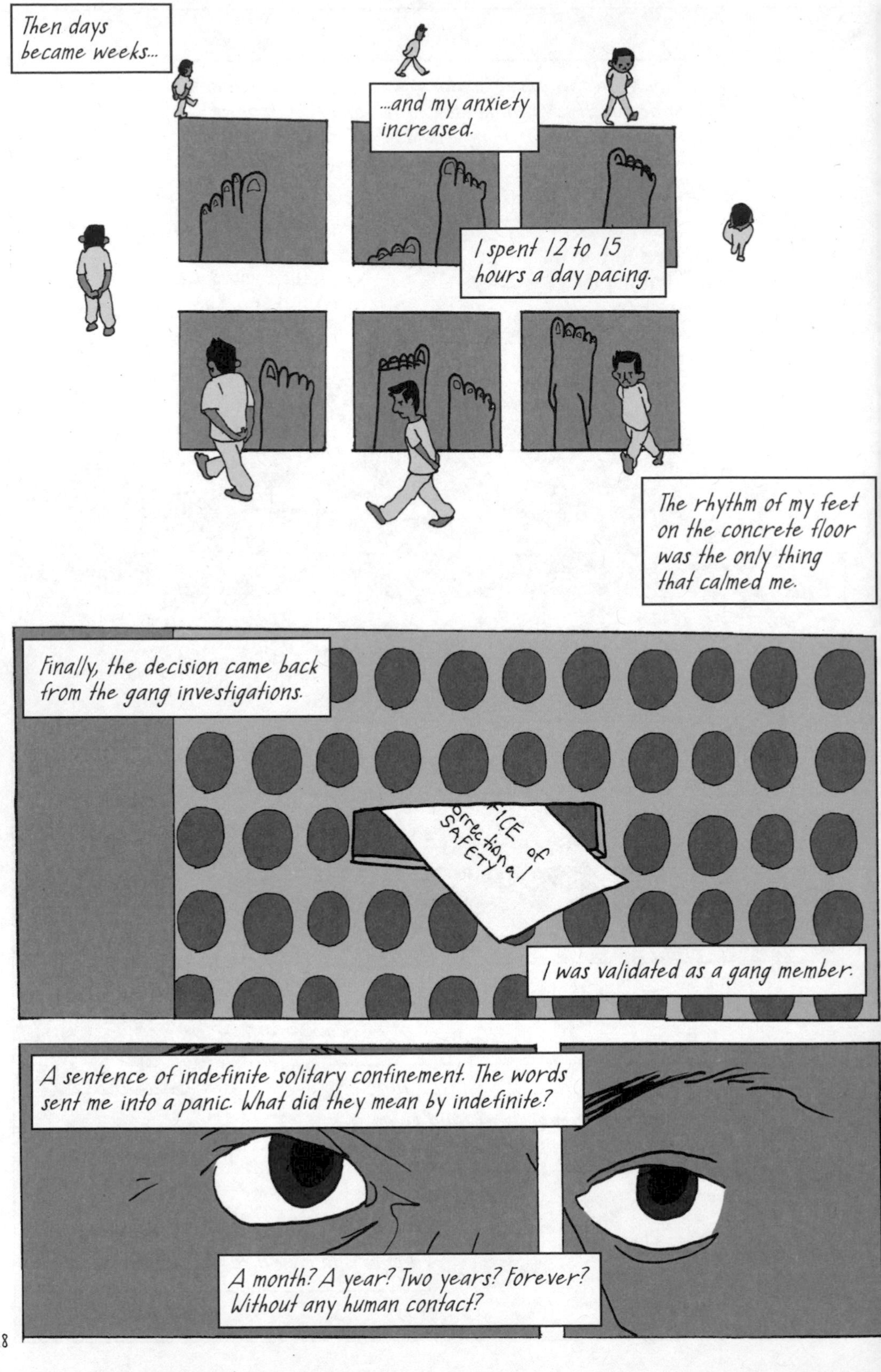
Then days became weeks...
...and my anxiety increased.
I spent 12 to 15 hours a day pacing.
The rhythm of my feet on the concrete floor was the only thing that calmed me.
Finally, the decision came back from the gang investigations.
FICE of orrectional SAFETY
I was validated as a gang member.
A sentence of indefinite solitary confinement. The words sent me into a panic. What did they mean by indefinite?
A month? A year? Two years? Forever? Without any human contact?

That's when I snapped.

YOU CAN'T DO THIS!

GET ME OUT OF THIS FUCKING HOLE!

I WILL KILL YOU!!!

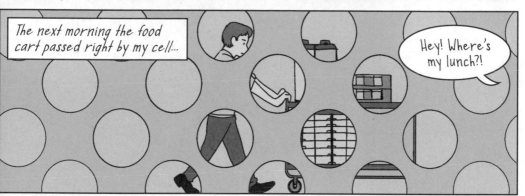

The next morning the food cart passed right by my cell...

Hey! Where's my lunch?!

...and later that day, the guards came back with tear gas.

HELP ME! NO! SOMEONE HELP!!

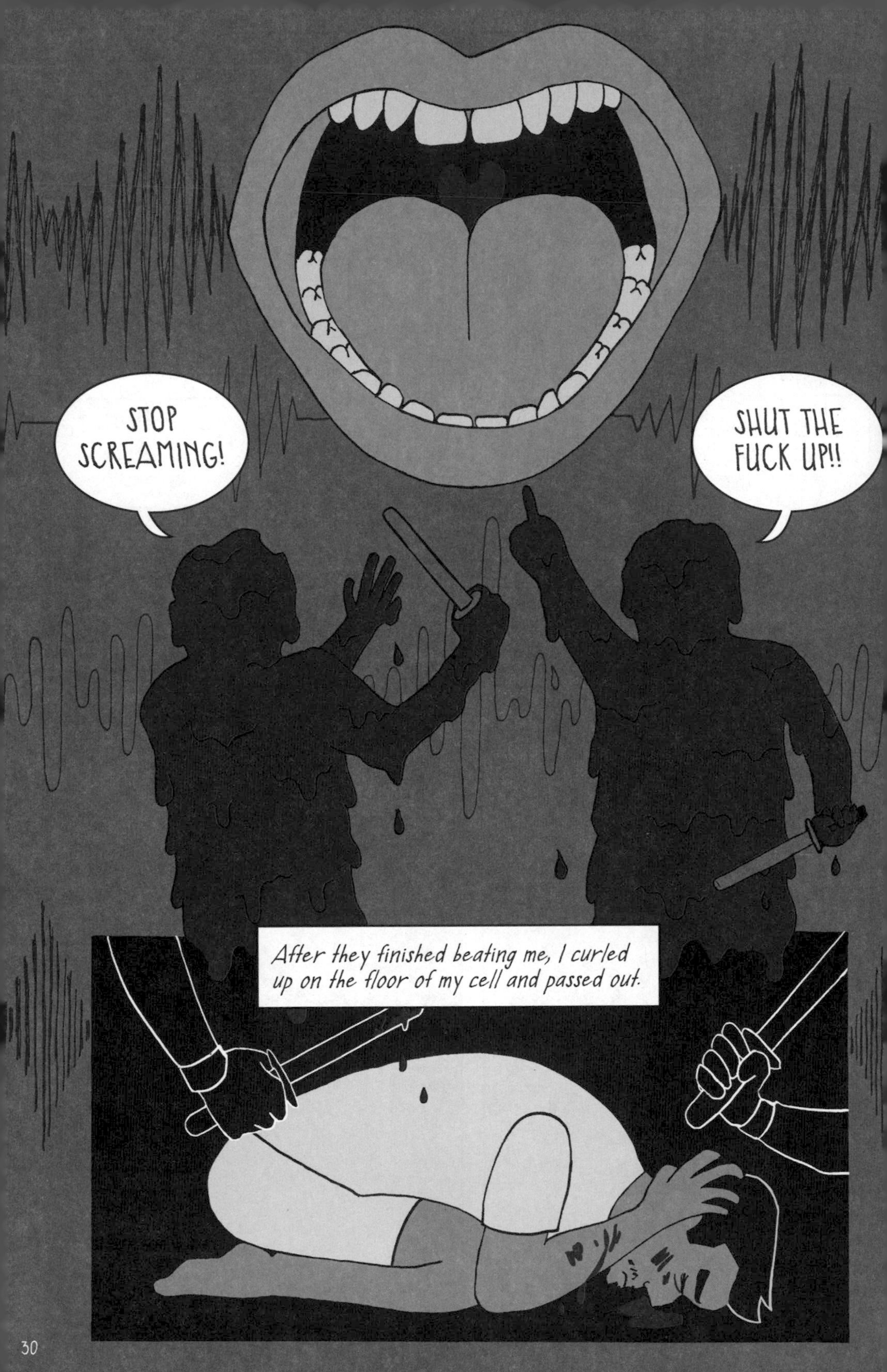
STOP SCREAMING!
SHUT THE FUCK UP!!
After they finished beating me, I curled up on the floor of my cell and passed out.

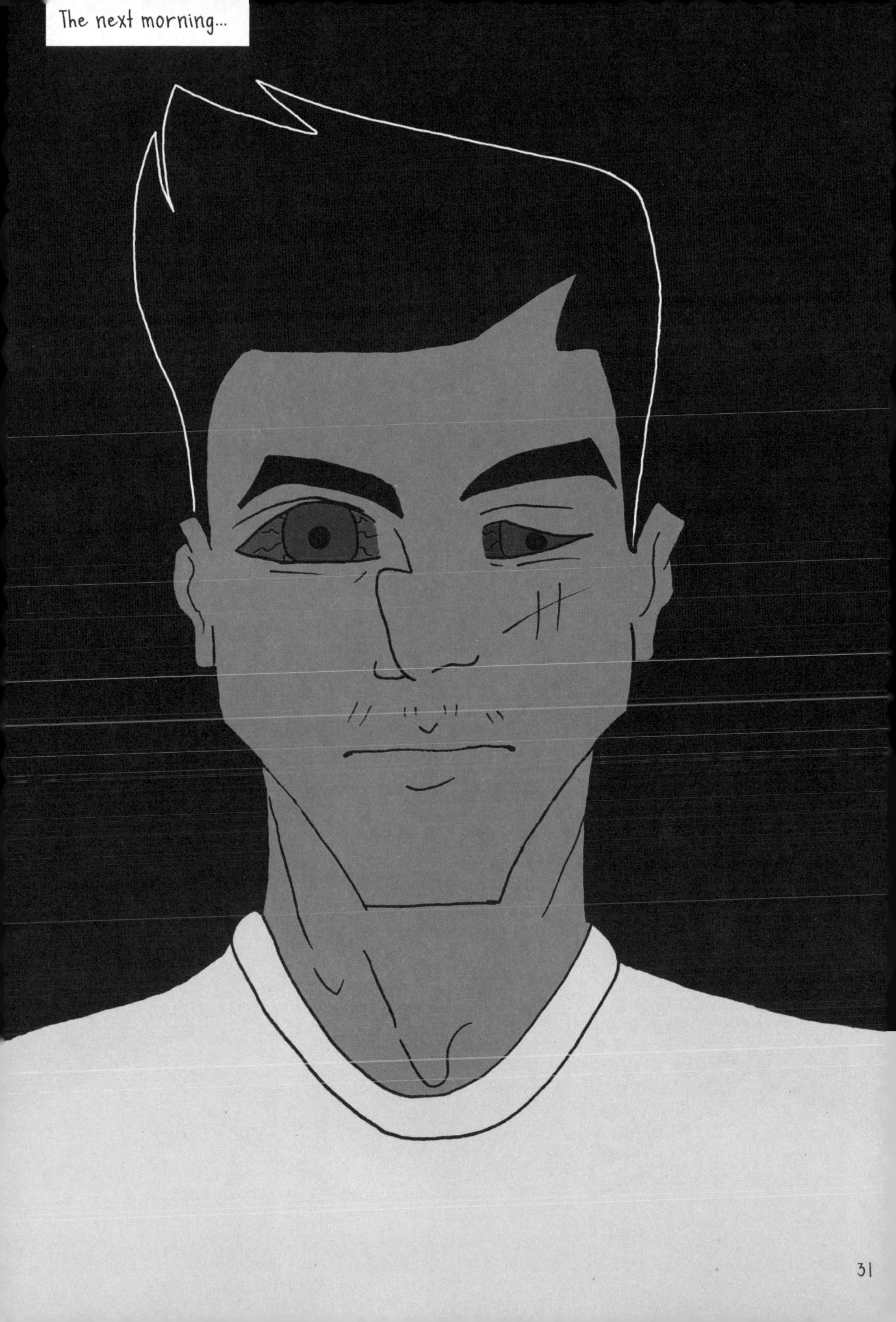
The next morning...

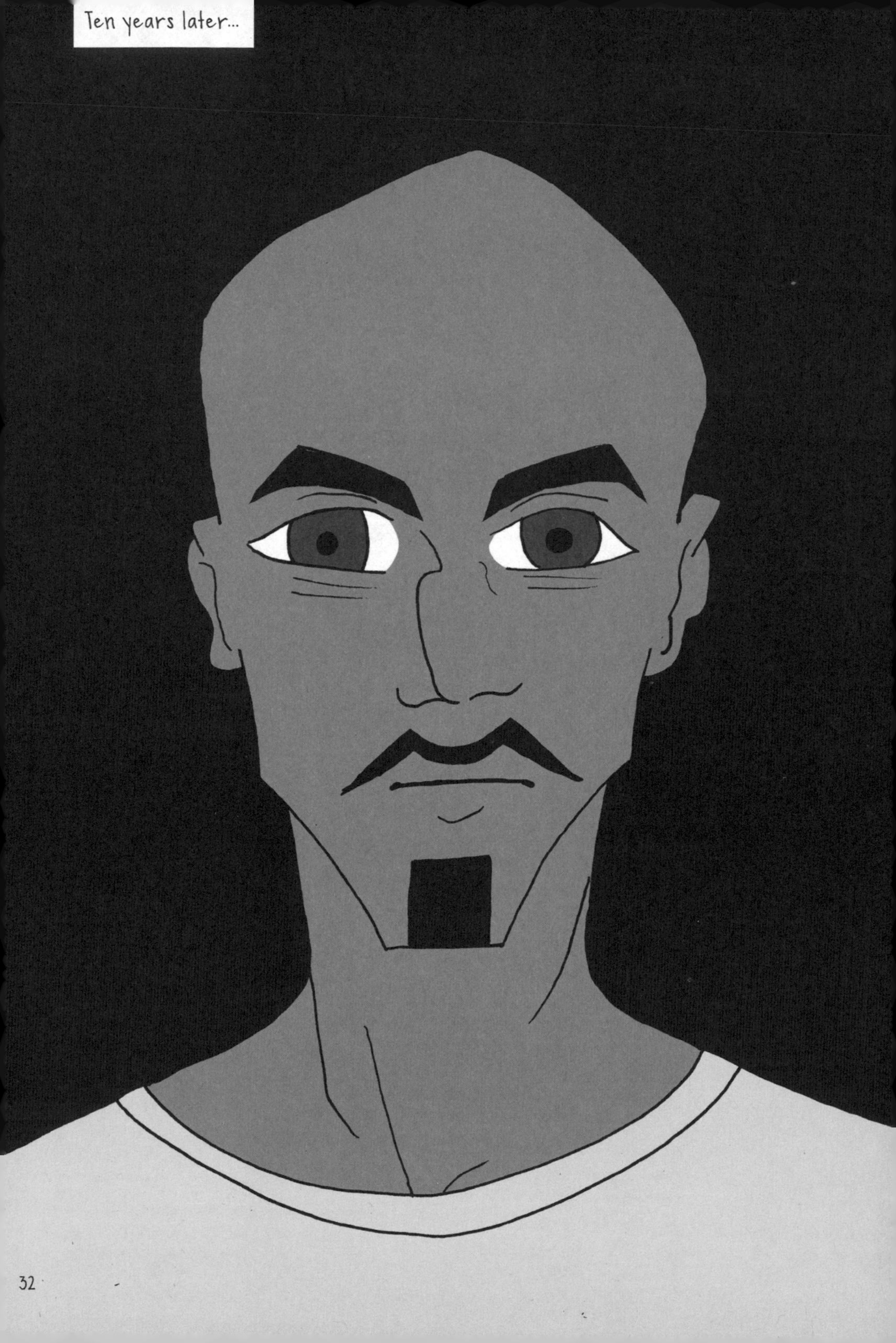
Ten years later...

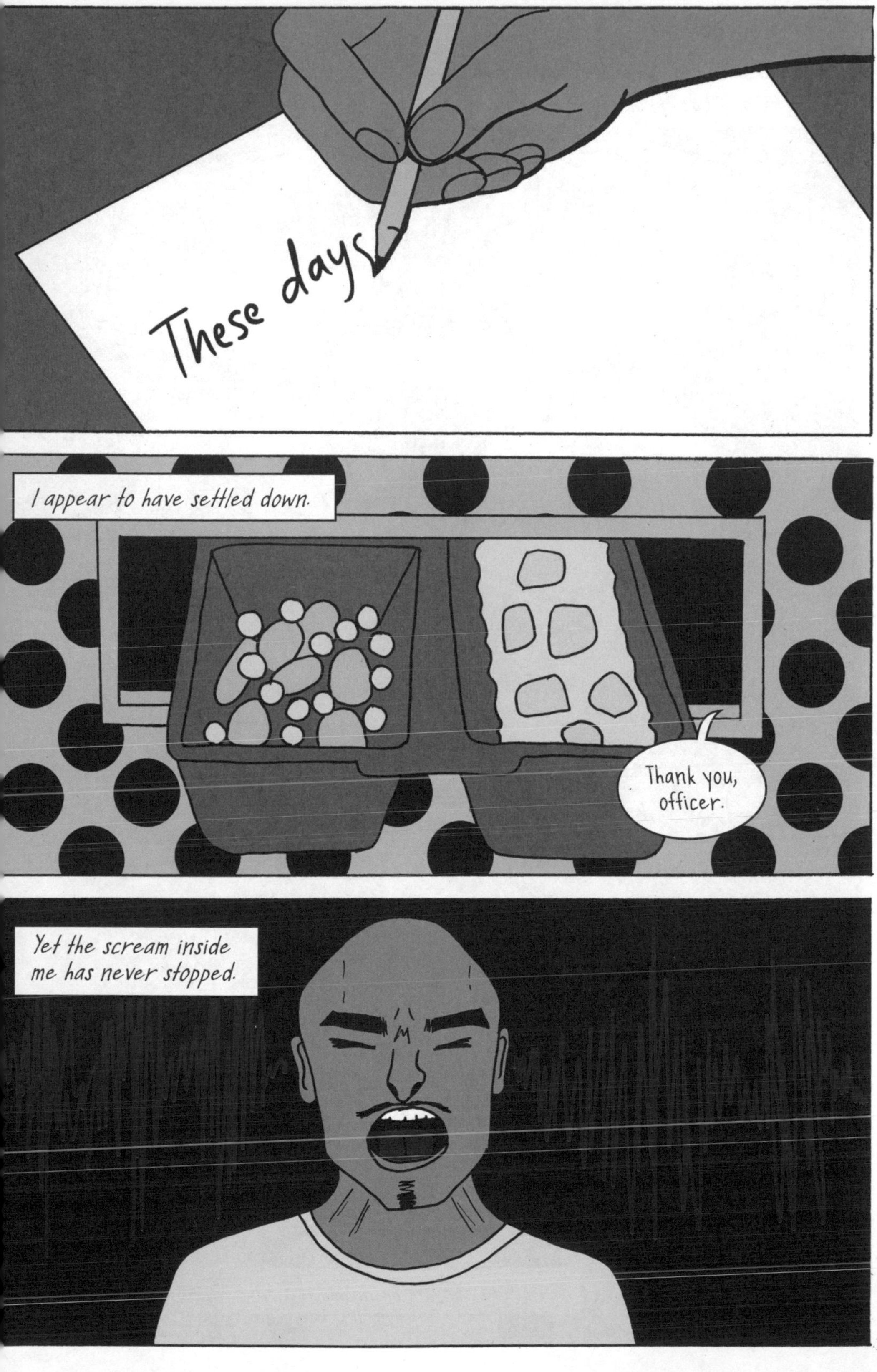
These days
I appear to have settled down.
Thank you, officer.
Yet the scream inside me has never stopped.

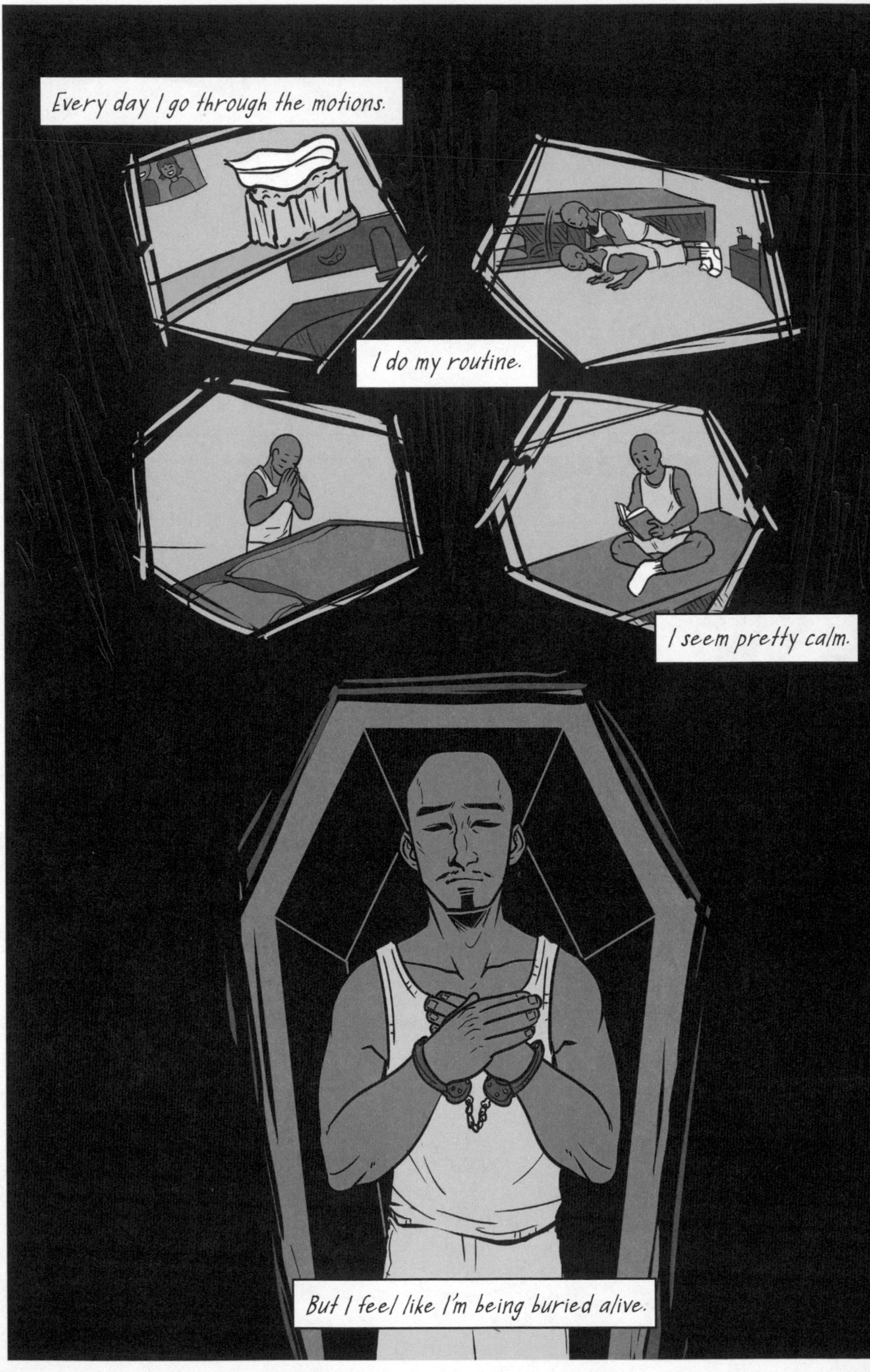
Every day I go through the motions.
I do my routine.
I seem pretty calm.
But I feel like I'm being buried alive.

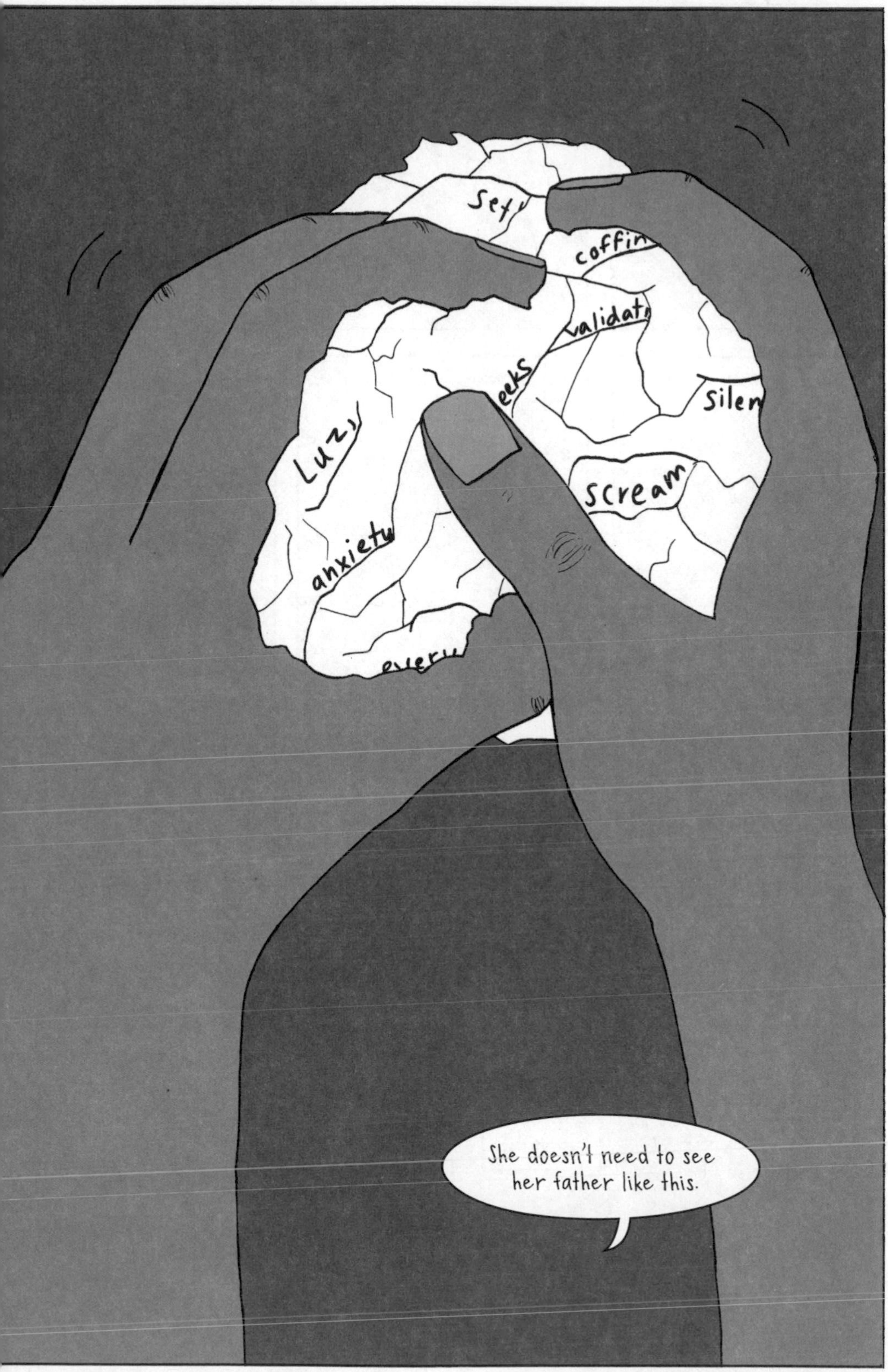
scream
She doesn't need to see her father like this.

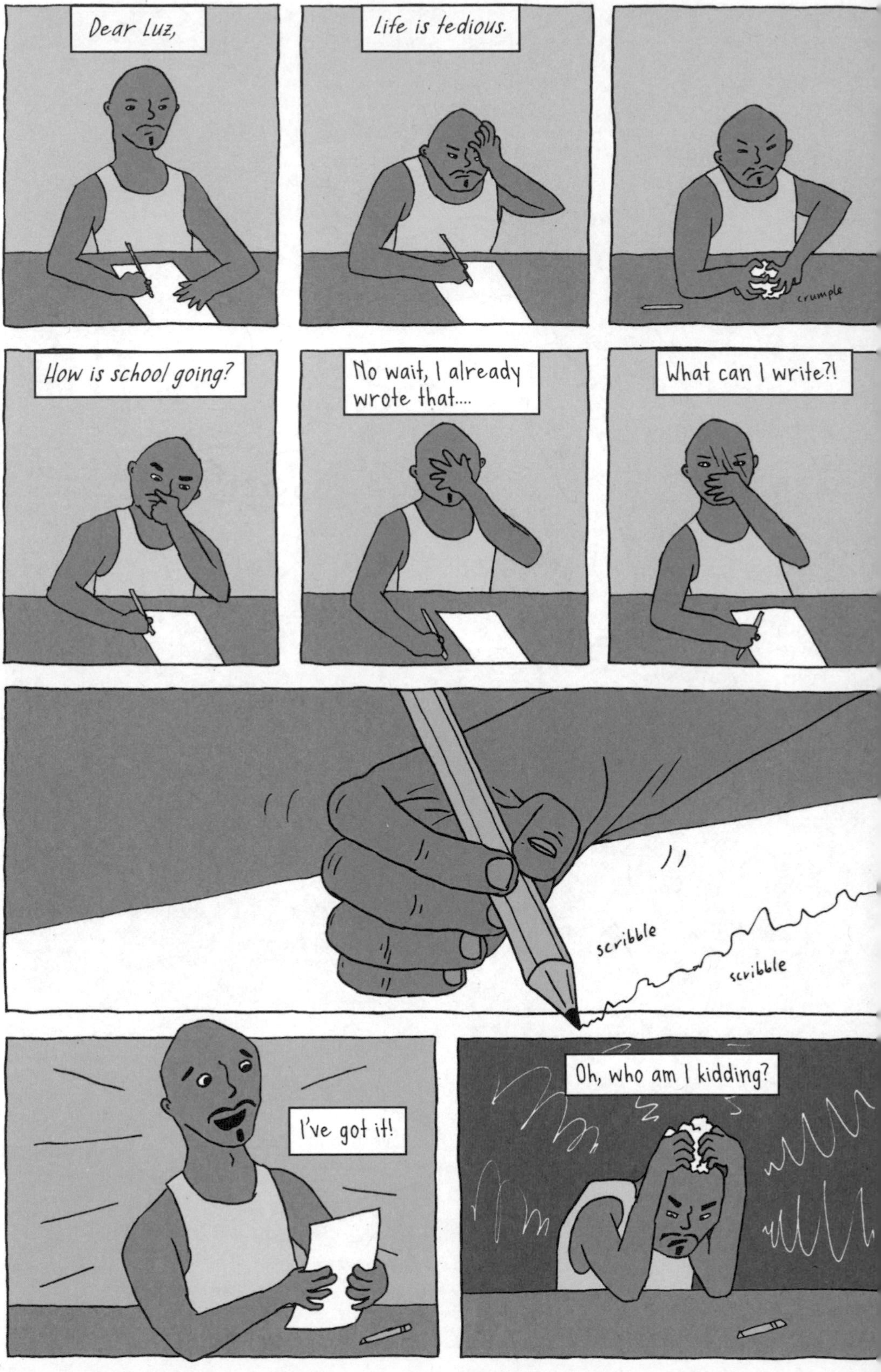

Dear Luz,
Life is tedious.
crumple
How is school going?
No wait, I already wrote that....
What can I write?!
scribble
scribble
I've got it!
Oh, who am I kidding?

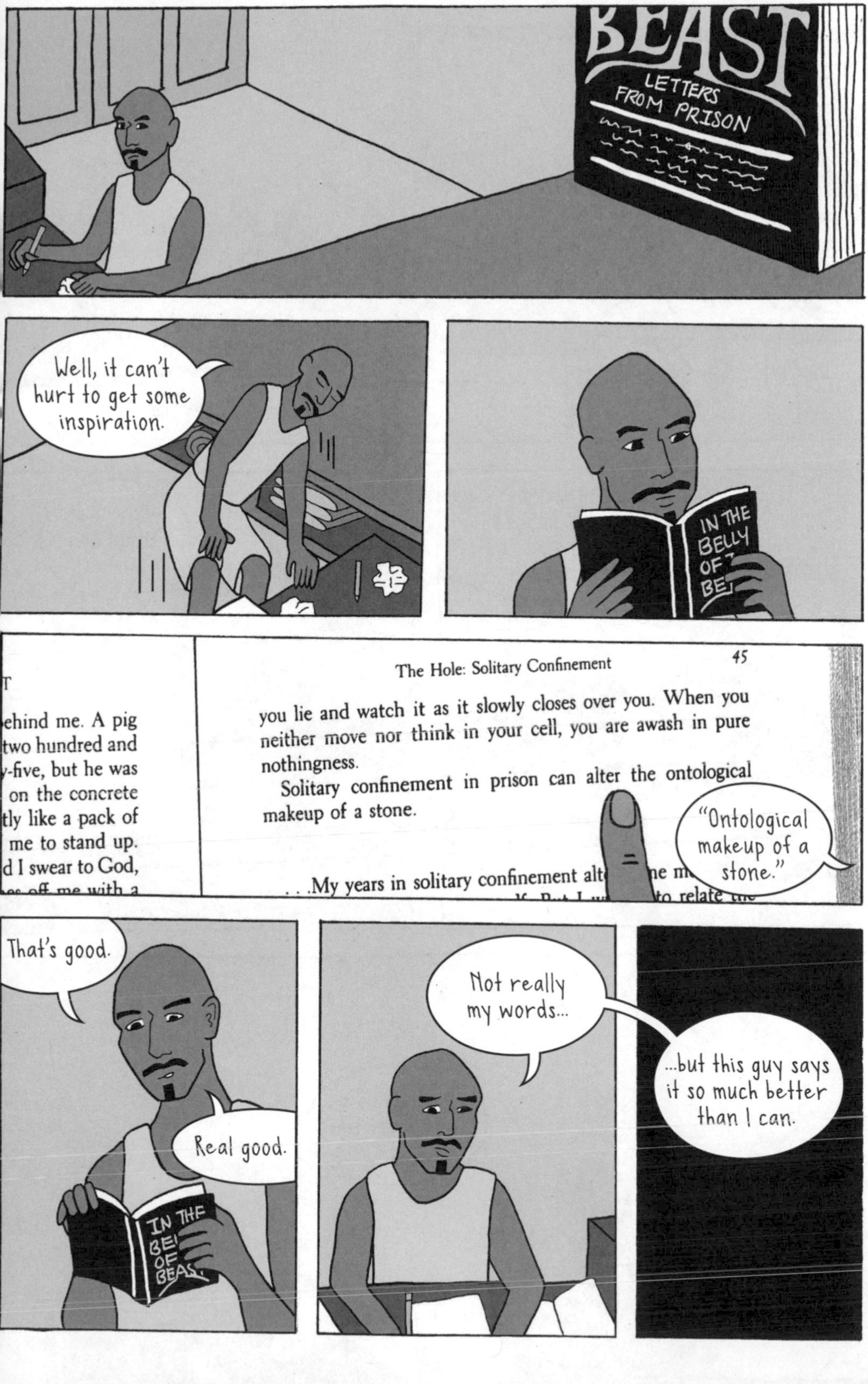
BEAST
LETTERS FROM PRISON
Well, it can't hurt to get some inspiration.
IN THE BELLY OF
ehind me. A pig
two hundred and
-five, but he was
on the concrete
tly like a pack of
me to stand up.
d I swear to God,
The Hole: Solitary Confinement 45
you lie and watch it as it slowly closes over you. When you neither move nor think in your cell, you are awash in pure nothingness.
Solitary confinement in prison can alter the ontological makeup of a stone.
. . .My years in solitary confinement alt
"Ontological makeup of a stone."
That's good.
Real good.
IN THE
OF
Not really my words...
...but this guy says it so much better than I can.

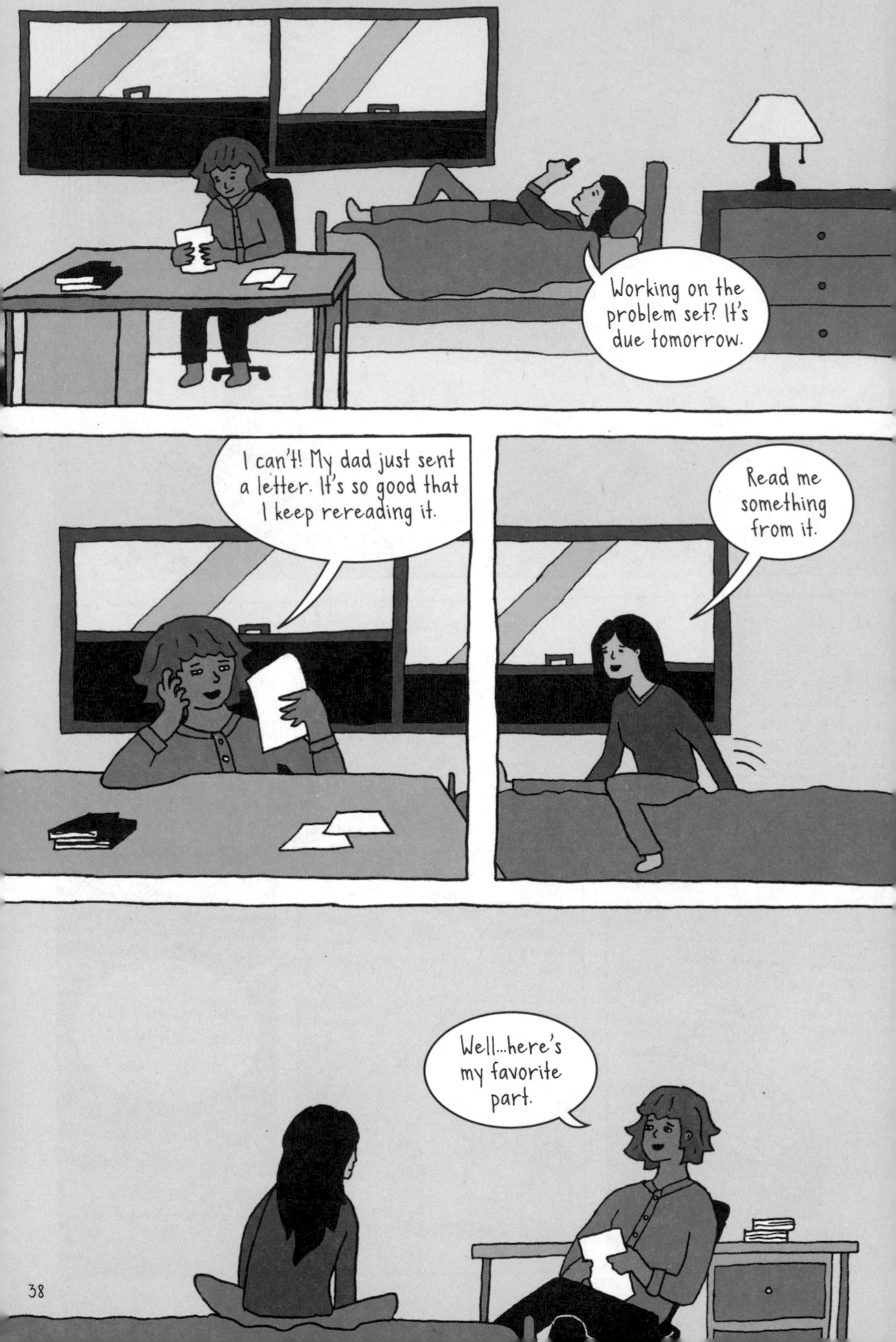
Working on the problem set? It's due tomorrow.
I can't! My dad just sent a letter. It's so good that I keep rereading it.
Read me something from it.
Well...here's my favorite part.

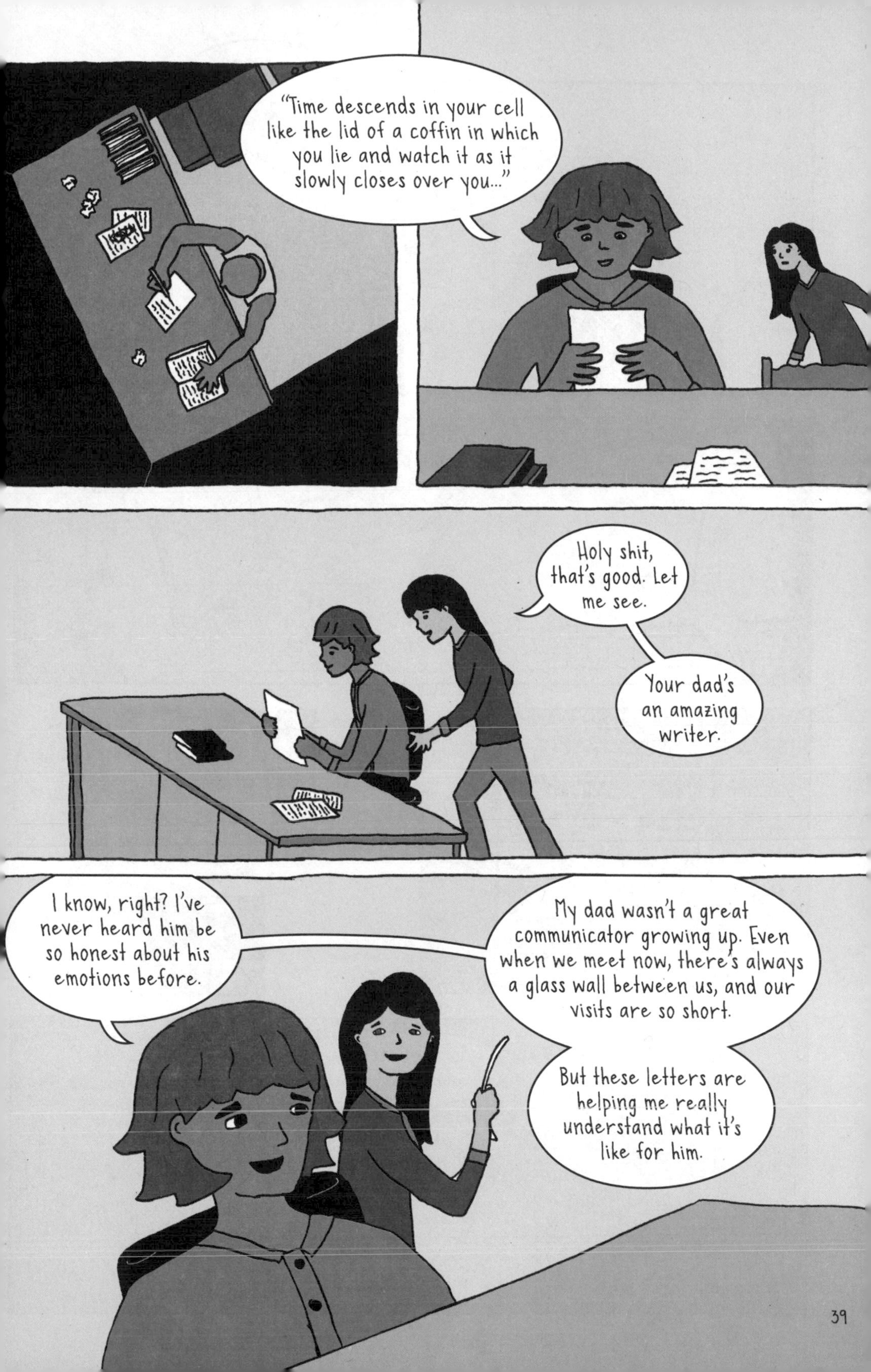
"Time descends in your cell like the lid of a coffin in which you lie and watch it as it slowly closes over you..."
Holy shit, that's good. Let me see.
Your dad's an amazing writer.
I know, right? I've never heard him be so honest about his emotions before.
My dad wasn't a great communicator growing up. Even when we meet now, there's always a glass wall between us, and our visits are so short.
But these letters are helping me really understand what it's like for him.

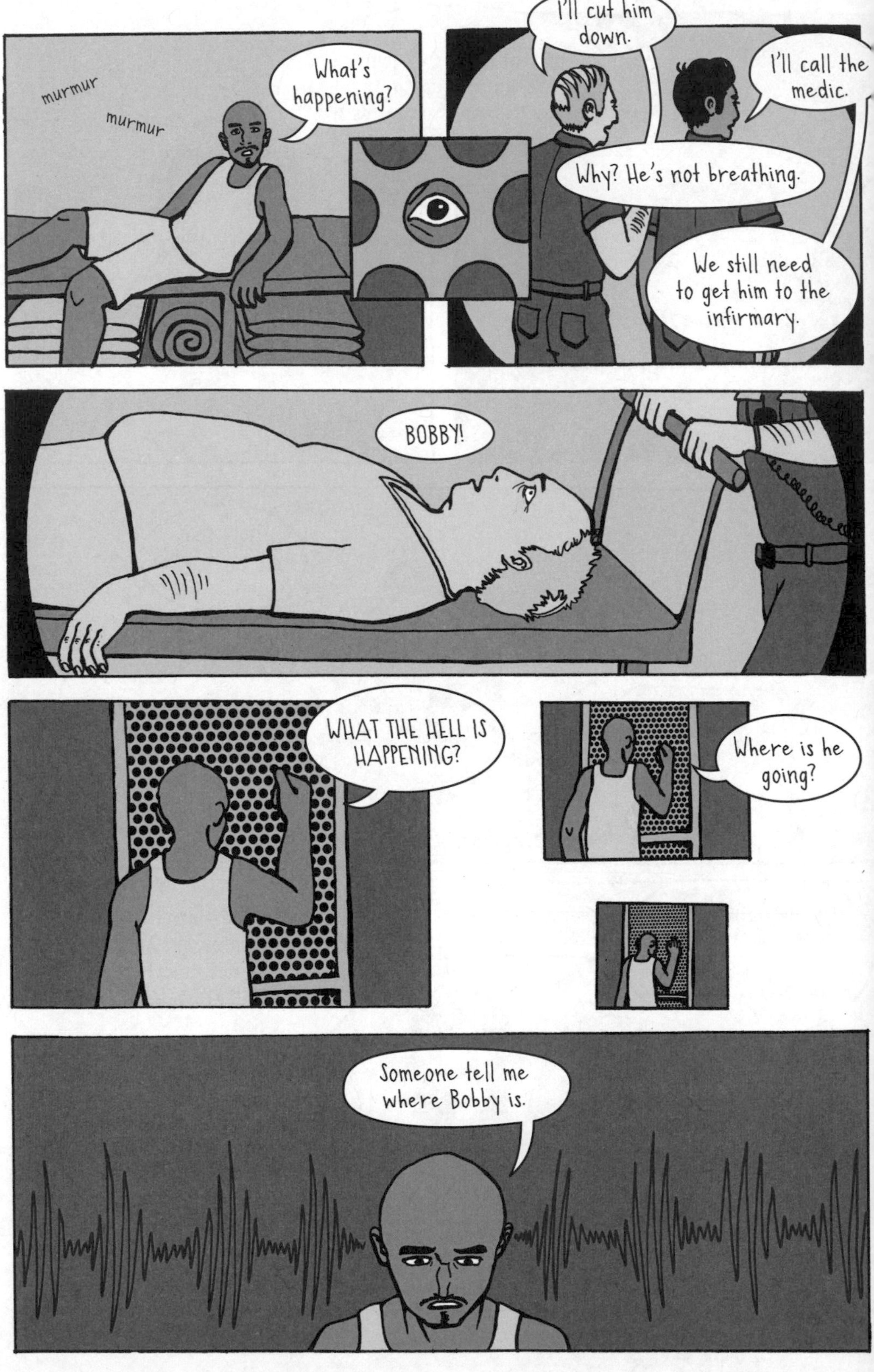
murmur
murmur
What's happening?
I'll cut him down.
I'll call the medic.
Why? He's not breathing.
We still need to get him to the infirmary.
BOBBY!
WHAT THE HELL IS HAPPENING?
Where is he going?
Someone tell me where Bobby is.

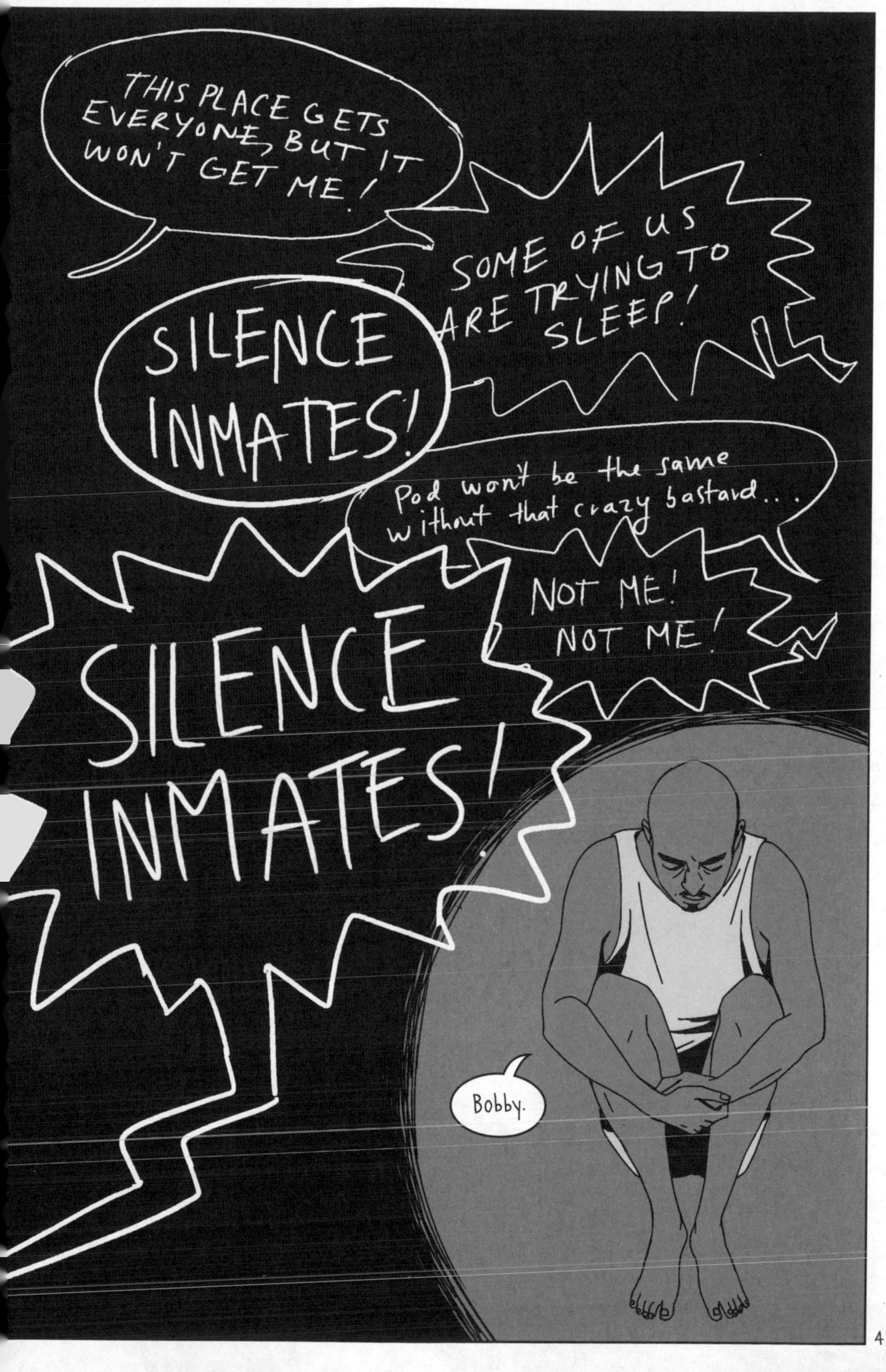
THIS PLACE GETS EVERYONE, BUT IT WON'T GET ME!
SOME OF US ARE TRYING TO SLEEP!
SILENCE INMATES!
Pod won't be the same without that crazy bastard...
NOT ME! NOT ME!
SILENCE INMATES!
Bobby.

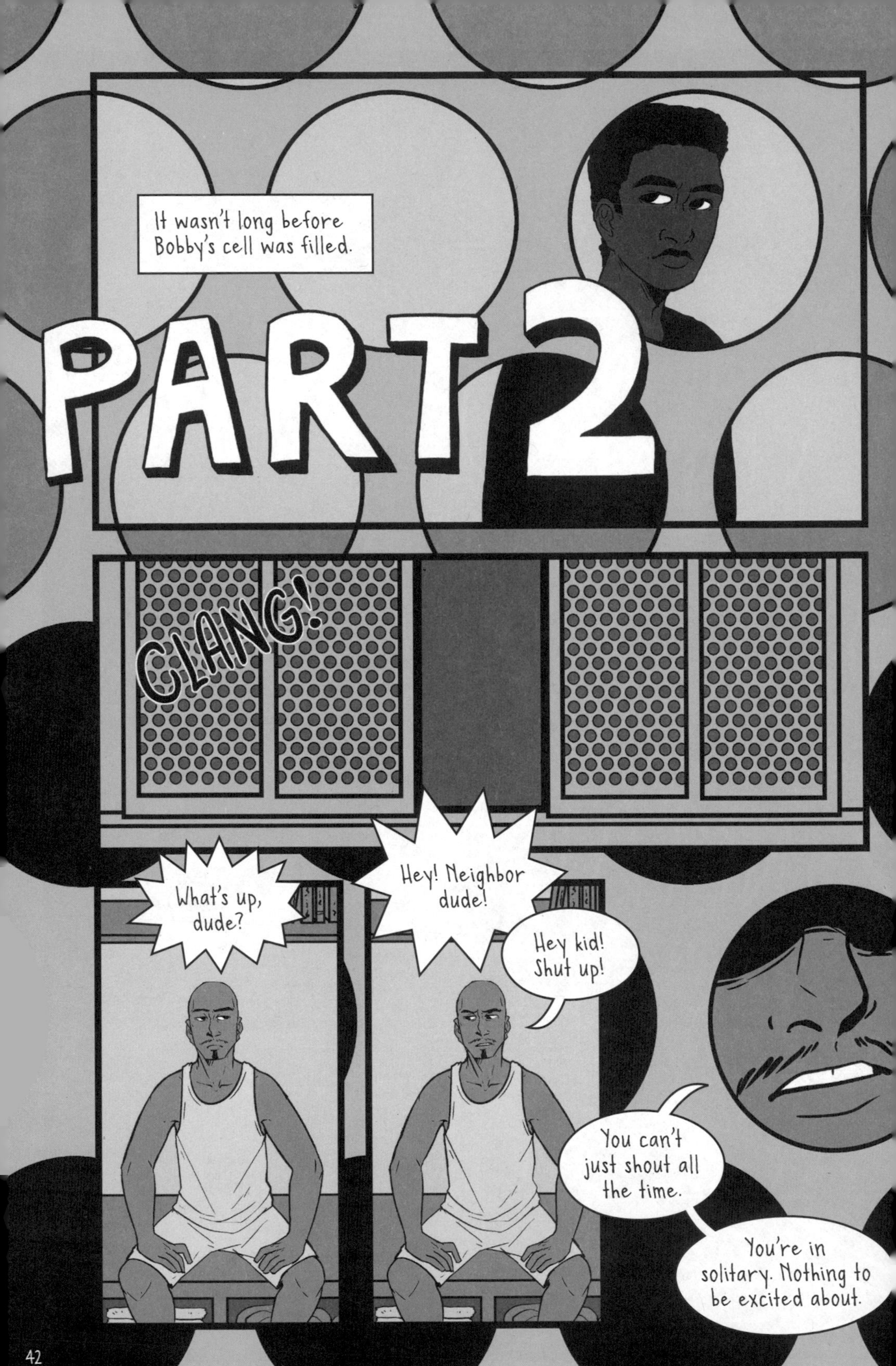

It wasn't long before Bobby's cell was filled.
PART 2
CLANG!
What's up, dude?
Hey! Neighbor dude!
Hey kid! Shut up!
You can't just shout all the time.
You're in solitary. Nothing to be excited about.

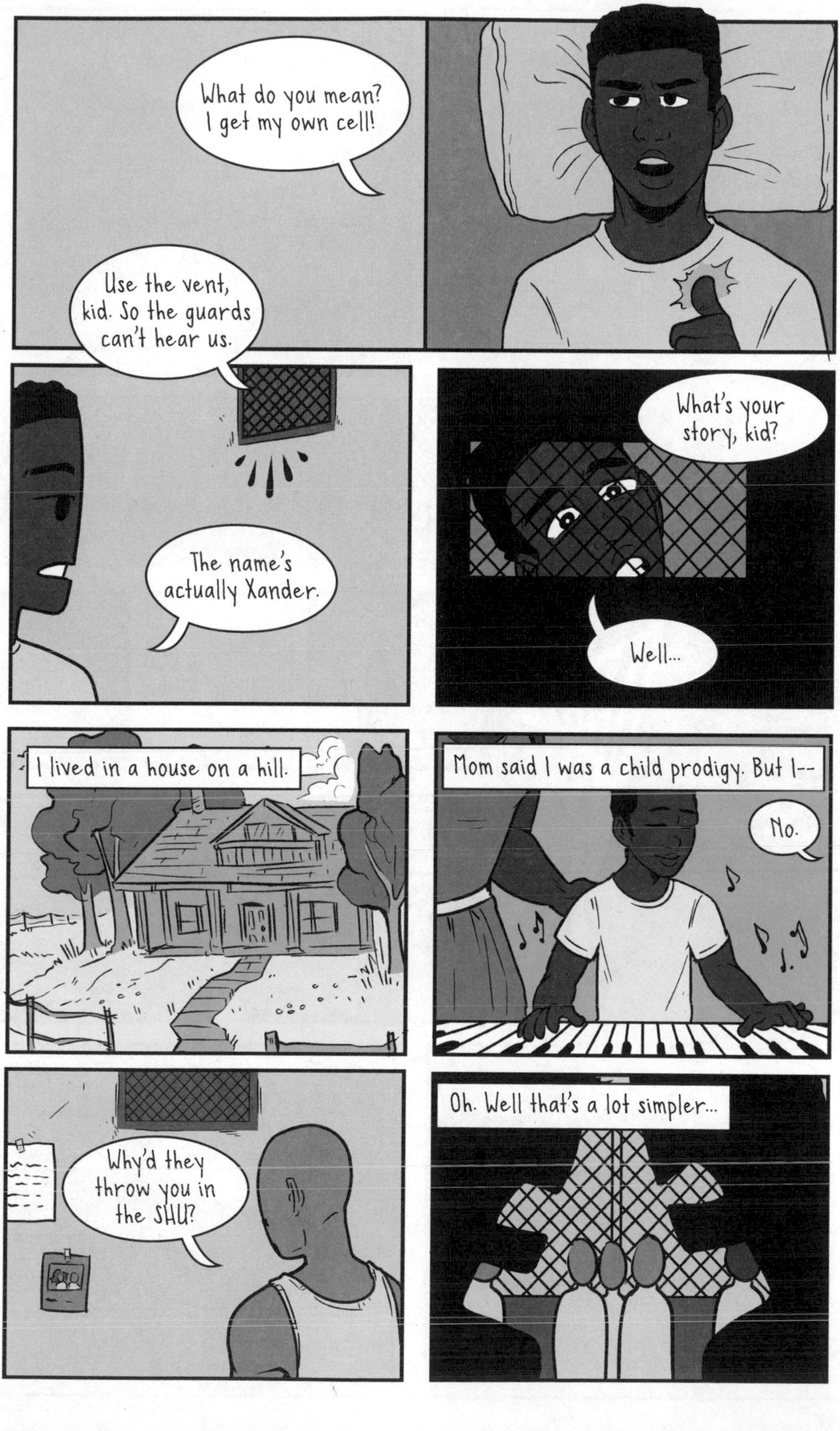

What do you mean? I get my own cell!
Use the vent, kid. So the guards can't hear us.
The name's actually Xander.
What's your story, kid?
Well...
I lived in a house on a hill.
Mom said I was a child prodigy. But I--
No.
Why'd they throw you in the SHU?
Oh. Well that's a lot simpler...

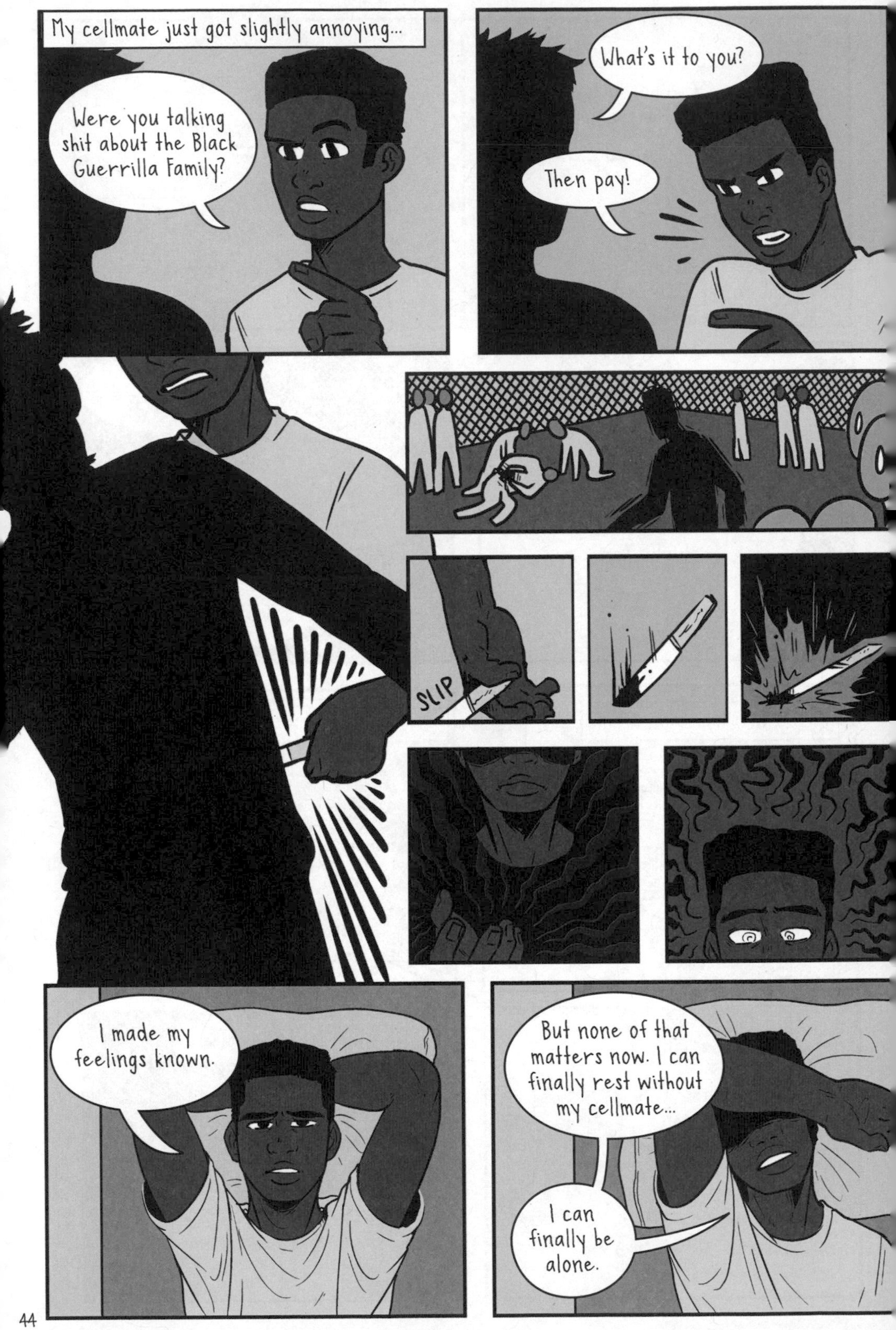
My cellmate just got slightly annoying...
Were you talking shit about the Black Guerrilla Family?
What's it to you?
Then pay!
SLIP
I made my feelings known.
But none of that matters now. I can finally rest without my cellmate...
I can finally be alone.

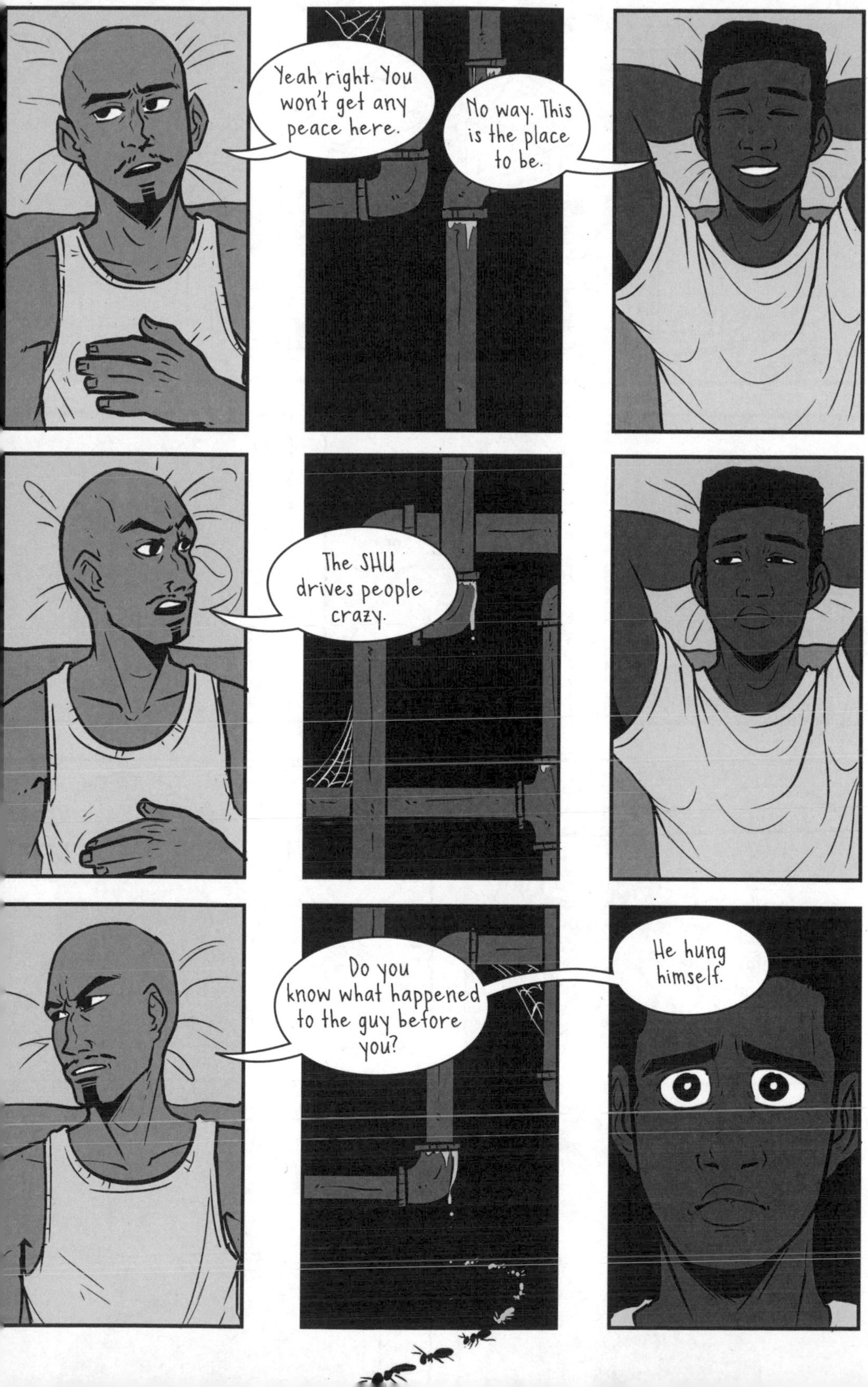

Yeah right. You won't get any peace here.
No way. This is the place to be.
The SHU drives people crazy.
Do you know what happened to the guy before you?
He hung himself.

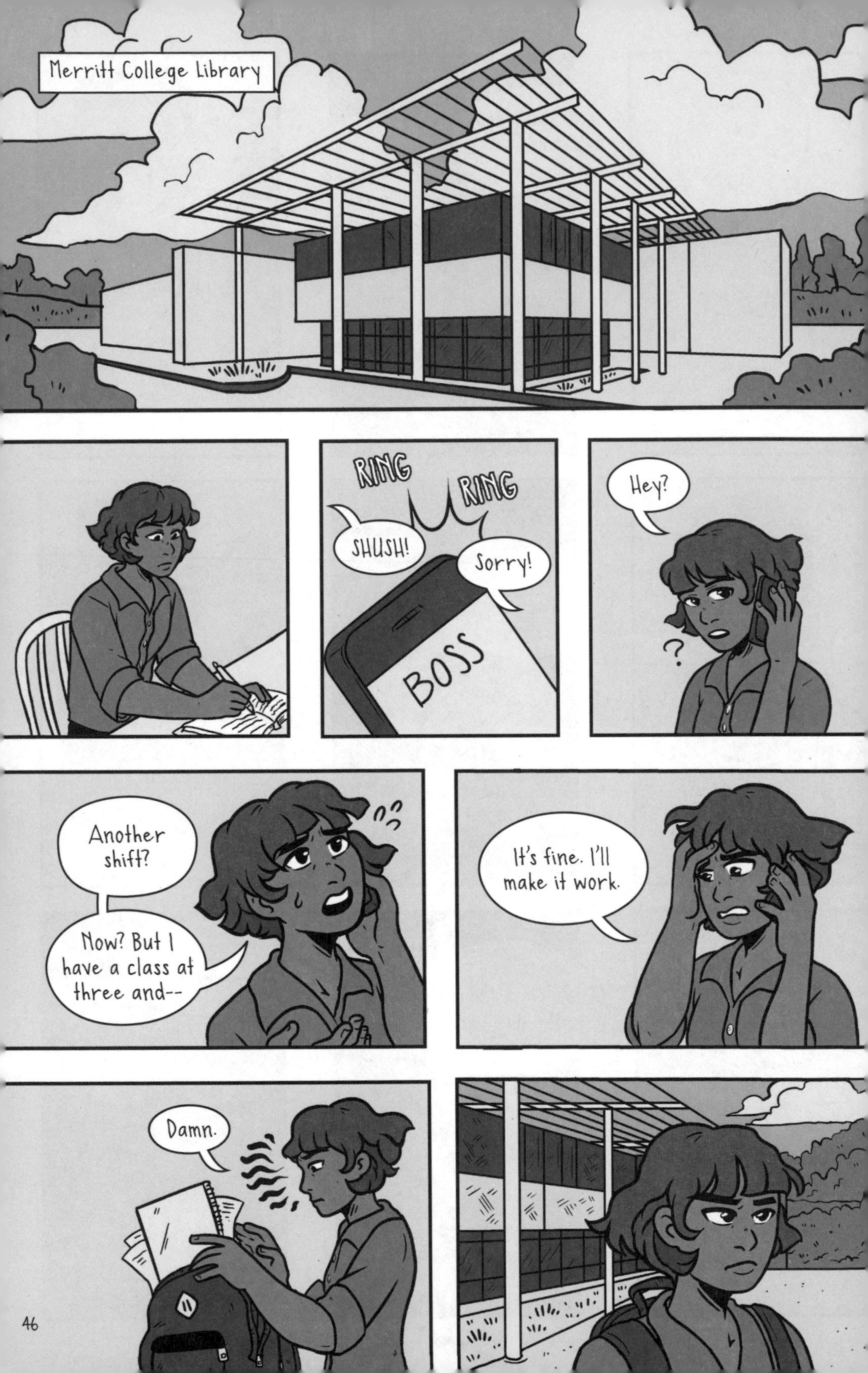
Merritt College Library
RING
RING
SHUSH!
Sorry!
BOSS
Hey?
?
Another shift?
Now? But I have a class at three and--
It's fine. I'll make it work.
Damn.

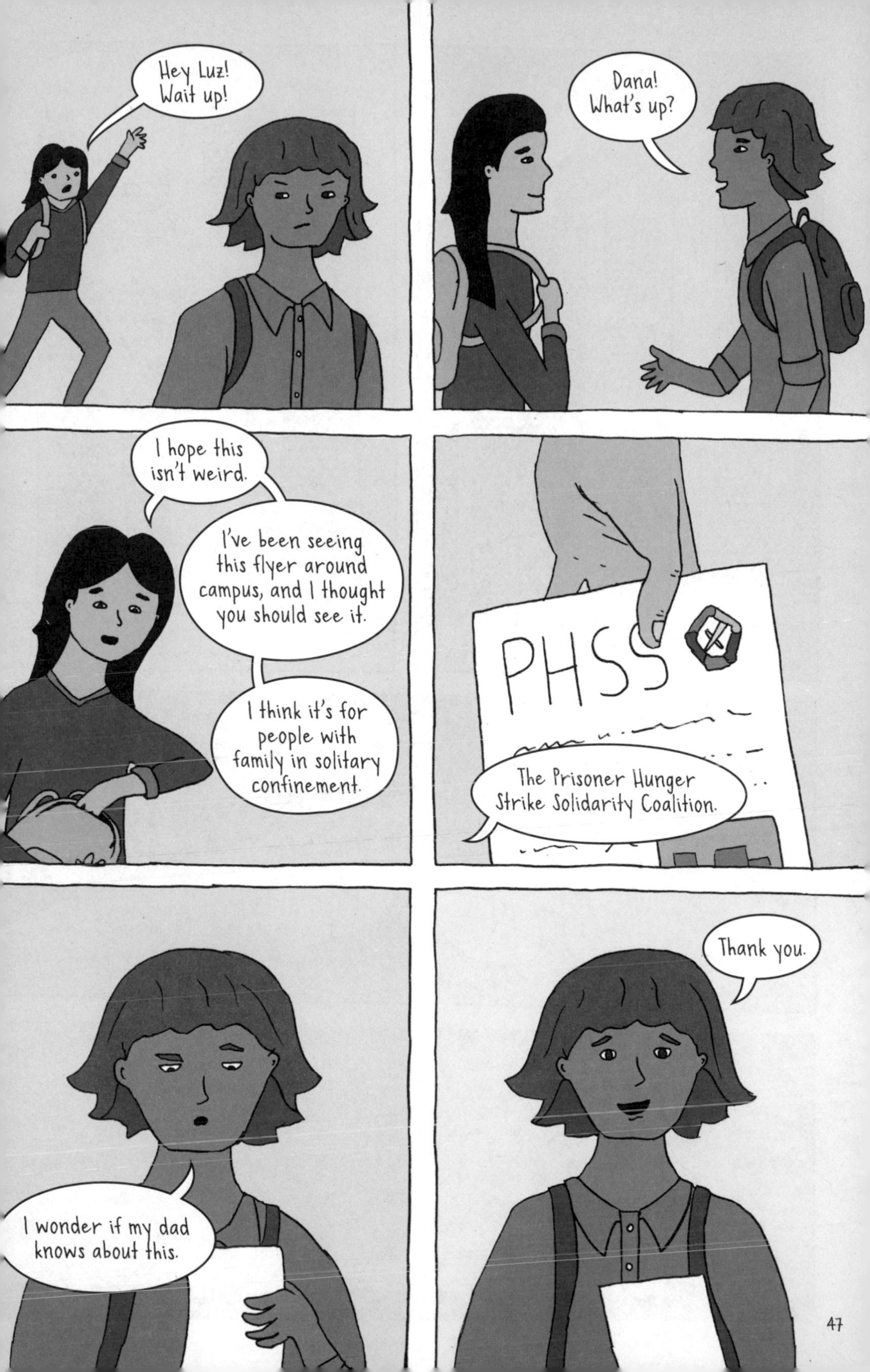
Hey Luz!
Wait up!
Dana!
What's up?
I hope this isn't weird.
I've been seeing this flyer around campus, and I thought you should see it.
I think it's for people with family in solitary confinement.
PHSS
The Prisoner Hunger Strike Solidarity Coalition.
I wonder if my dad knows about this.
Thank you.

Rodrigo! Incoming!
Why are you sending me a line? We don't talk.
It's important. Don't let the guards see.

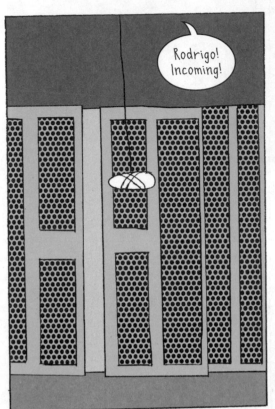

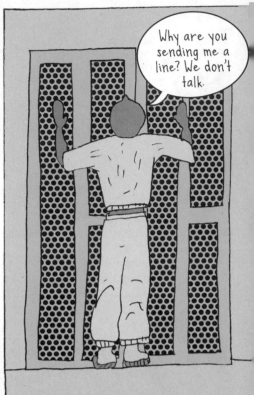

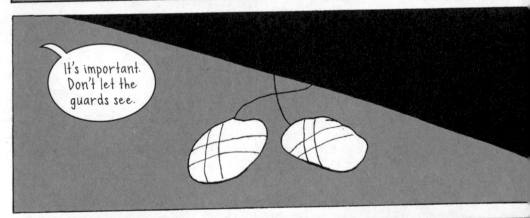

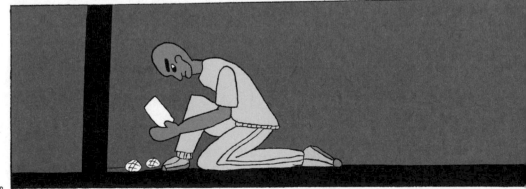

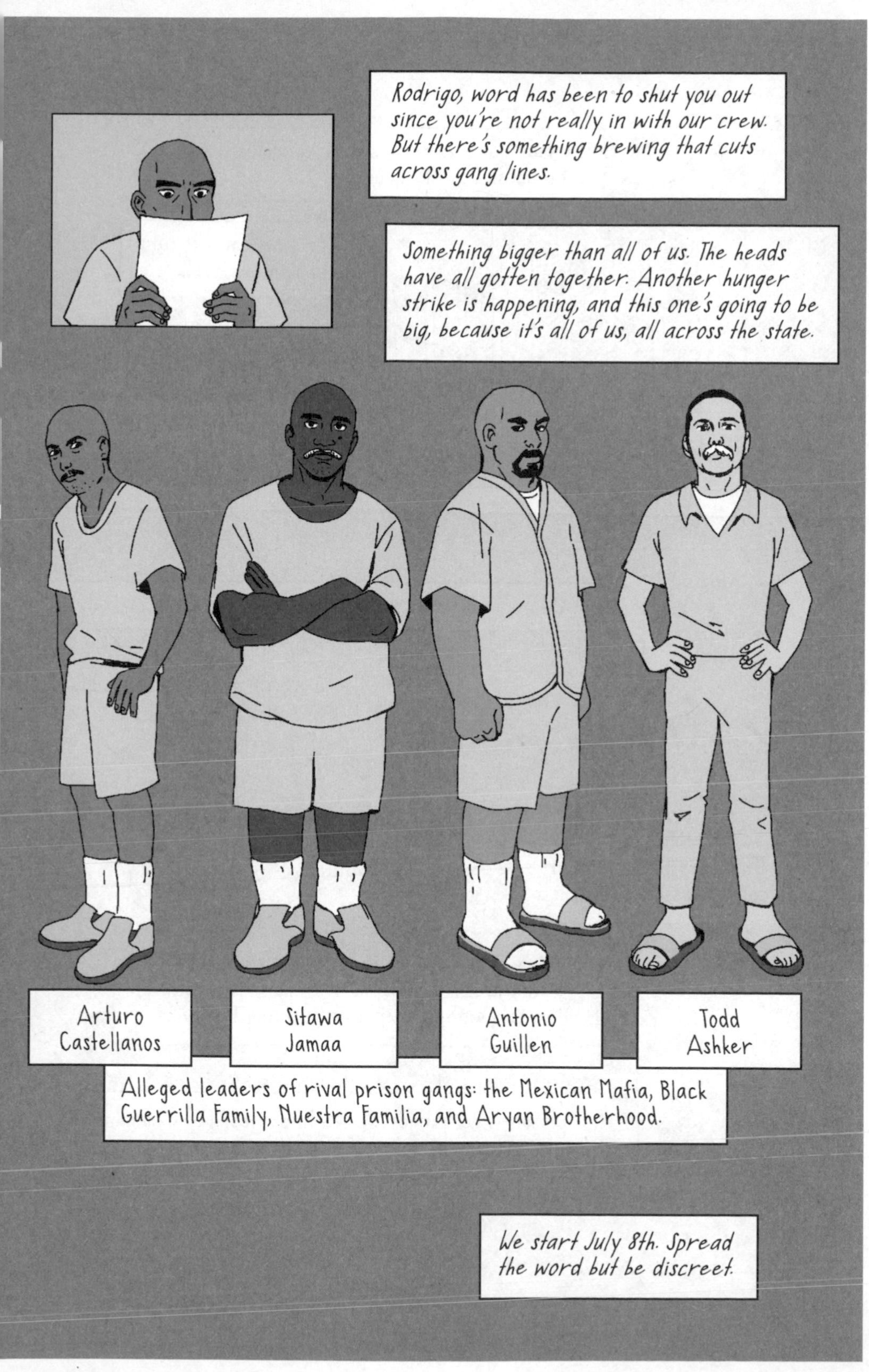
Rodrigo, word has been to shut you out since you're not really in with our crew. But there's something brewing that cuts across gang lines.
Something bigger than all of us. The heads have all gotten together. Another hunger strike is happening, and this one's going to be big, because it's all of us, all across the state.
Arturo Castellanos
Sitawa Jamaa
Antonio Guillen
Todd Ashker
Alleged leaders of rival prison gangs: the Mexican Mafia, Black Guerrilla Family, Nuestra Familia, and Aryan Brotherhood.
We start July 8th. Spread the word but be discreet.

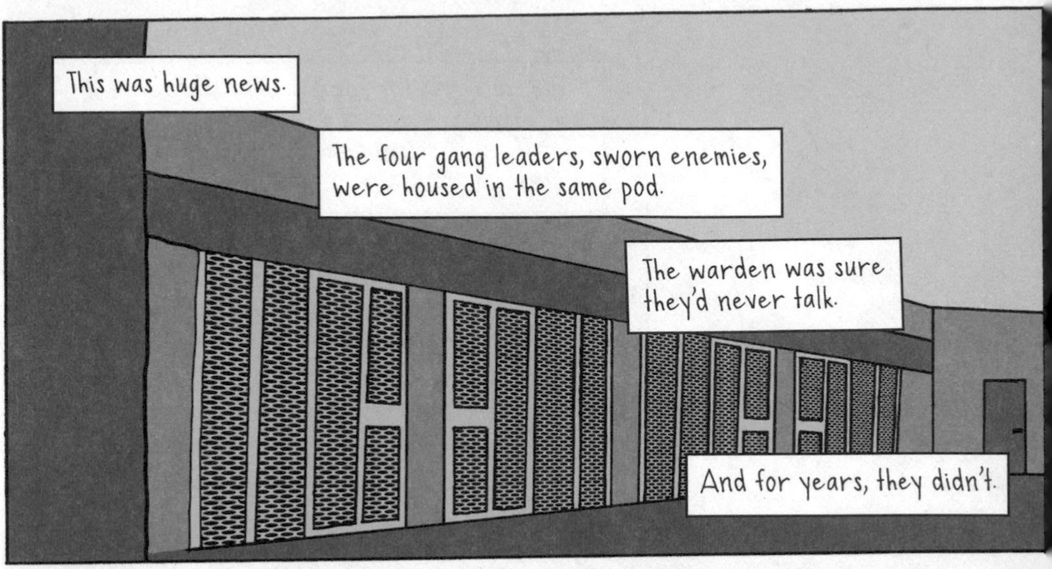
This was huge news.
The four gang leaders, sworn enemies, were housed in the same pod.
The warden was sure they'd never talk.
And for years, they didn't.

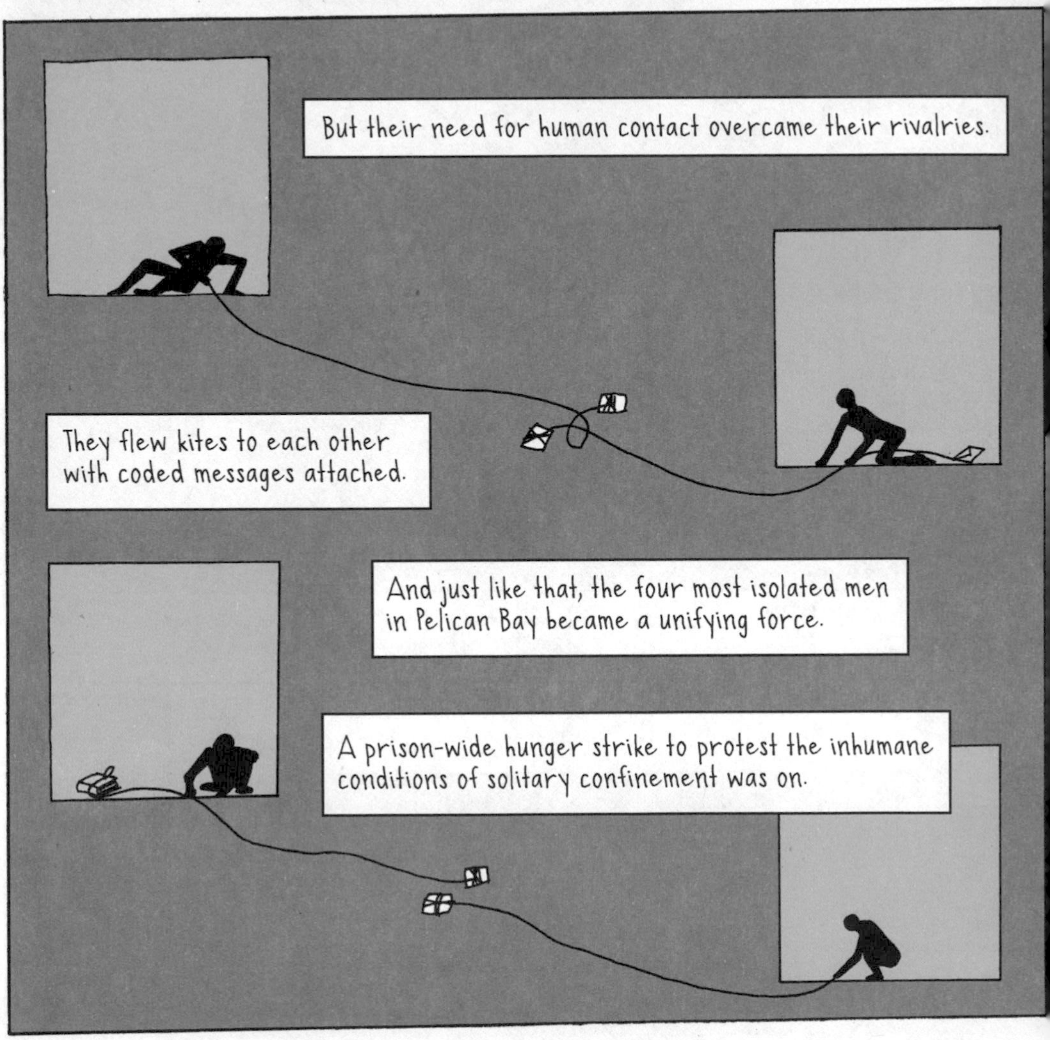
But their need for human contact overcame their rivalries.
They flew kites to each other with coded messages attached.
And just like that, the four most isolated men in Pelican Bay became a unifying force.
A prison-wide hunger strike to protest the inhumane conditions of solitary confinement was on.

Whoa.
A hunger strike?
"All races"? Shit. That's a big fucking deal!
Hey Xander.
Yeah?
I've got something to tell you.
Something big!

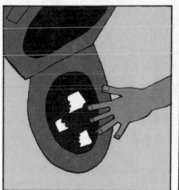

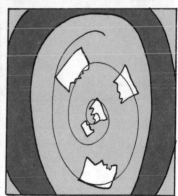

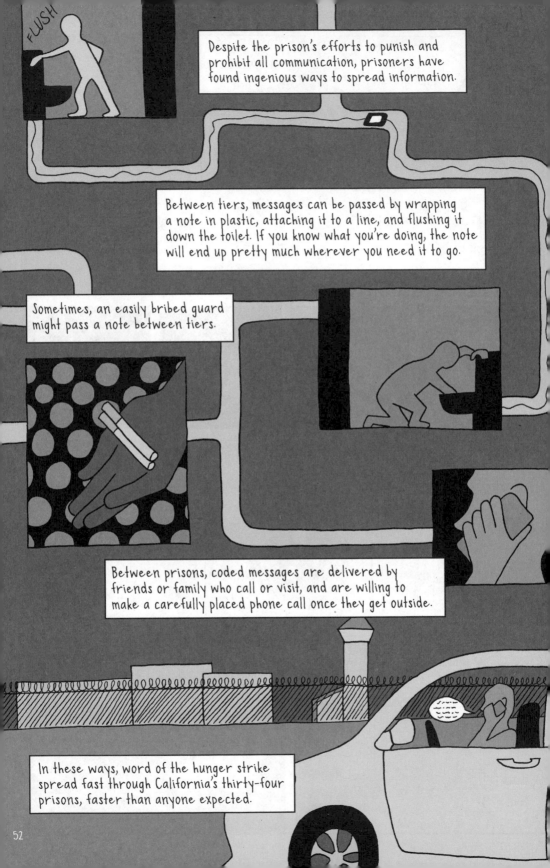

Despite the prison's efforts to punish and prohibit all communication, prisoners have found ingenious ways to spread information.

Between tiers, messages can be passed by wrapping a note in plastic, attaching it to a line, and flushing it down the toilet. If you know what you're doing, the note will end up pretty much wherever you need it to go.

Sometimes, an easily bribed guard might pass a note between tiers.

Between prisons, coded messages are delivered by friends or family who call or visit, and are willing to make a carefully placed phone call once they get outside.

In these ways, word of the hunger strike spread fast through California's thirty-four prisons, faster than anyone expected.

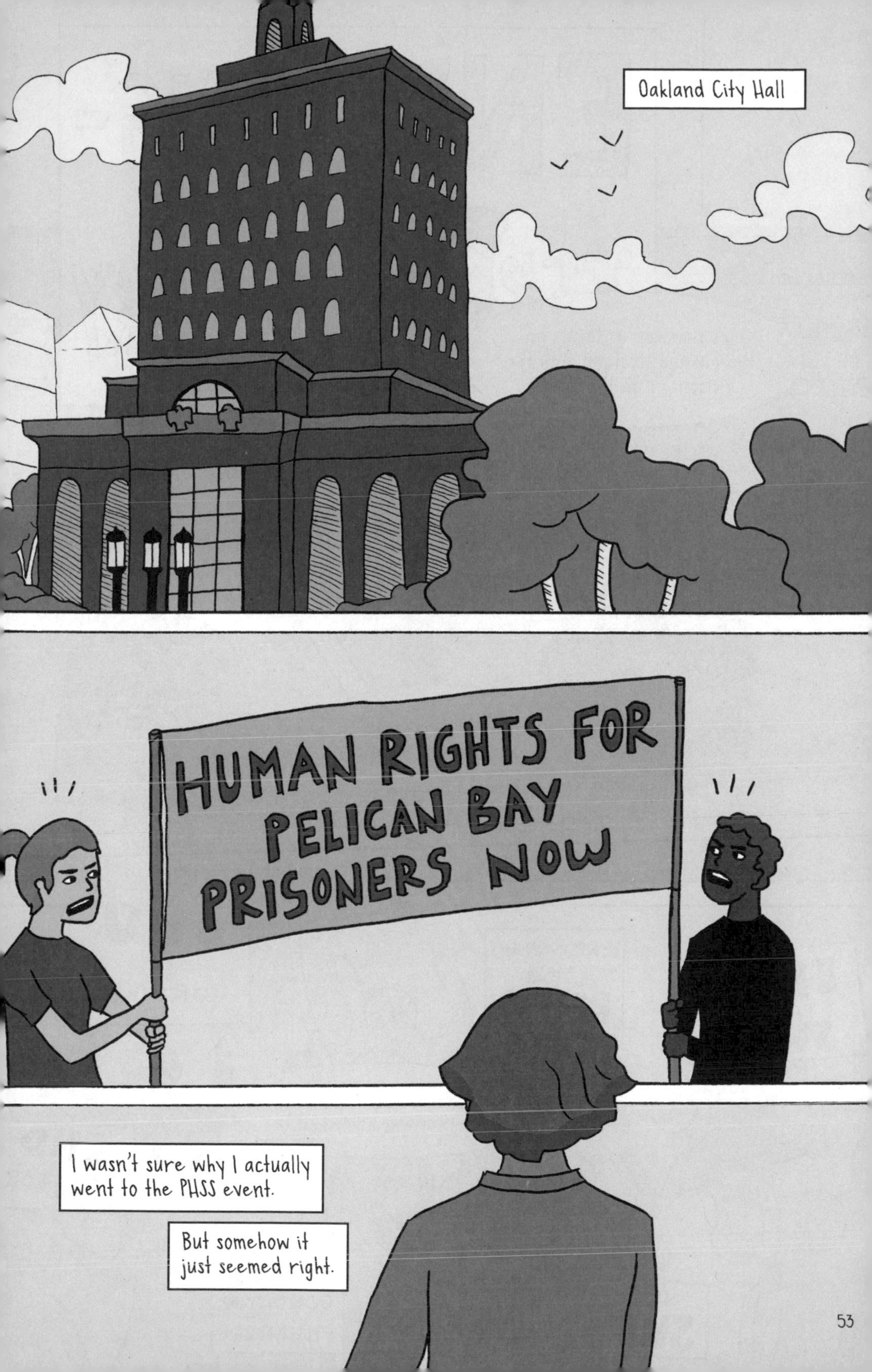
Oakland City Hall
HUMAN RIGHTS FOR PELICAN BAY PRISONERS NOW
I wasn't sure why I actually went to the PHSS event.
But somehow it just seemed right.

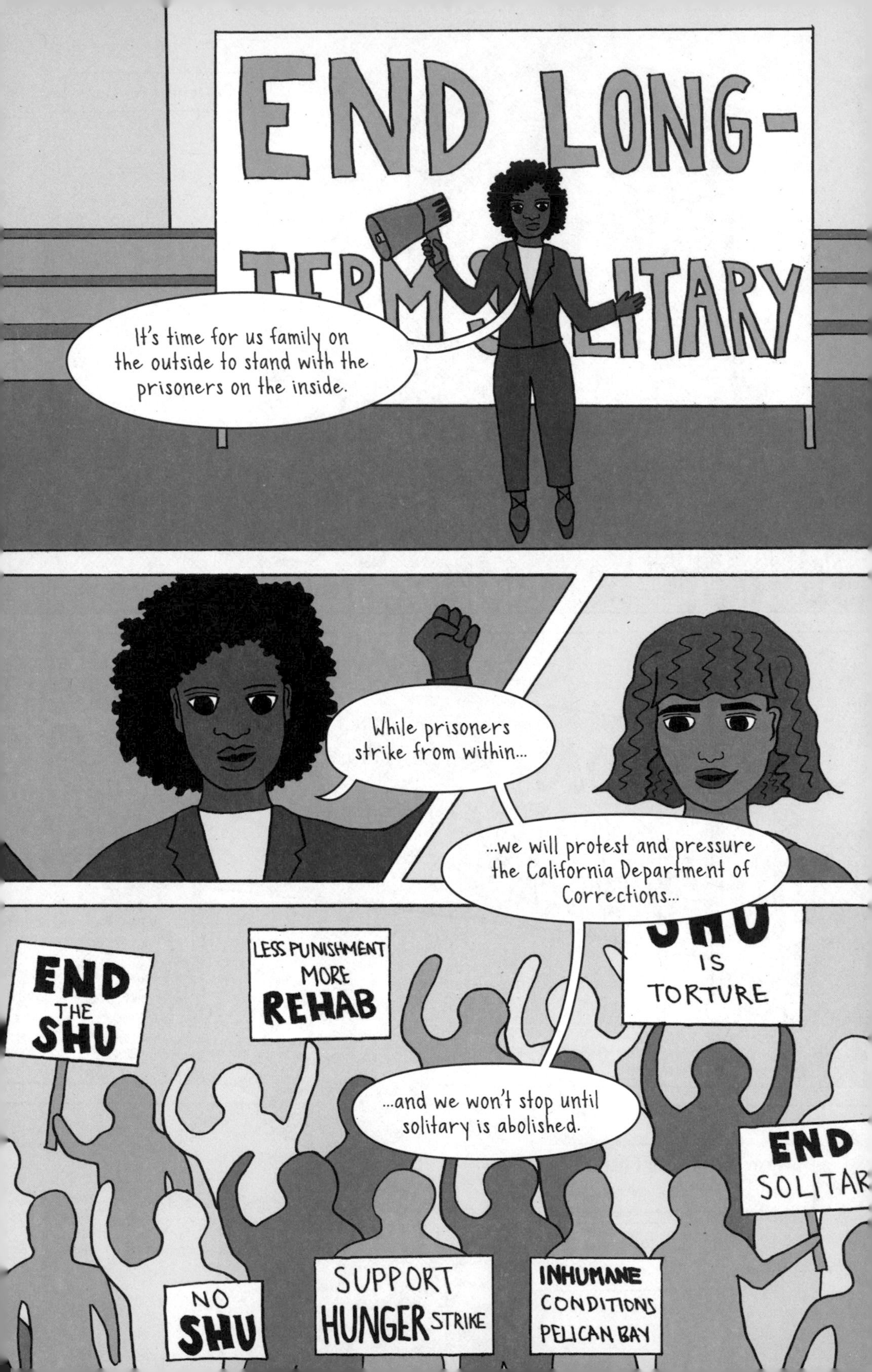
END LONG-TERM SOLITARY
It's time for us family on the outside to stand with the prisoners on the inside.
While prisoners strike from within...
...we will protest and pressure the California Department of Corrections...
END THE SHU
LESS PUNISHMENT MORE REHAB
IS TORTURE
...and we won't stop until solitary is abolished.
END SOLITAR
NO SHU
SUPPORT HUNGER STRIKE
INHUMANE CONDITIONS PELICAN BAY

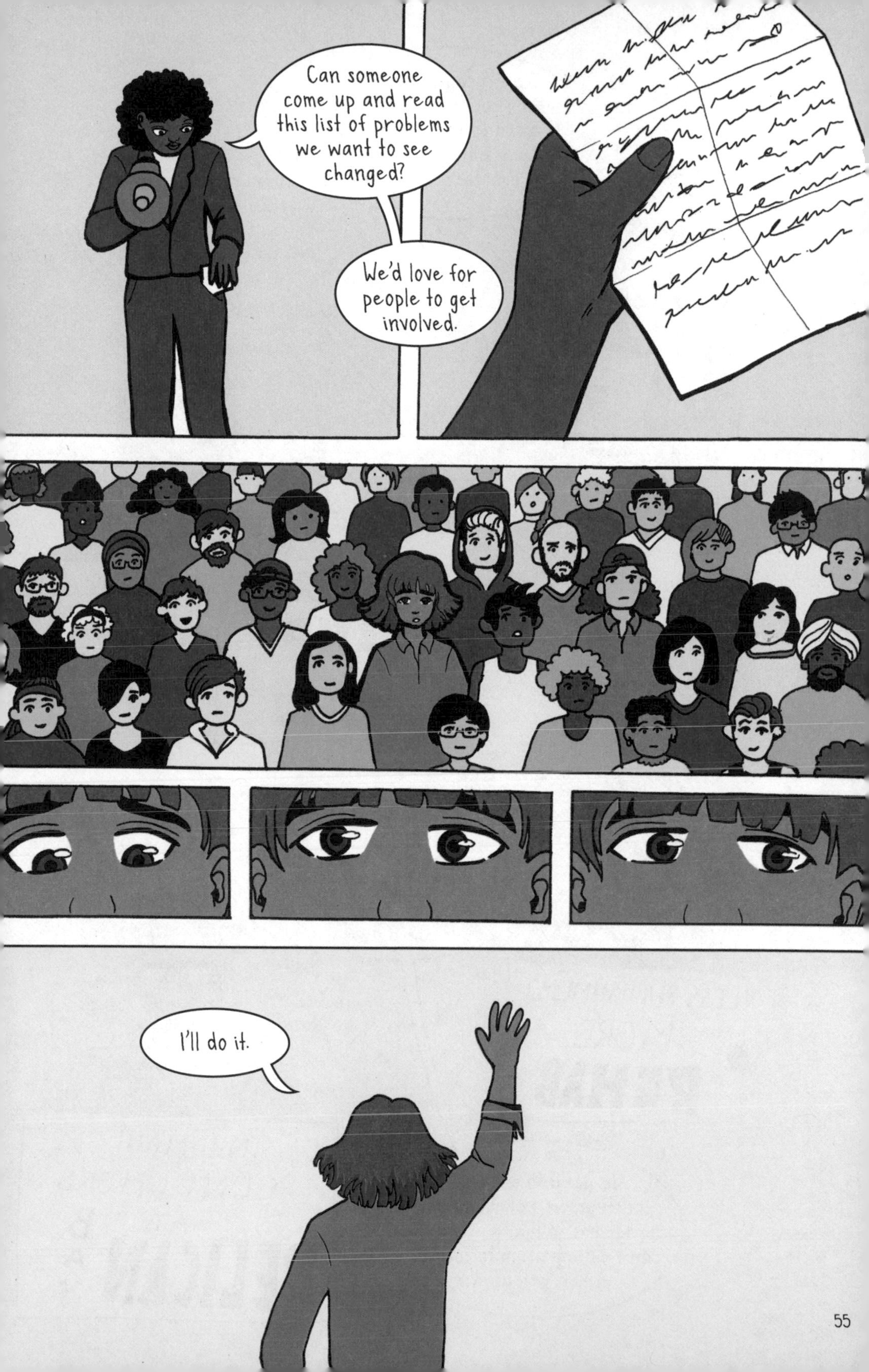

Can someone come up and read this list of problems we want to see changed?
We'd love for people to get involved.
I'll do it.

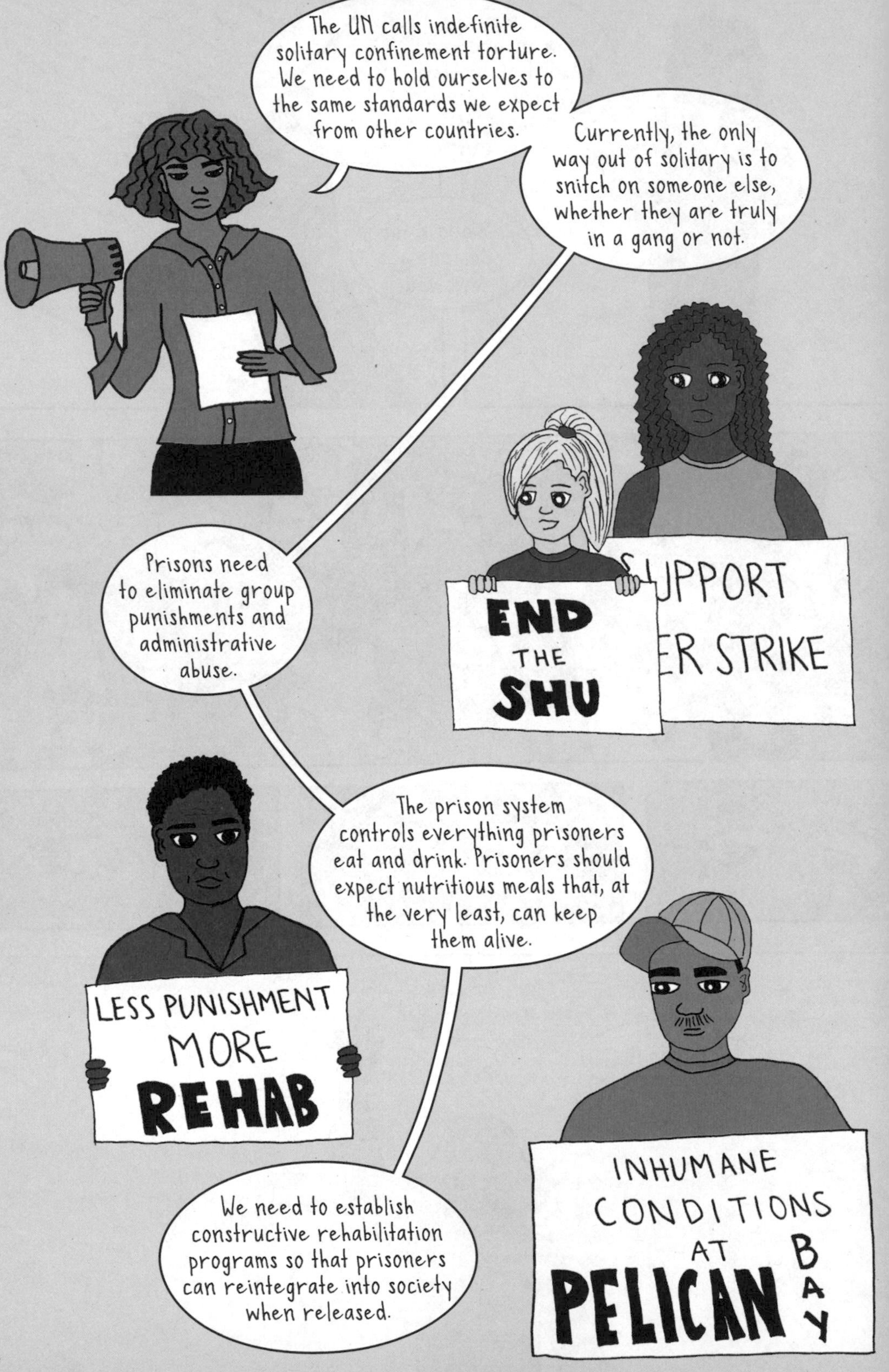
The UN calls indefinite solitary confinement torture. We need to hold ourselves to the same standards we expect from other countries.
Currently, the only way out of solitary is to snitch on someone else, whether they are truly in a gang or not.
END THE SHU
SUPPORT
ER STRIKE
Prisons need to eliminate group punishments and administrative abuse.
The prison system controls everything prisoners eat and drink. Prisoners should expect nutritious meals that, at the very least, can keep them alive.
LESS PUNISHMENT MORE REHAB
We need to establish constructive rehabilitation programs so that prisoners can reintegrate into society when released.
INHUMANE CONDITIONS AT PELICAN BAY

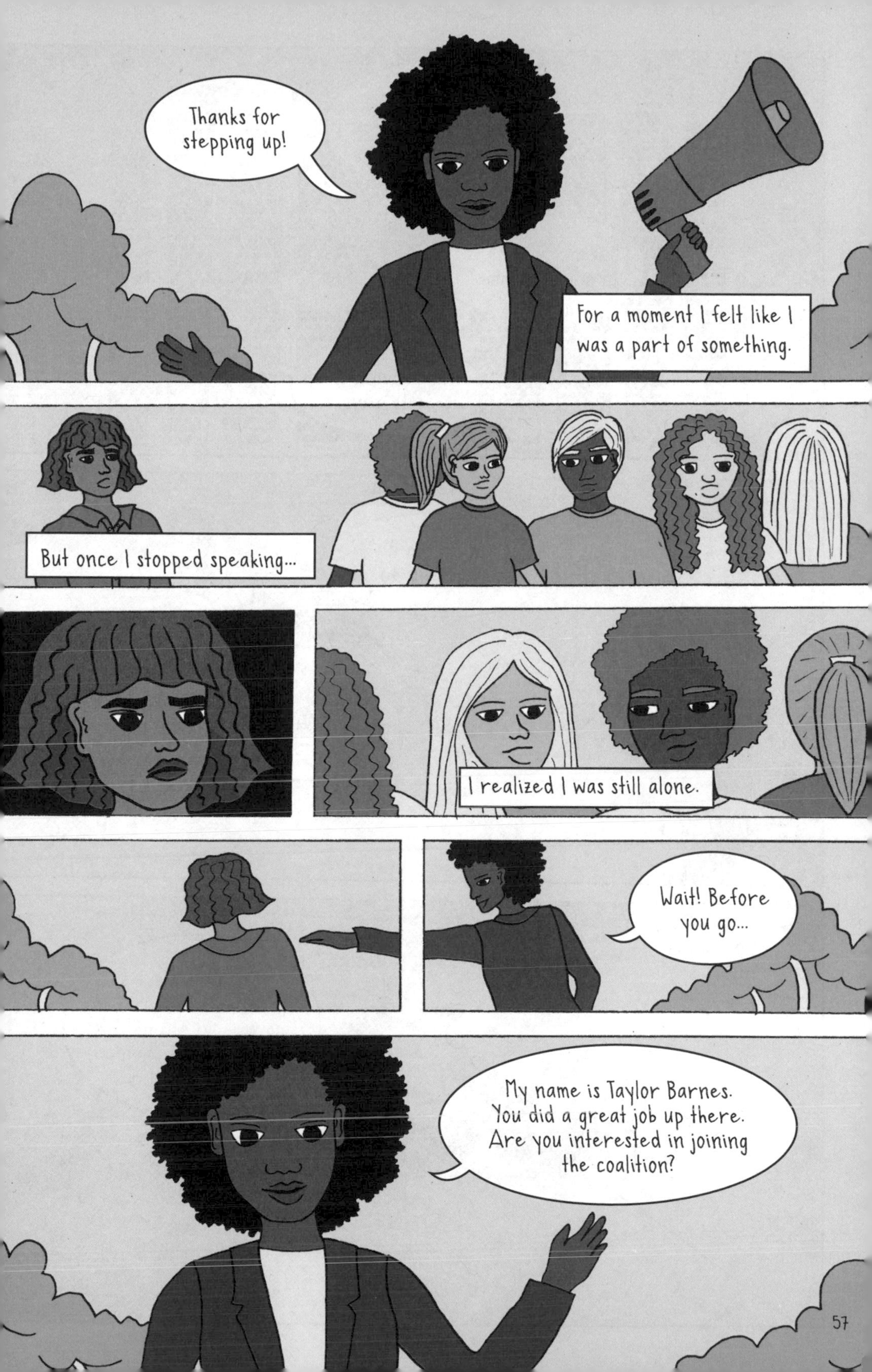
Thanks for stepping up!
For a moment I felt like I was a part of something.
But once I stopped speaking...
I realized I was still alone.
Wait! Before you go...
My name is Taylor Barnes. You did a great job up there. Are you interested in joining the coalition?

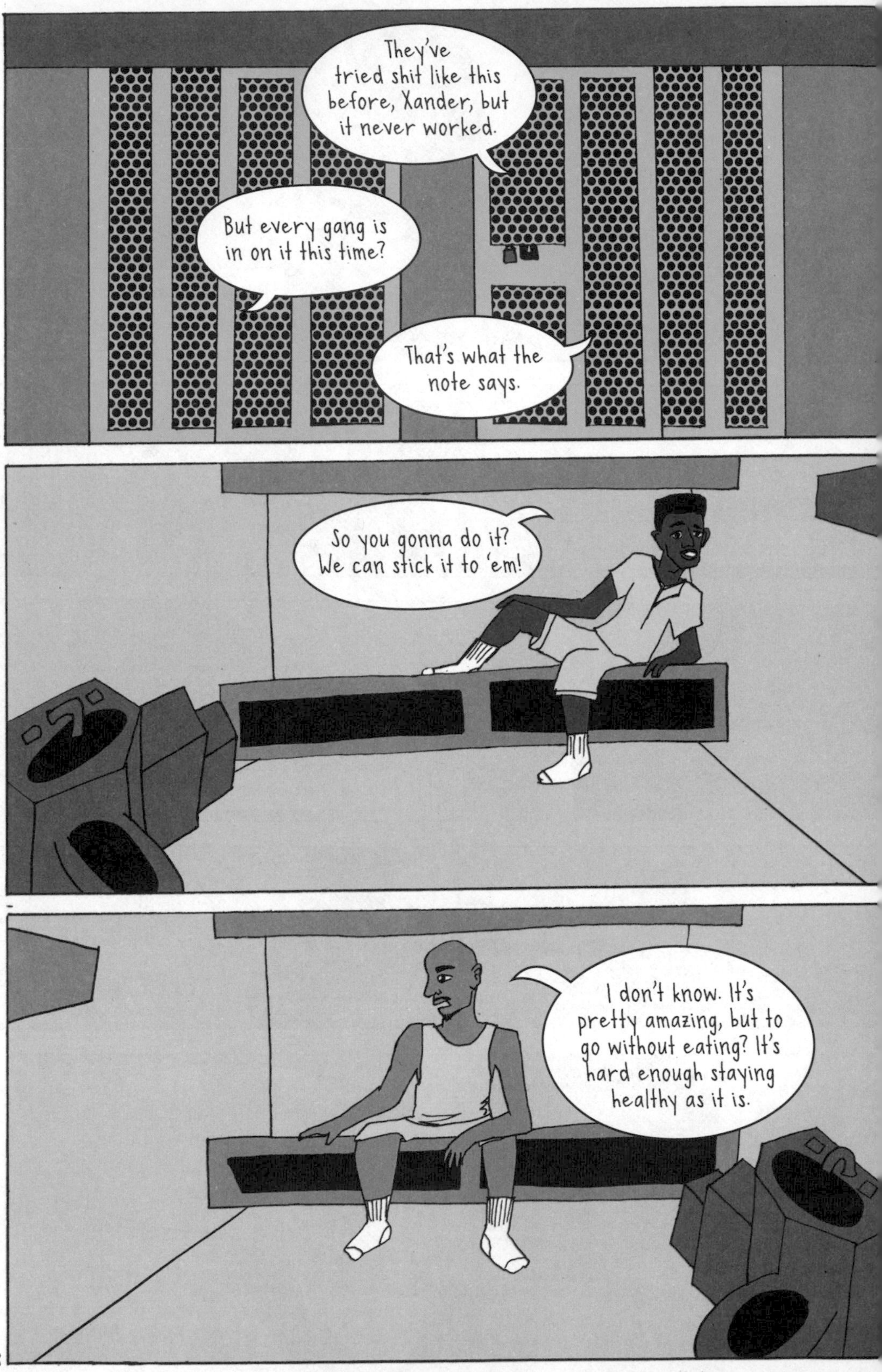
They've tried shit like this before, Xander, but it never worked.
But every gang is in on it this time?
That's what the note says.
So you gonna do it? We can stick it to 'em!
I don't know. It's pretty amazing, but to go without eating? It's hard enough staying healthy as it is.

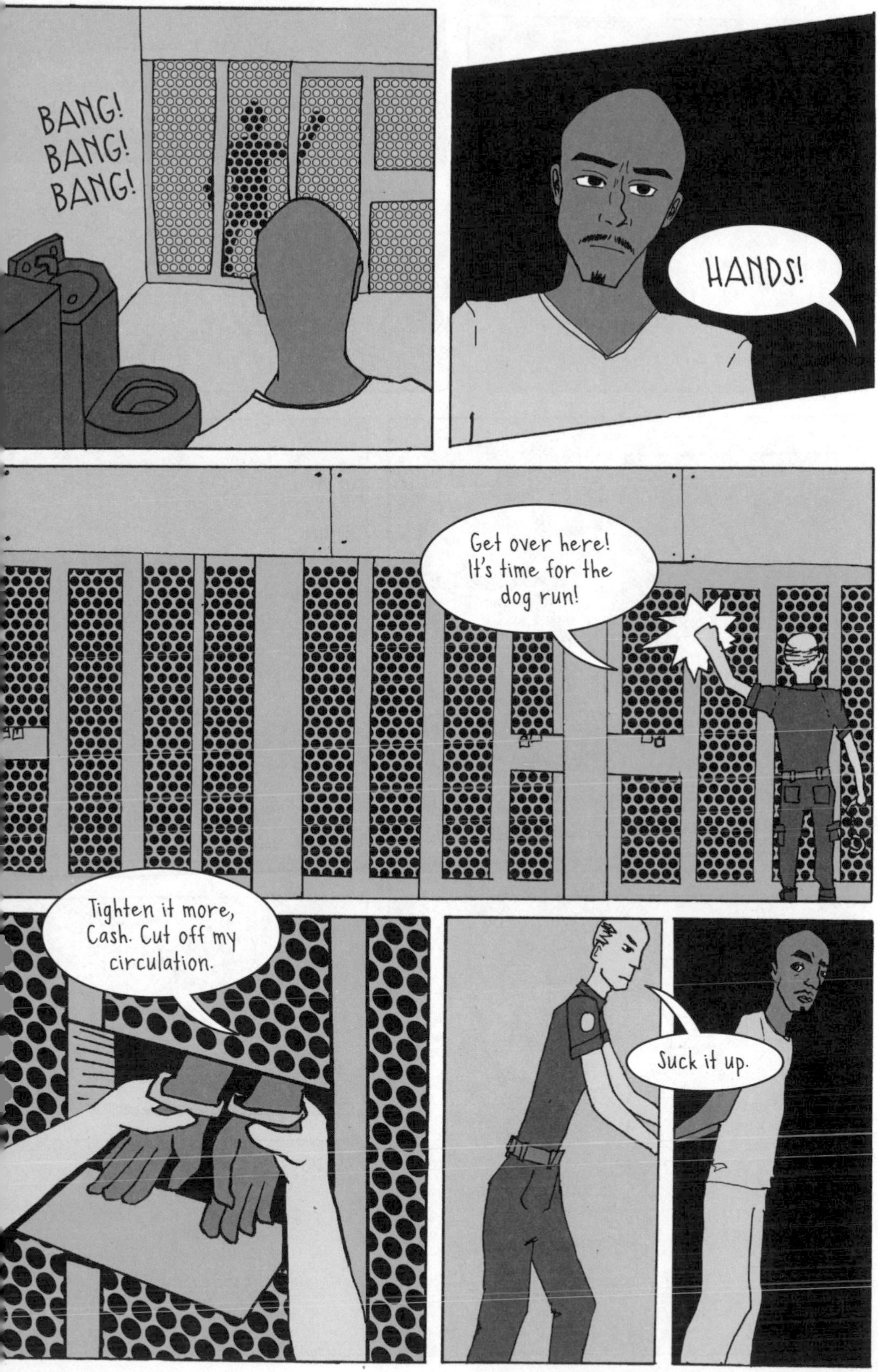
BANG! BANG! BANG!
HANDS!
Get over here! It's time for the dog run!
Tighten it more, Cash. Cut off my circulation.
Suck it up.

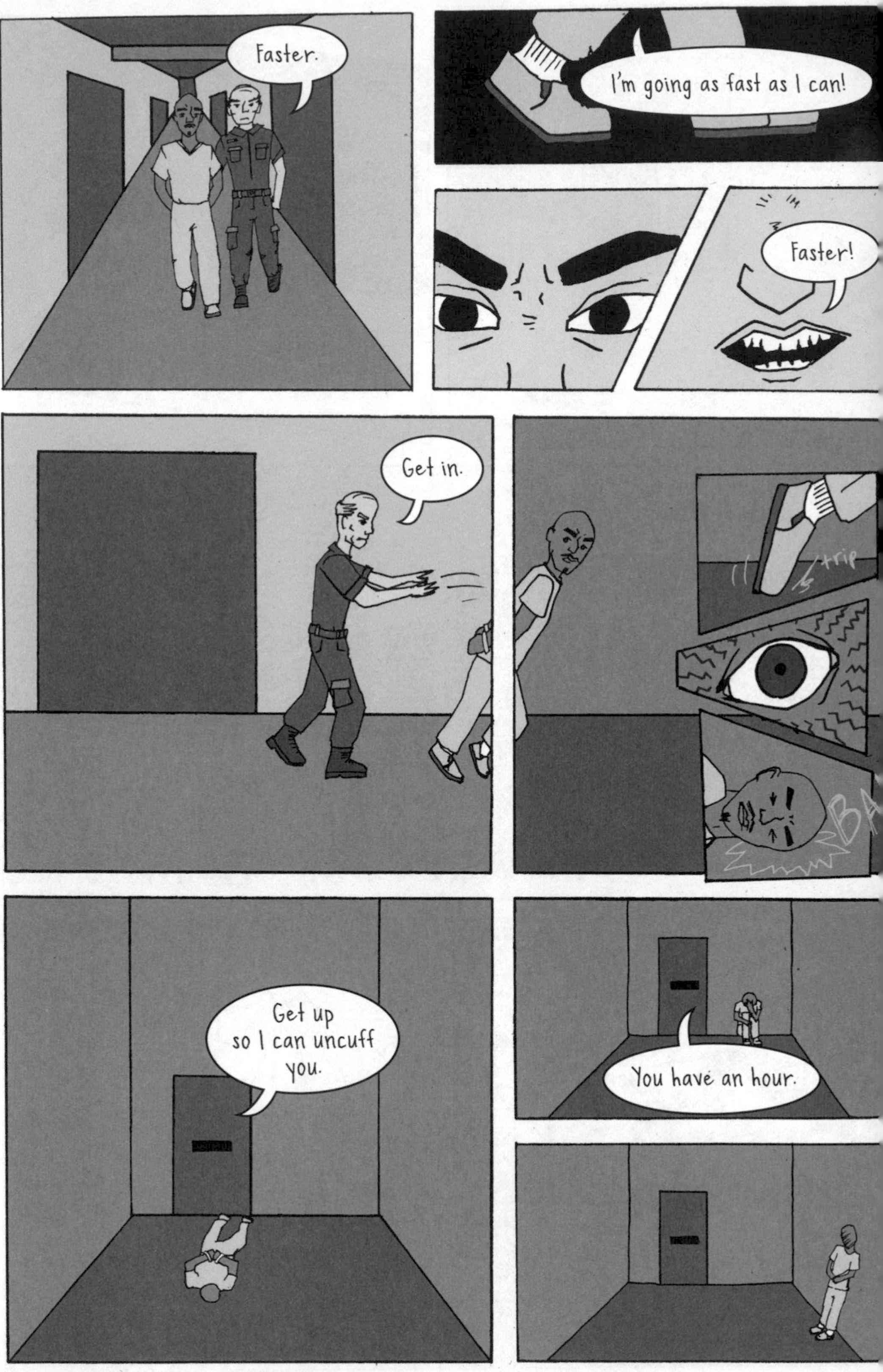
Faster.
I'm going as fast as I can!
Faster!
Get in.
trip
Get up so I can uncuff you.
You have an hour.

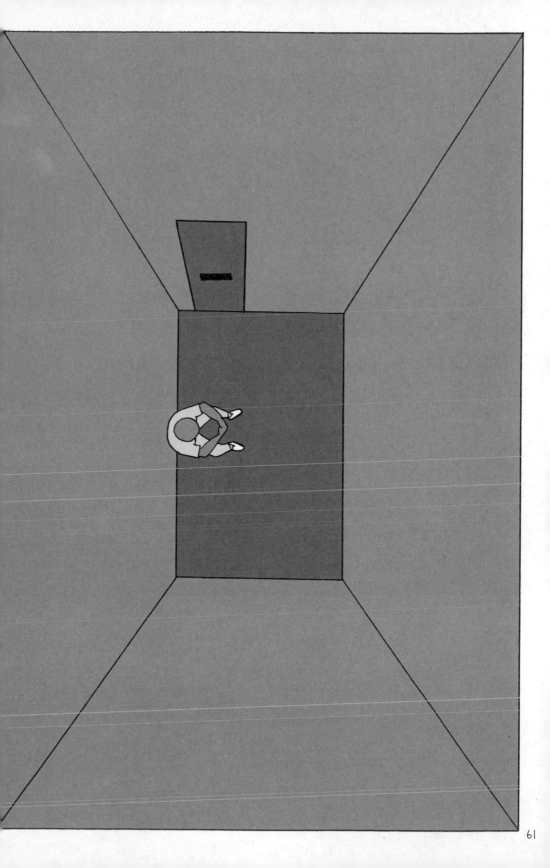

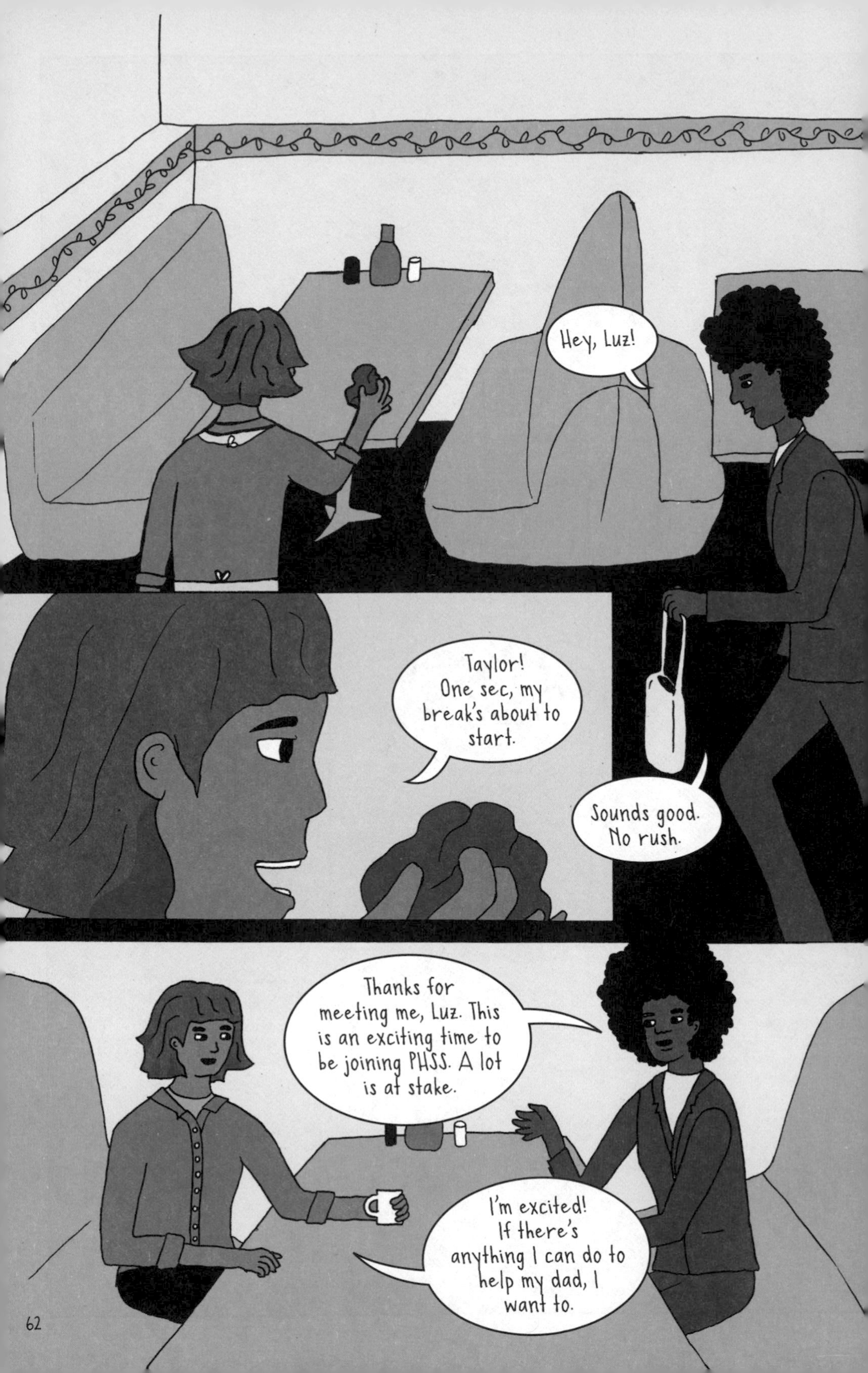
Hey, Luz!
Taylor! One sec, my break's about to start.
Sounds good. No rush.
Thanks for meeting me, Luz. This is an exciting time to be joining PHSS. A lot is at stake.
I'm excited! If there's anything I can do to help my dad, I want to.

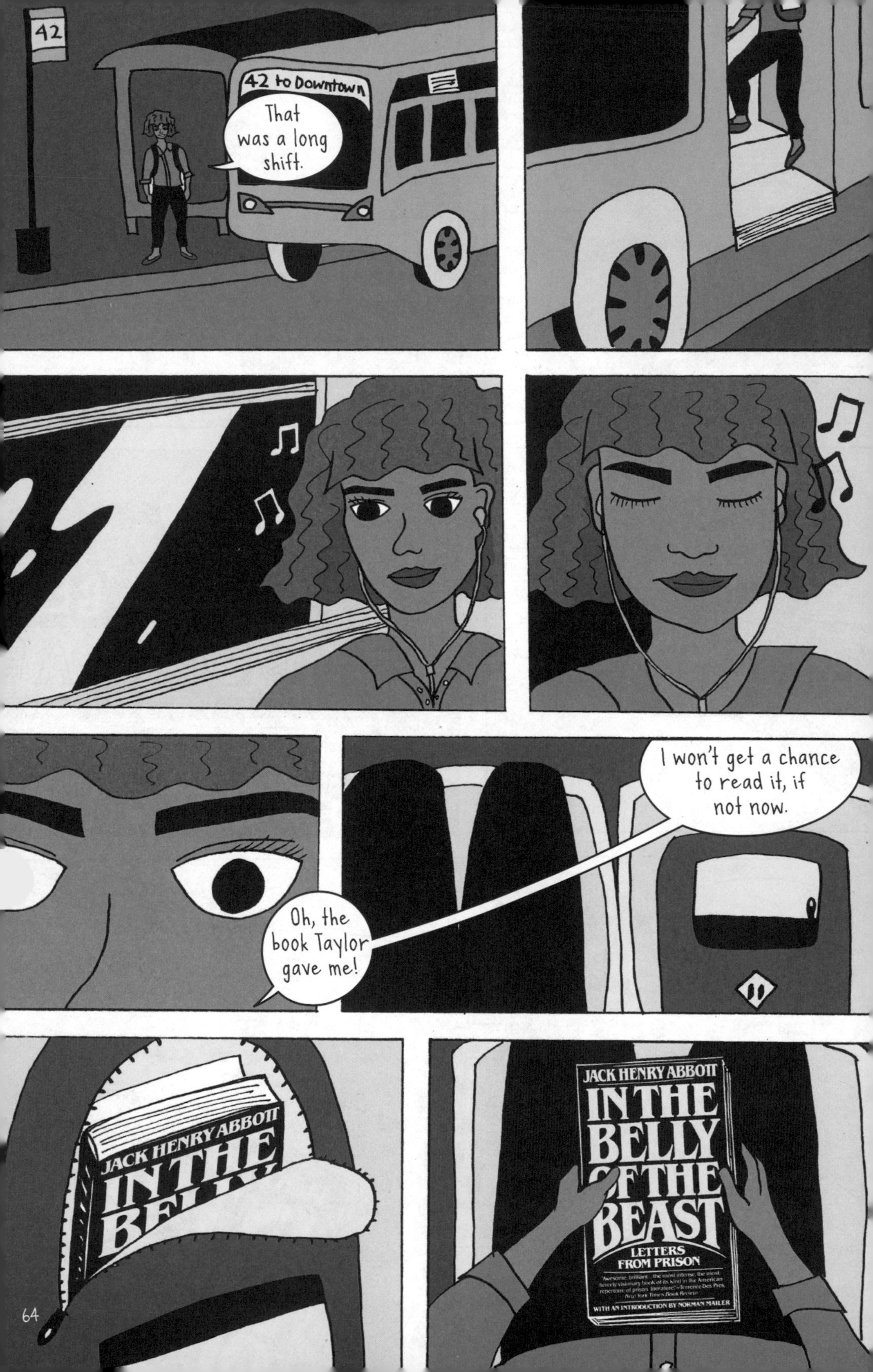
42
42 to Downtown
That was a long shift.
Oh, the book Taylor gave me!
I won't get a chance to read it, if not now.
JACK HENRY ABBOTT
IN THE BELLY
JACK HENRY ABBOTT
IN THE BELLY OF THE BEAST
LETTERS FROM PRISON
WITH AN INTRODUCTION BY NORMAN MAILER

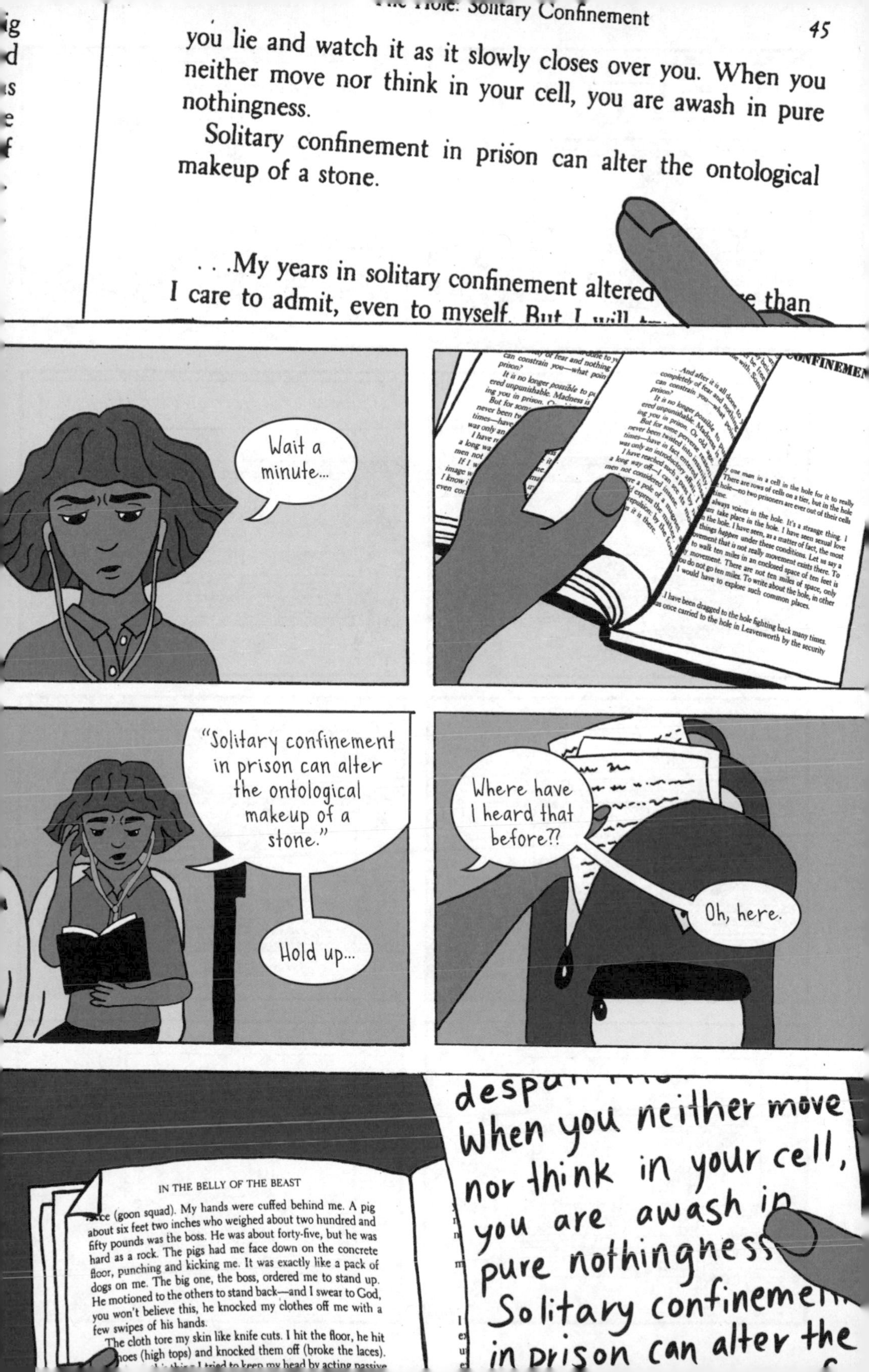
Solitary Confinement
45
you lie and watch it as it slowly closes over you. When you neither move nor think in your cell, you are awash in pure nothingness.
Solitary confinement in prison can alter the ontological makeup of a stone.
. . .My years in solitary confinement altered
I care to admit, even to myself.
Wait a minute...
"Solitary confinement in prison can alter the ontological makeup of a stone."
Hold up...
Where have I heard that before??
Oh, here.
IN THE BELLY OF THE BEAST
(goon squad). My hands were cuffed behind me. A pig about six feet two inches who weighed about two hundred and fifty pounds was the boss. He was about forty-five, but he was hard as a rock. The pigs had me face down on the concrete floor, punching and kicking me. It was exactly like a pack of dogs on me. The big one, the boss, ordered me to stand up. He motioned to the others to stand back—and I swear to God, you won't believe this, he knocked my clothes off me with a few swipes of his hands.
The cloth tore my skin like knife cuts. I hit the floor, he hit
(high tops) and knocked them off (broke the laces).
When you neither move nor think in your cell, you are awash in pure nothingness
Solitary confineme
in prison can alter the

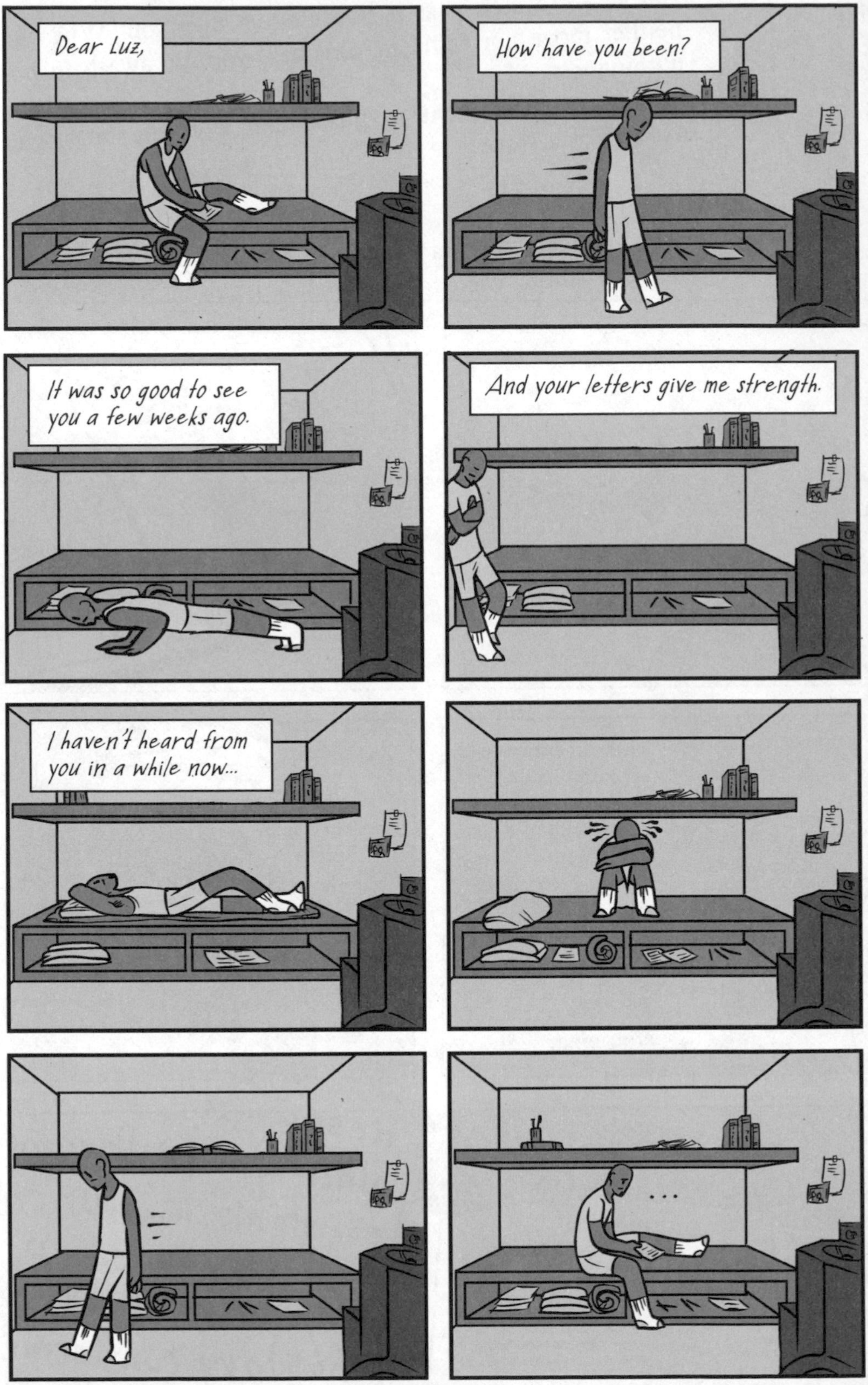
Dear Luz,
How have you been?
It was so good to see you a few weeks ago.
And your letters give me strength.
I haven't heard from you in a while now...
. . .

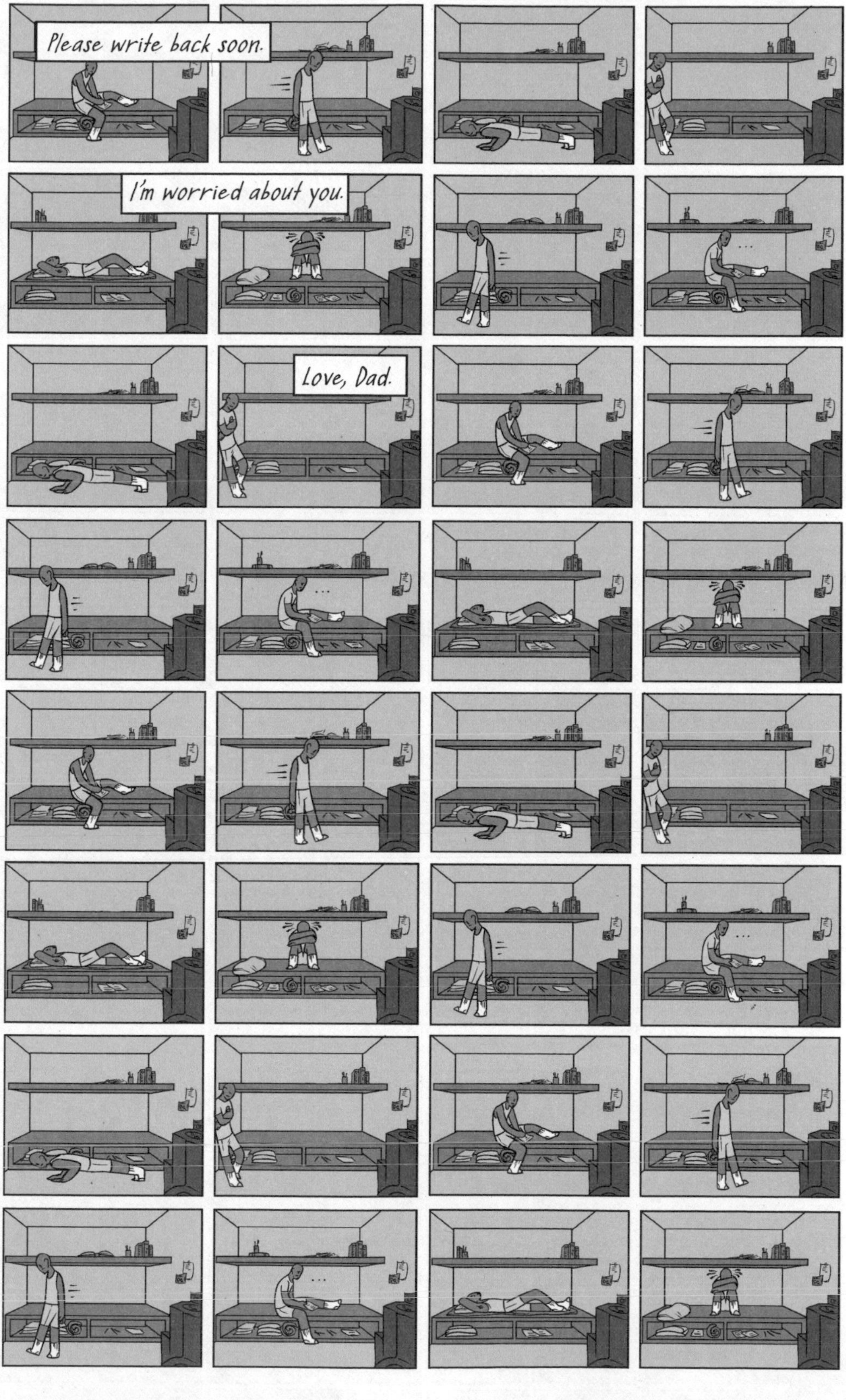
Please write back soon.
I'm worried about you.
Love, Dad.

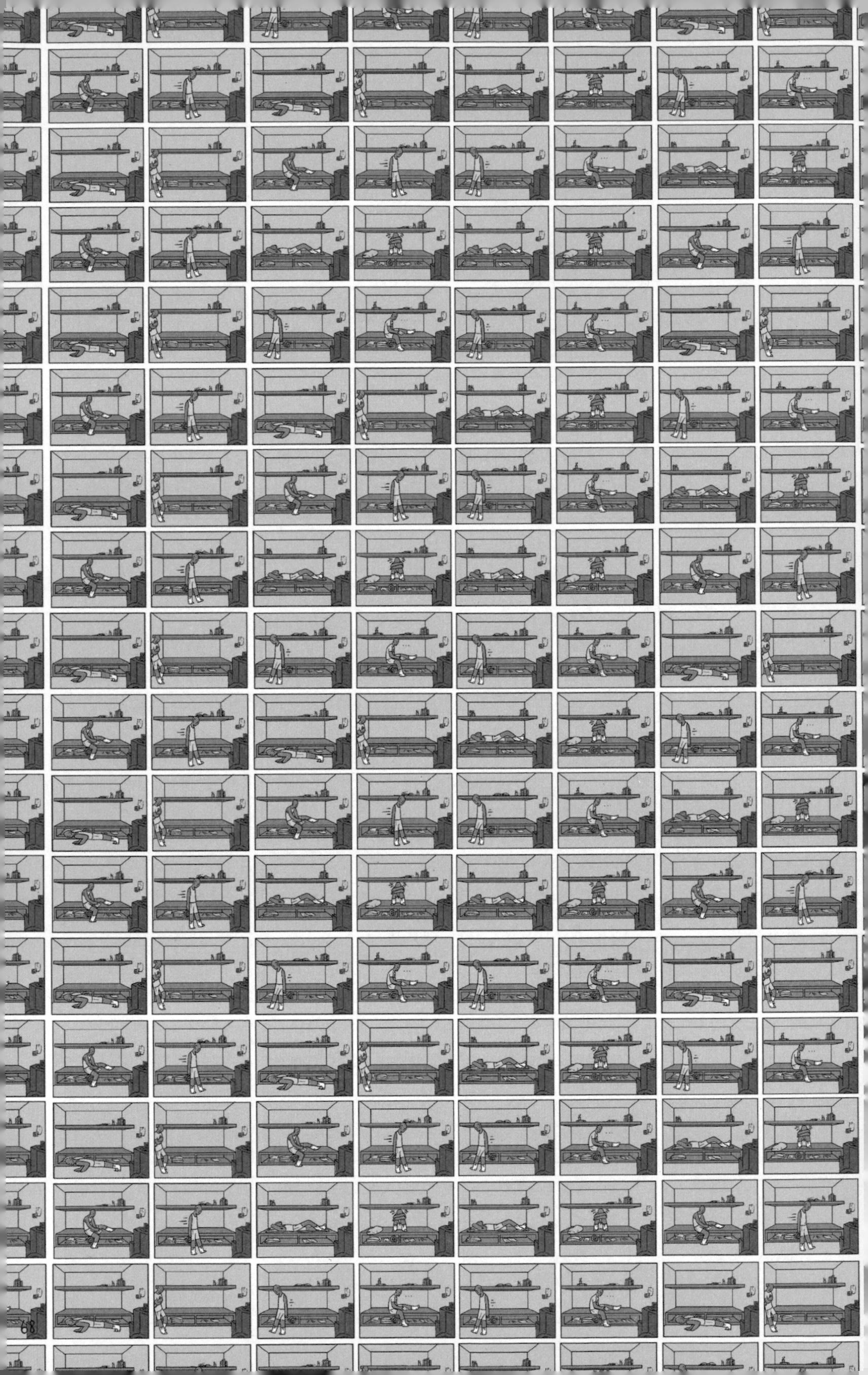

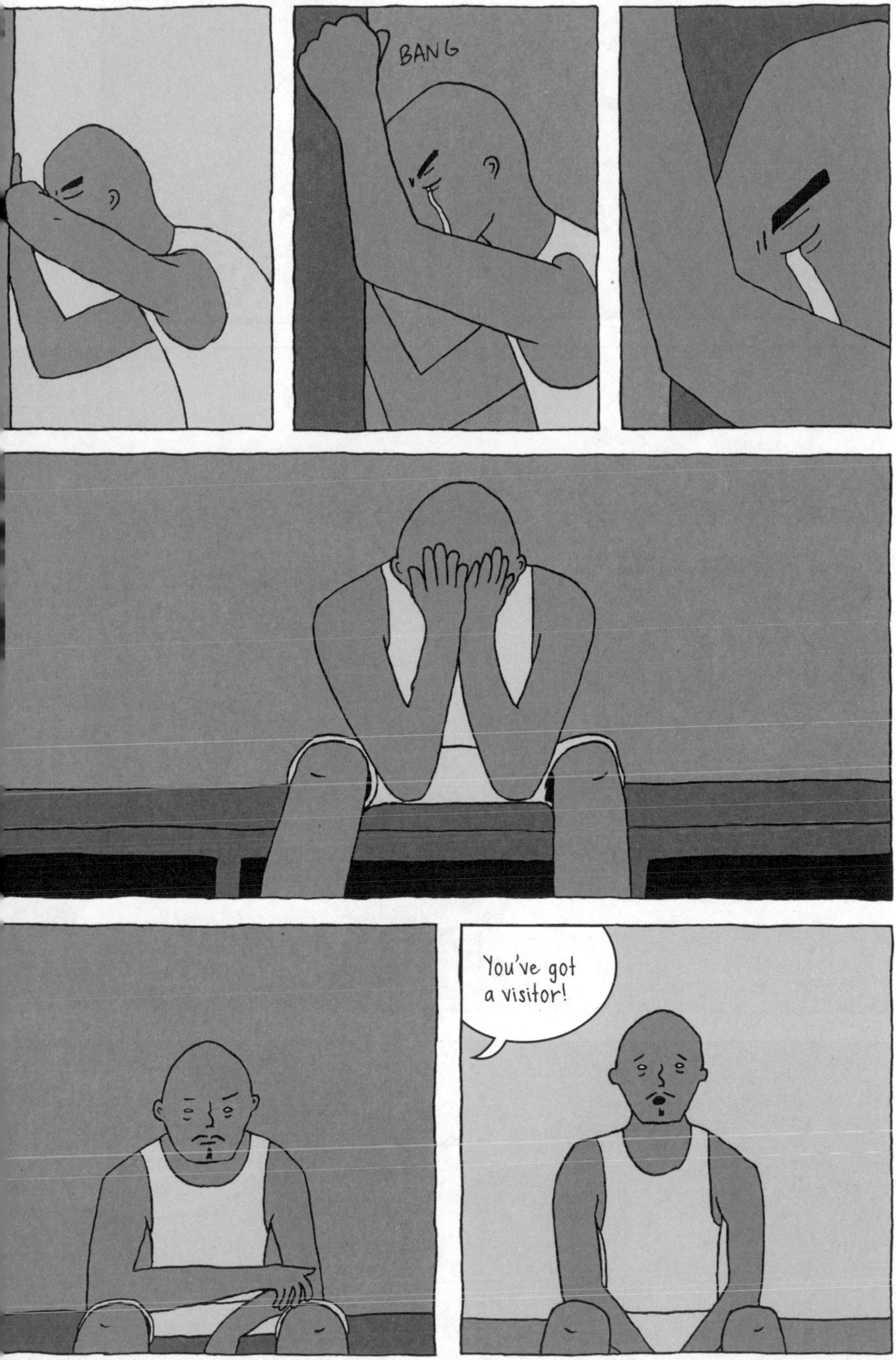
BANG
You've got a visitor!

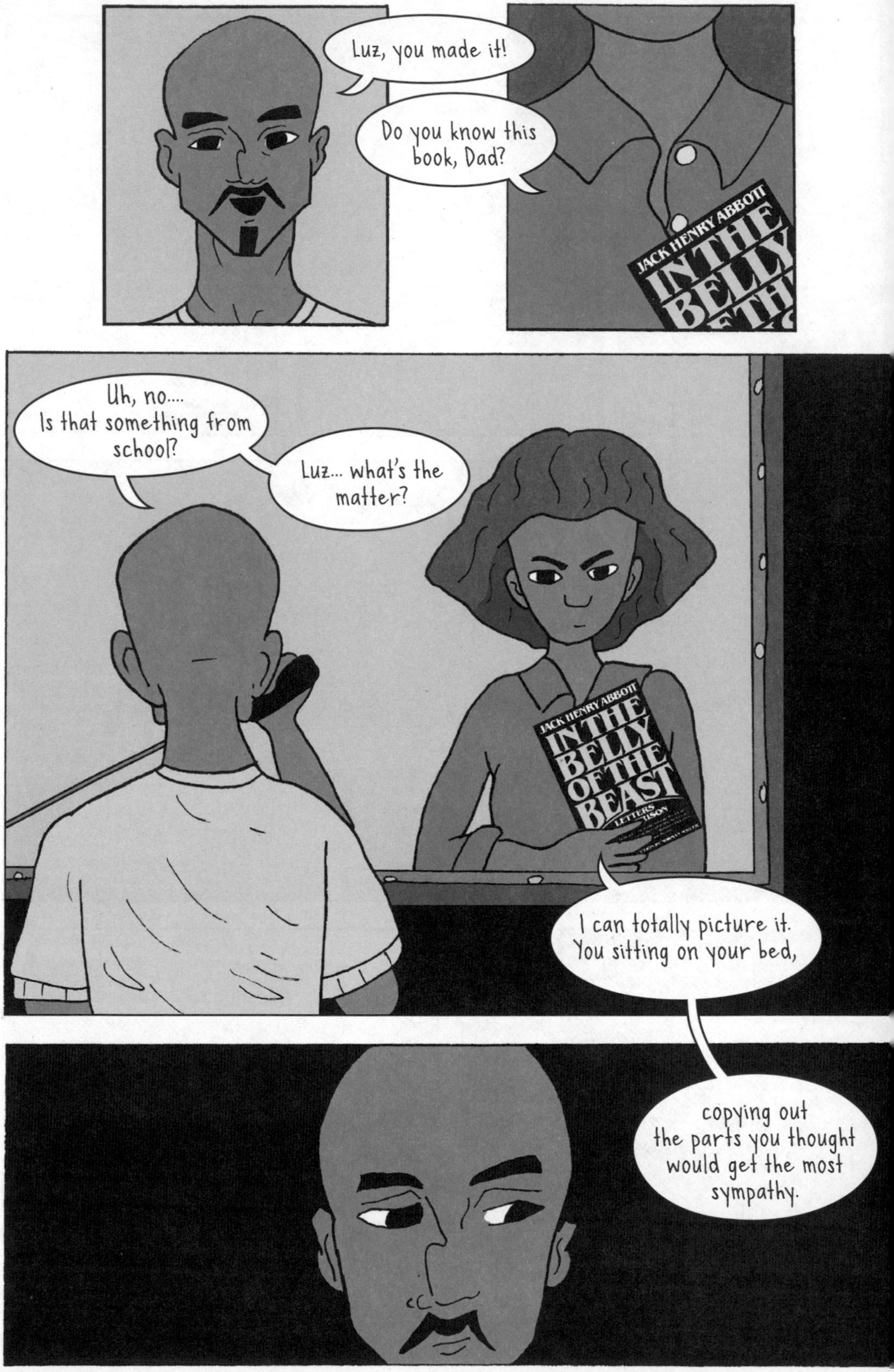
Luz, you made it!
Do you know this book, Dad?
JACK HENRY ABBOTT IN THE BELLY OF THE BEAST
Uh, no.... Is that something from school?
Luz... what's the matter?
I can totally picture it. You sitting on your bed,
copying out the parts you thought would get the most sympathy.

"Solitary confinement can alter the ontological makeup of a stone."

Jack Henry Abbott. A prisoner from the 70s. He wrote that, not you.

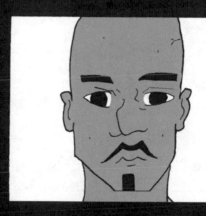

I thought I knew you.

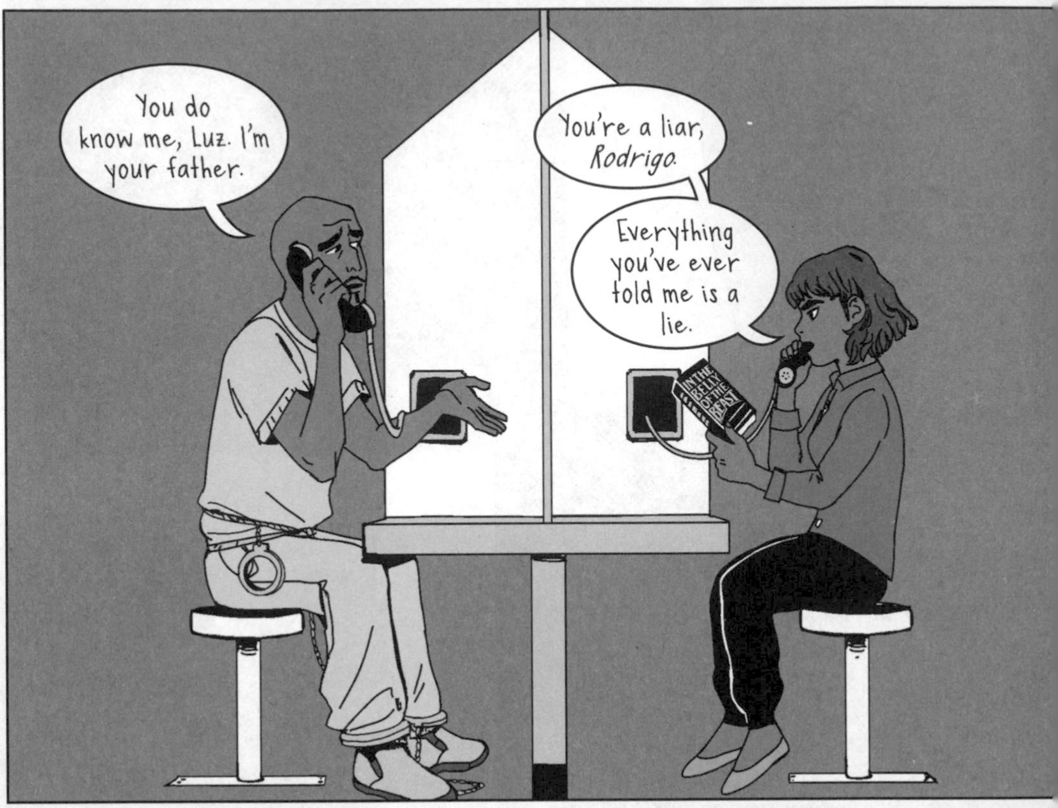
You do know me, Luz. I'm your father.
You're a liar, *Rodrigo.*
Everything you've ever told me is a lie.
IN THE BELLY OF THE BEAST

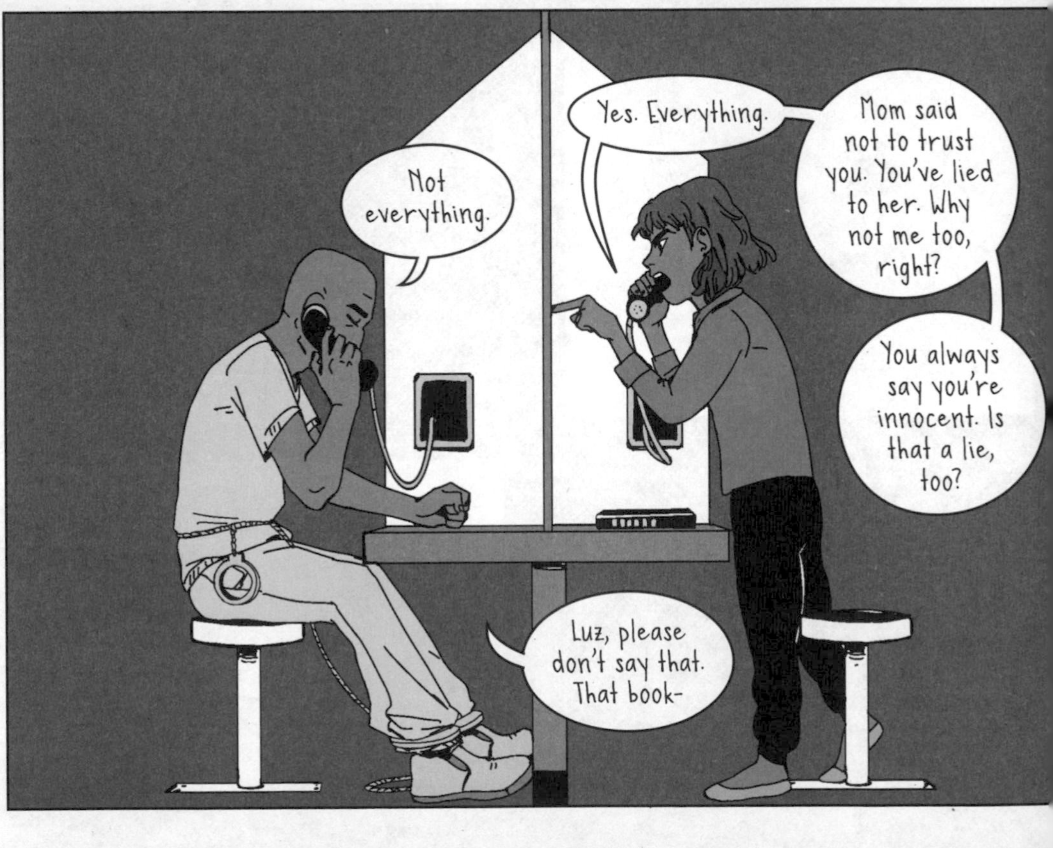
Yes. Everything.
Mom said not to trust you. You've lied to her. Why not me too, right?
You always say you're innocent. Is that a lie, too?
Not everything.
Luz, please don't say that. That book-

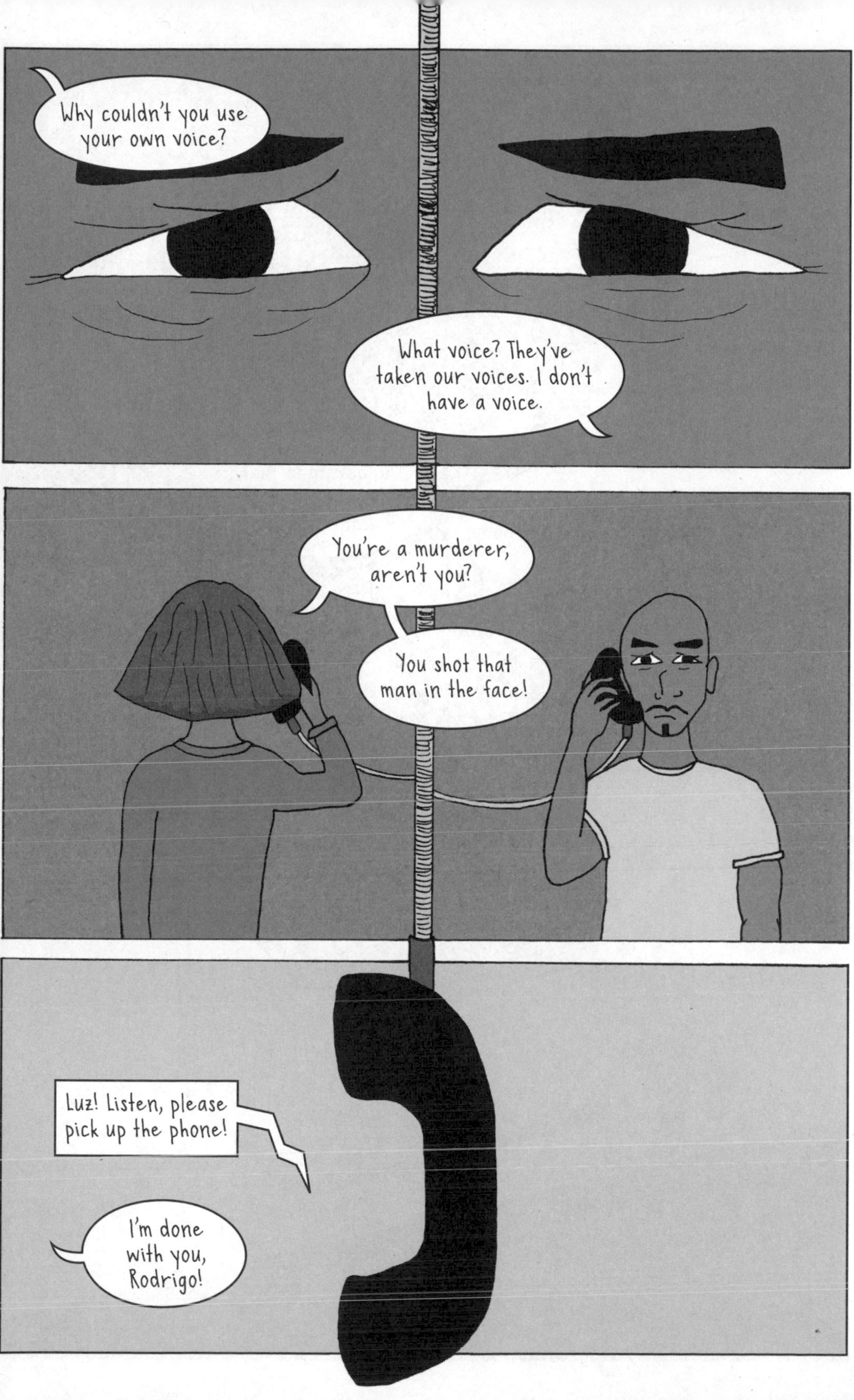

Why couldn't you use your own voice?
What voice? They've taken our voices. I don't have a voice.
You're a murderer, aren't you?
You shot that man in the face!
Luz! Listen, please pick up the phone!
I'm done with you, Rodrigo!

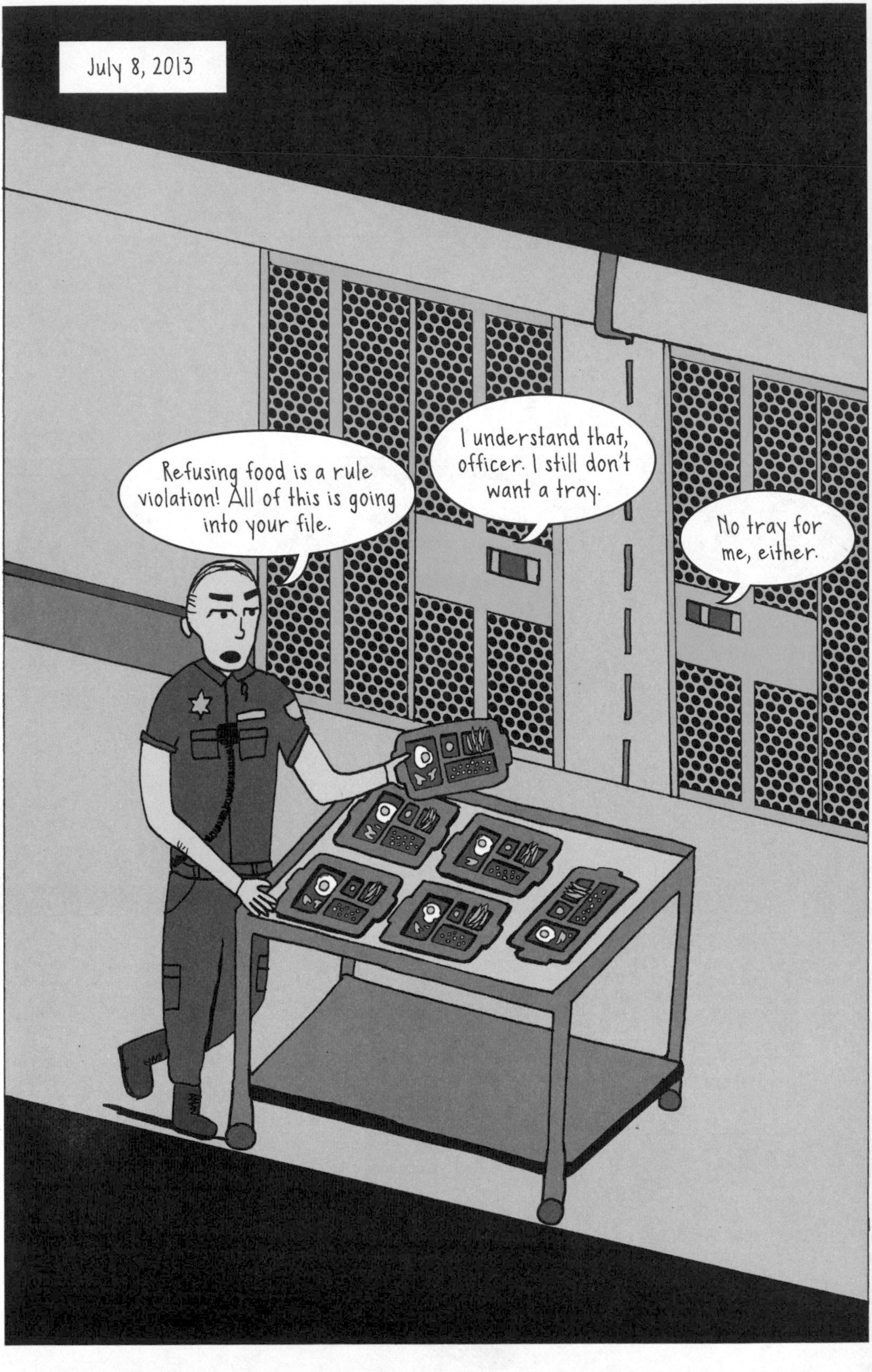
July 8, 2013
Refusing food is a rule violation! All of this is going into your file.
I understand that, officer. I still don't want a tray.
No tray for me, either.

Tray.
No.

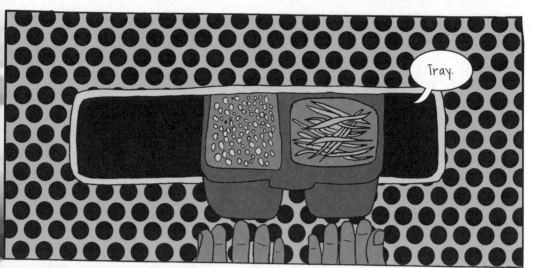

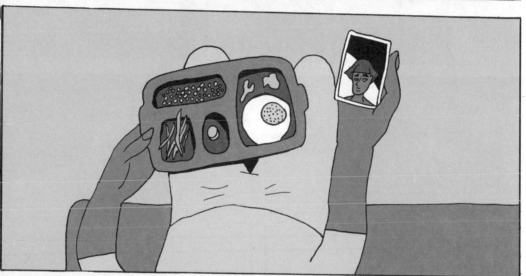

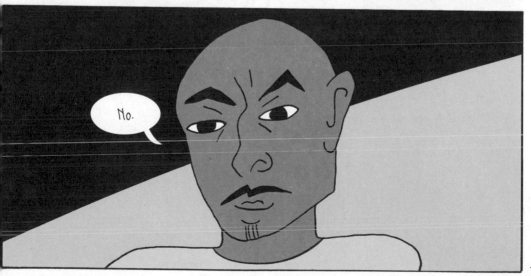

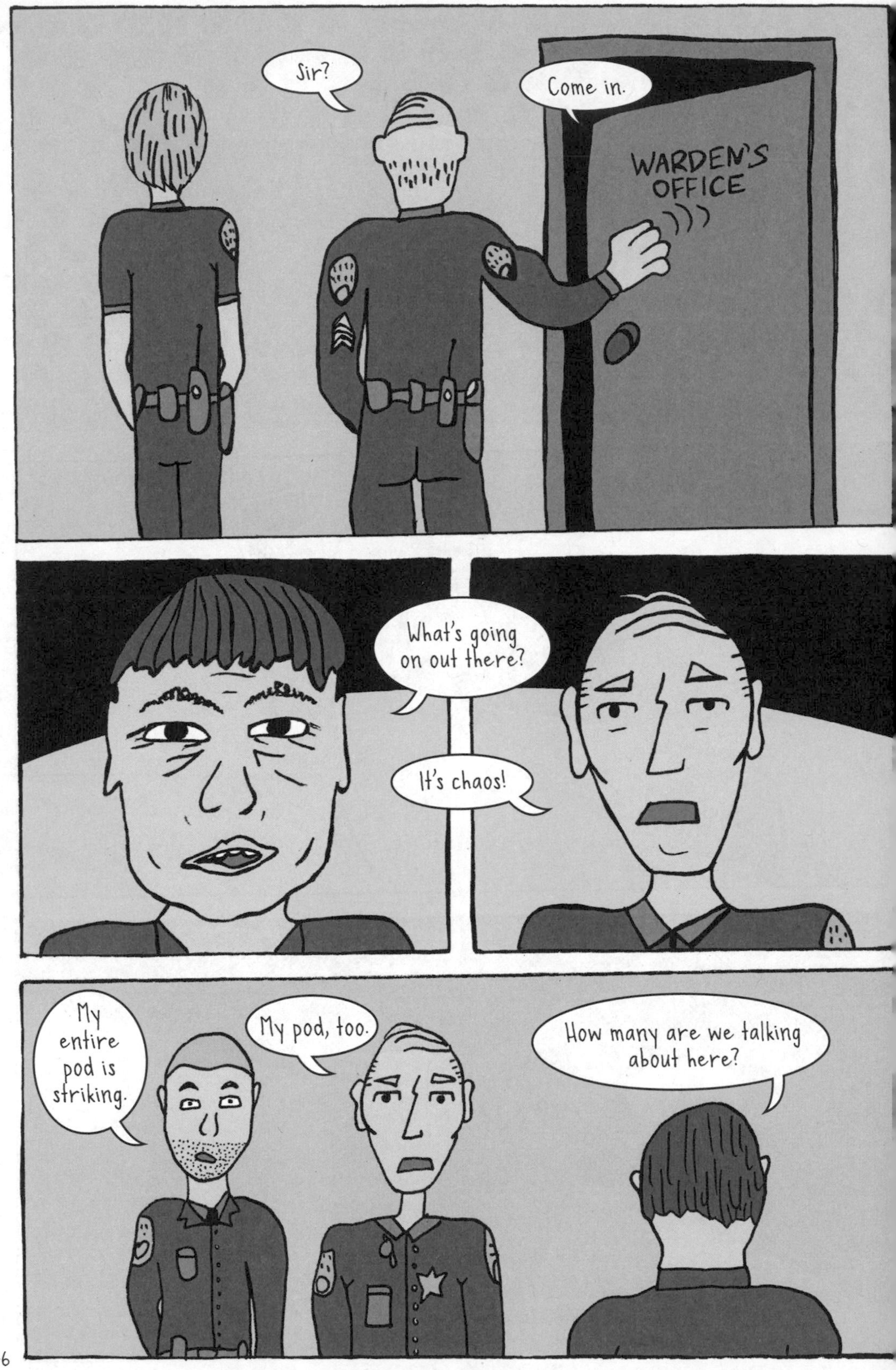
Sir?
Come in.
WARDEN'S OFFICE
What's going on out there?
It's chaos!
My entire pod is striking.
My pod, too.
How many are we talking about here?

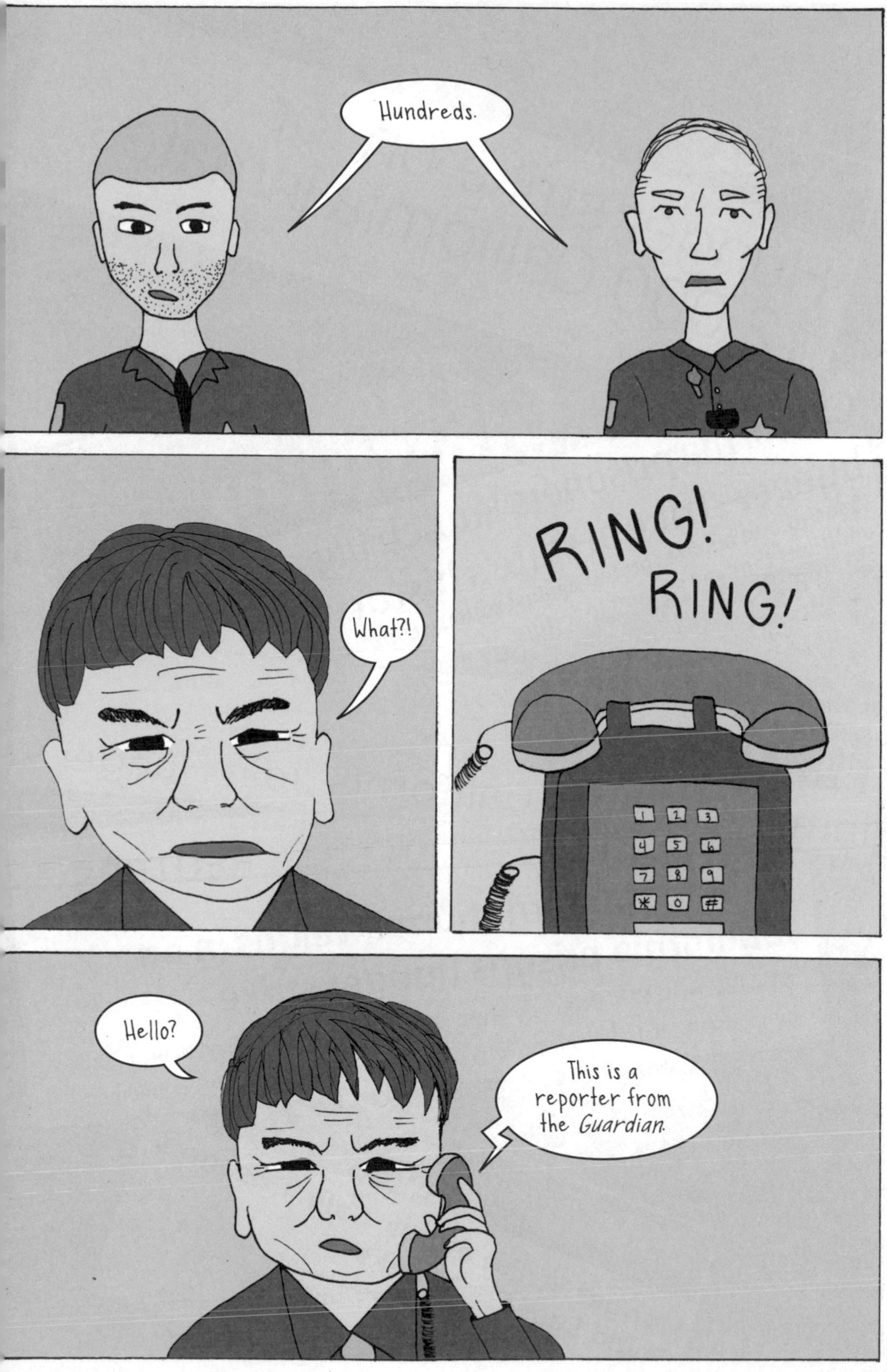
Hundreds.
What?!
RING!
RING!
Hello?
This is a reporter from the *Guardian*.

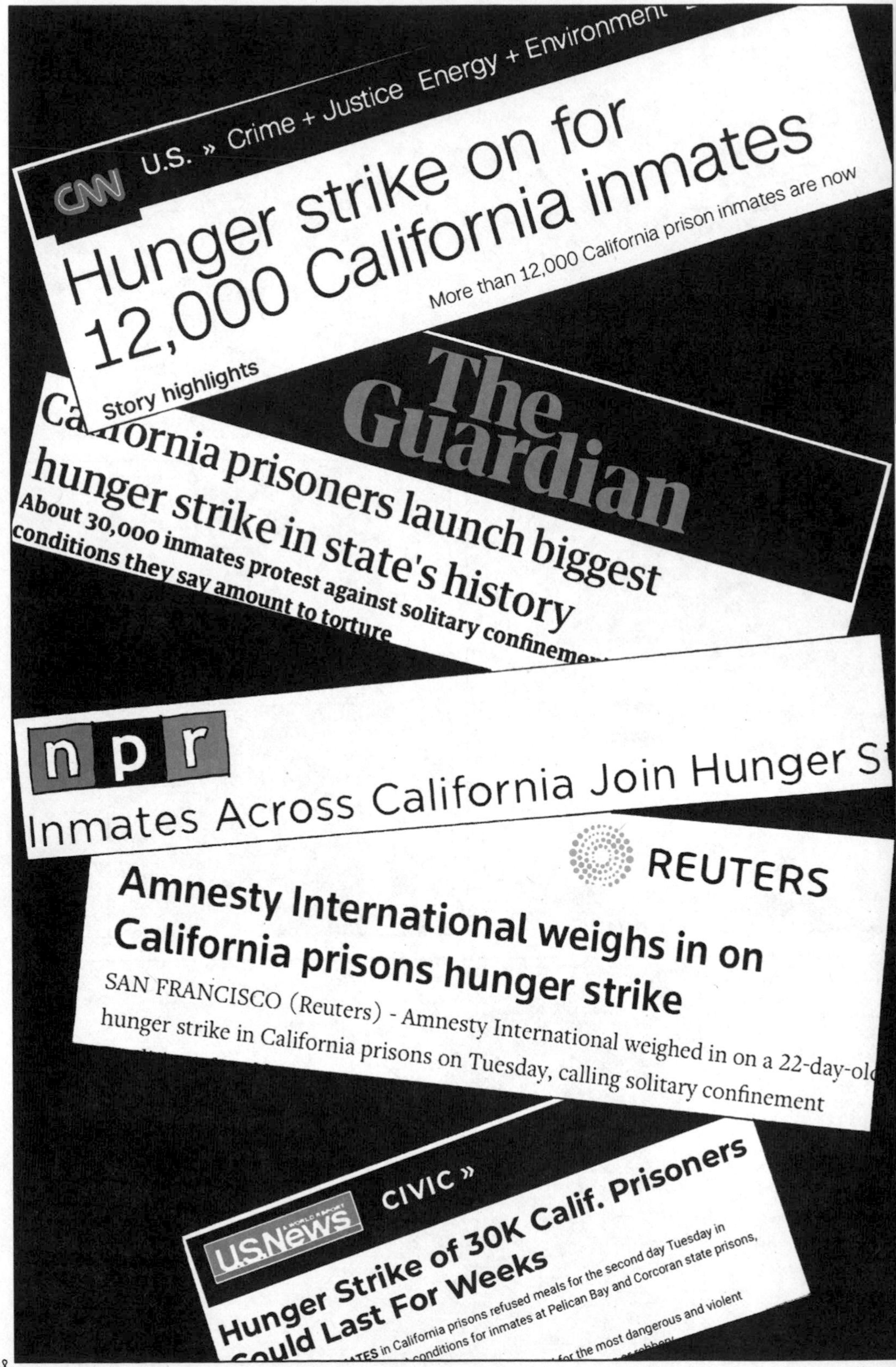
CNN U.S. » Crime + Justice Energy + Environment
Hunger strike on for 12,000 California inmates
More than 12,000 California prison inmates are now
Story highlights
The Guardian
California prisoners launch biggest hunger strike in state's history
About 30,000 inmates protest against solitary confinement conditions they say amount to torture
npr
Inmates Across California Join Hunger St
REUTERS
Amnesty International weighs in on California prisons hunger strike
SAN FRANCISCO (Reuters) - Amnesty International weighed in on a 22-day-old hunger strike in California prisons on Tuesday, calling solitary confinement
U.S.News & WORLD REPORT
CIVIC »
Hunger Strike of 30K Calif. Prisoners Could Last For Weeks
in California prisons refused meals for the second day Tuesday in conditions for inmates at Pelican Bay and Corcoran state prisons, for the most dangerous and violent

Thirty thousand prisoners collectively refused food to protest solitary confinement.

Whether it was out of personal motives...

...or political...

...they put aside their gang affiliations to unite.

SOUL ON ICE

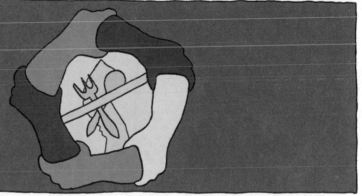

The war was waged not only within the prisons but also by various external organizations, including the PHSS.

As the days passed...

...and the stakes increased....

...the prisoners showed no sign of backing down.

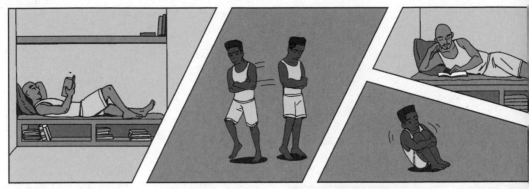

But we wondered how much longer we could keep it up.

40 DAYS AND 40 NIGHTS!

40 DAYS AND 40 NIGHTS!

40 DAYS AND 40 NIGHTS!

One day, Sitawa Jamaa was led down our corridor on his way to Administrative Segregation. He strengthened our resolve with a plan and a rallying cry. The energy that day was infectious.

40 DAYS AND 40 NIGHTS! Keep it up! We are making change!

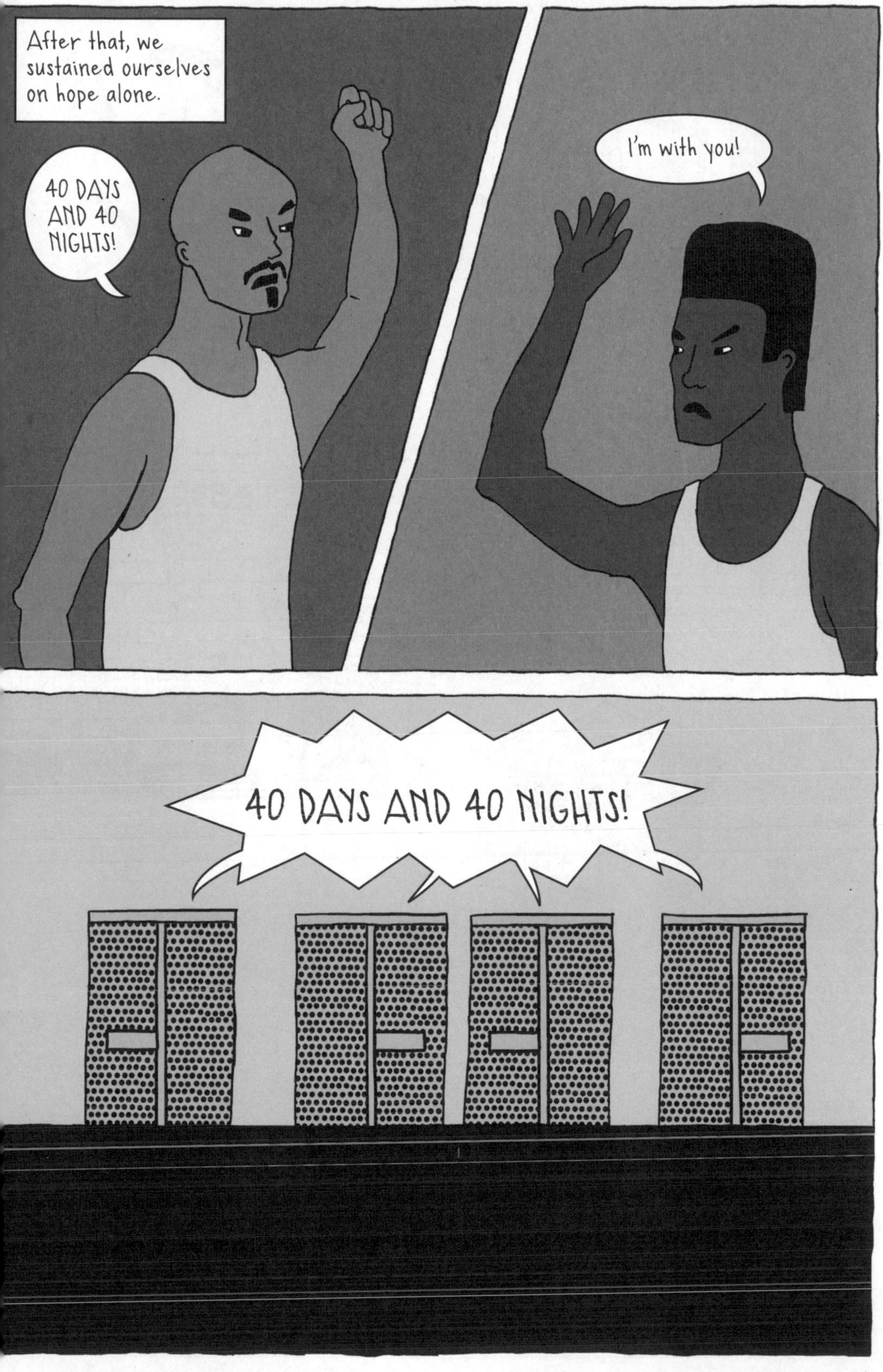
After that, we sustained ourselves on hope alone.
40 DAYS AND 40 NIGHTS!
I'm with you!
40 DAYS AND 40 NIGHTS!

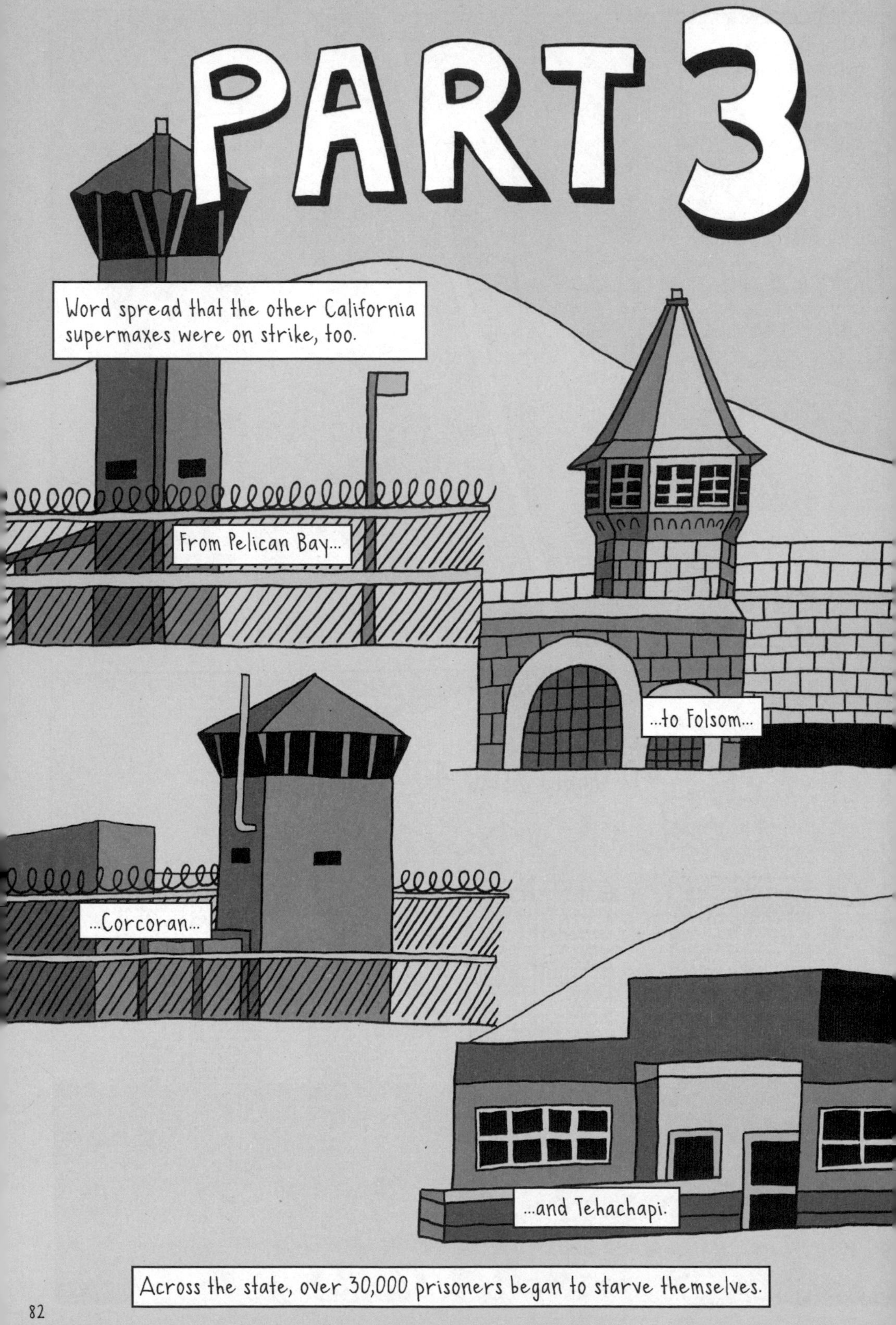
PART 3
Word spread that the other California supermaxes were on strike, too.
From Pelican Bay...
...to Folsom...
...Corcoran...
...and Tehachapi.
Across the state, over 30,000 prisoners began to starve themselves.

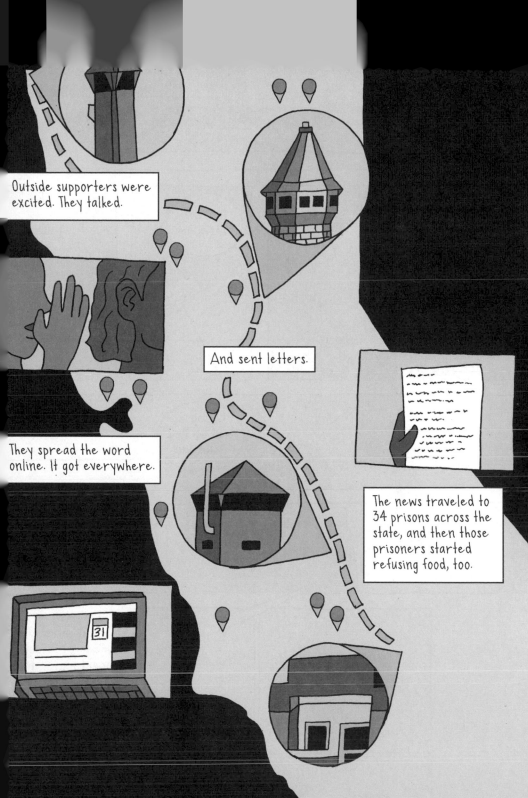

Outside supporters were excited. They talked.

And sent letters.

They spread the word online. It got everywhere.

The news traveled to 34 prisons across the state, and then those prisoners started refusing food, too.

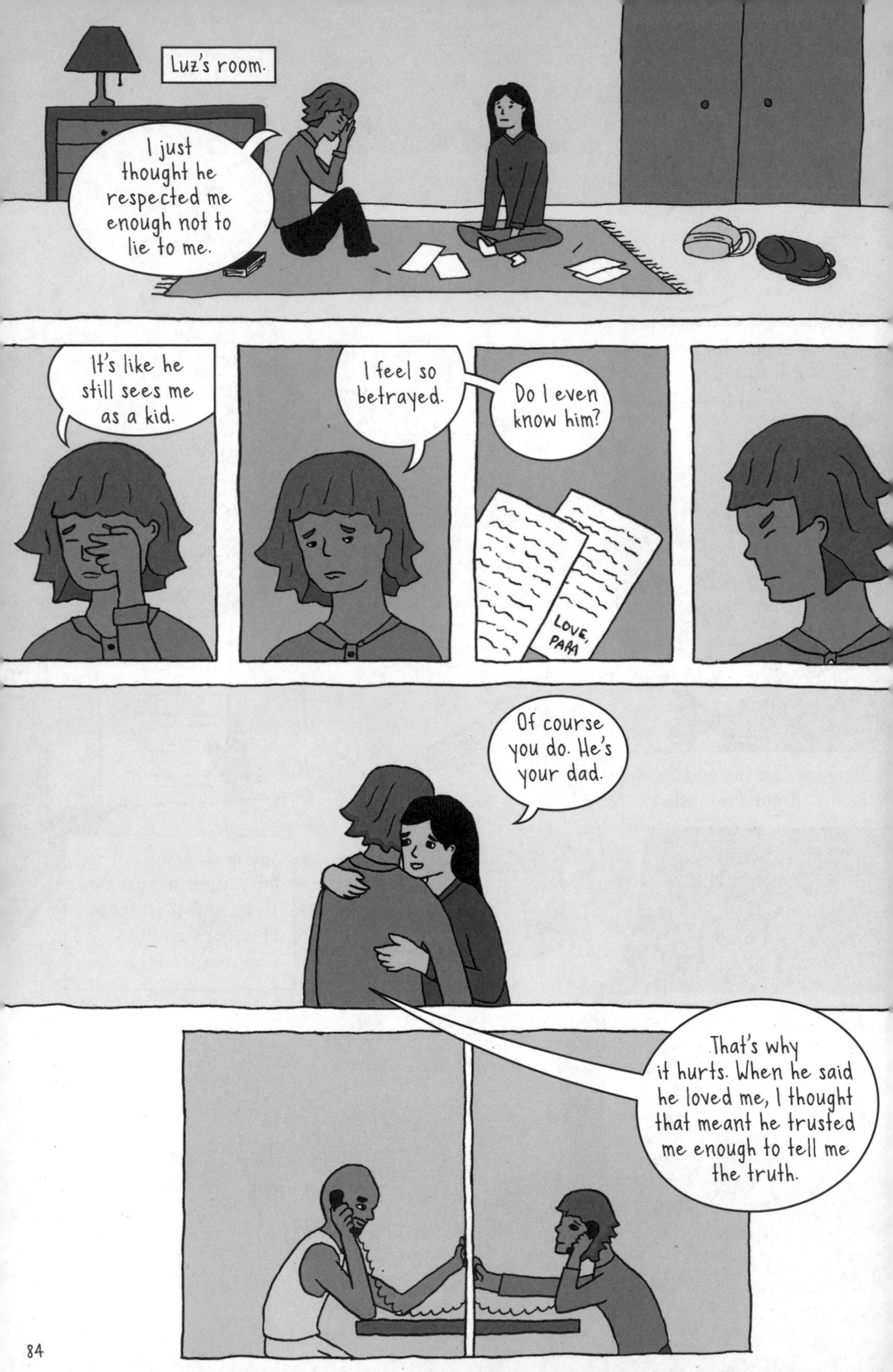

Luz's room.
I just thought he respected me enough not to lie to me.
It's like he still sees me as a kid.
I feel so betrayed.
Do I even know him?
LOVE, PAPA
Of course you do. He's your dad.
That's why it hurts. When he said he loved me, I thought that meant he trusted me enough to tell me the truth.

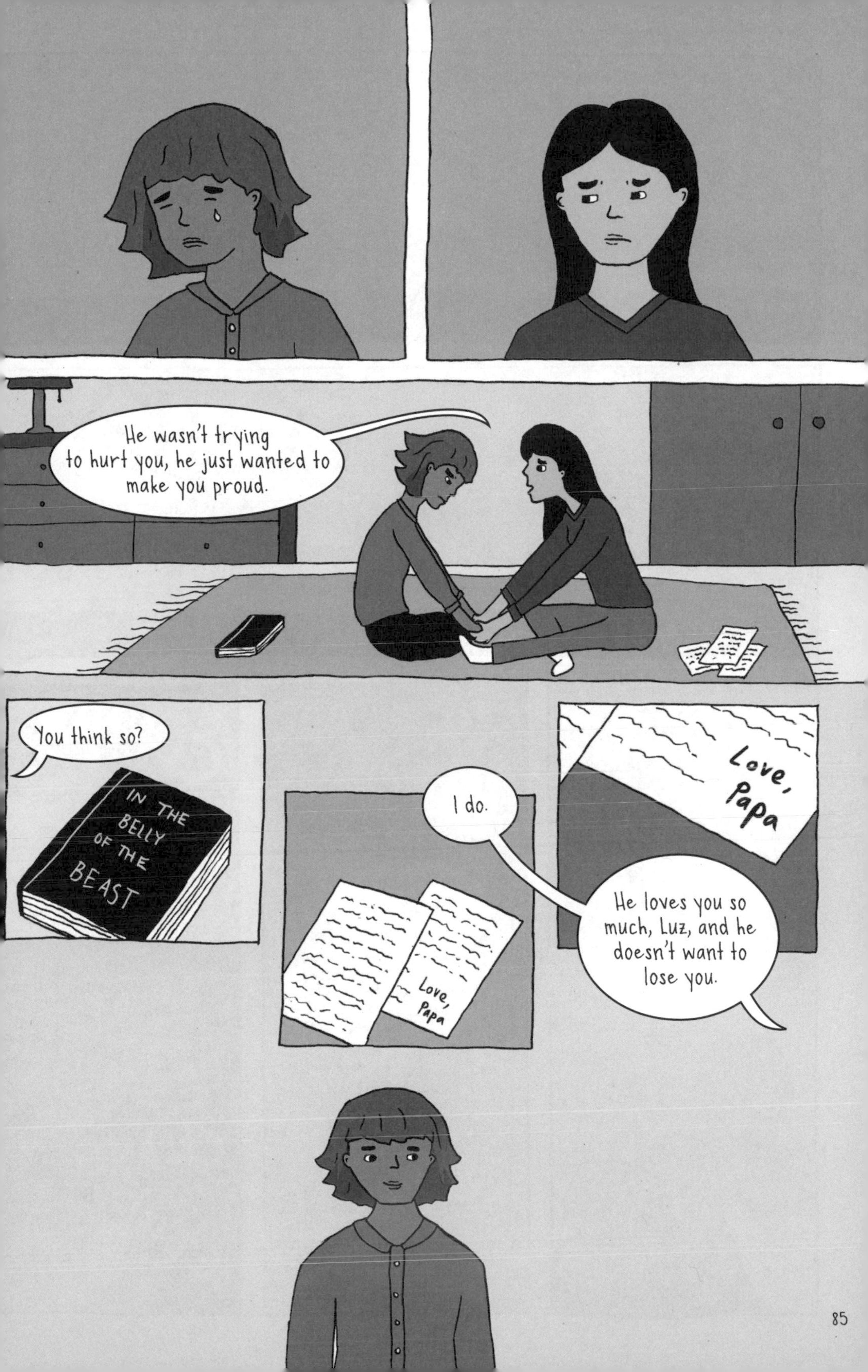
He wasn't trying to hurt you, he just wanted to make you proud.
You think so?
IN THE BELLY OF THE BEAST
I do.
Love, Papa
Love, Papa
He loves you so much, Luz, and he doesn't want to lose you.

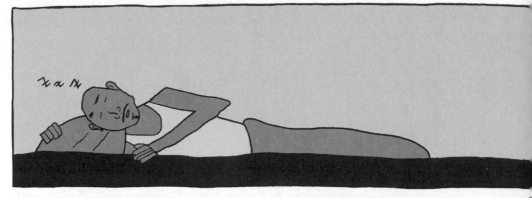

CLANG!

Inmate! Wake up!

Again with this? I'm sleeping!

Just seeing if you assholes are still alive.

CLANG
HEY

HEY
CLANG

GET UP

Hey, did you hear?
Hear what?
Heard the guards talking. We're down to a couple thousand.
Better than zero.
Damn, I'm hungry.
Me too, but we gotta hang in there. Forty days and forty nights, Sitawa said.
What if it doesn't even work? What's to say they'll even listen to us?
I don't know. But we gotta try. It's all we got.
How you holding up, man?
Okay. Trying to sleep off the hunger, distract myself. How many are left?
From what I heard, a couple hundred now.
Shit. Dropping like flies.
I can barely move. My body feels all wrong. I can't think. What if it's just us, man?
Hello? Yo, anybody there?

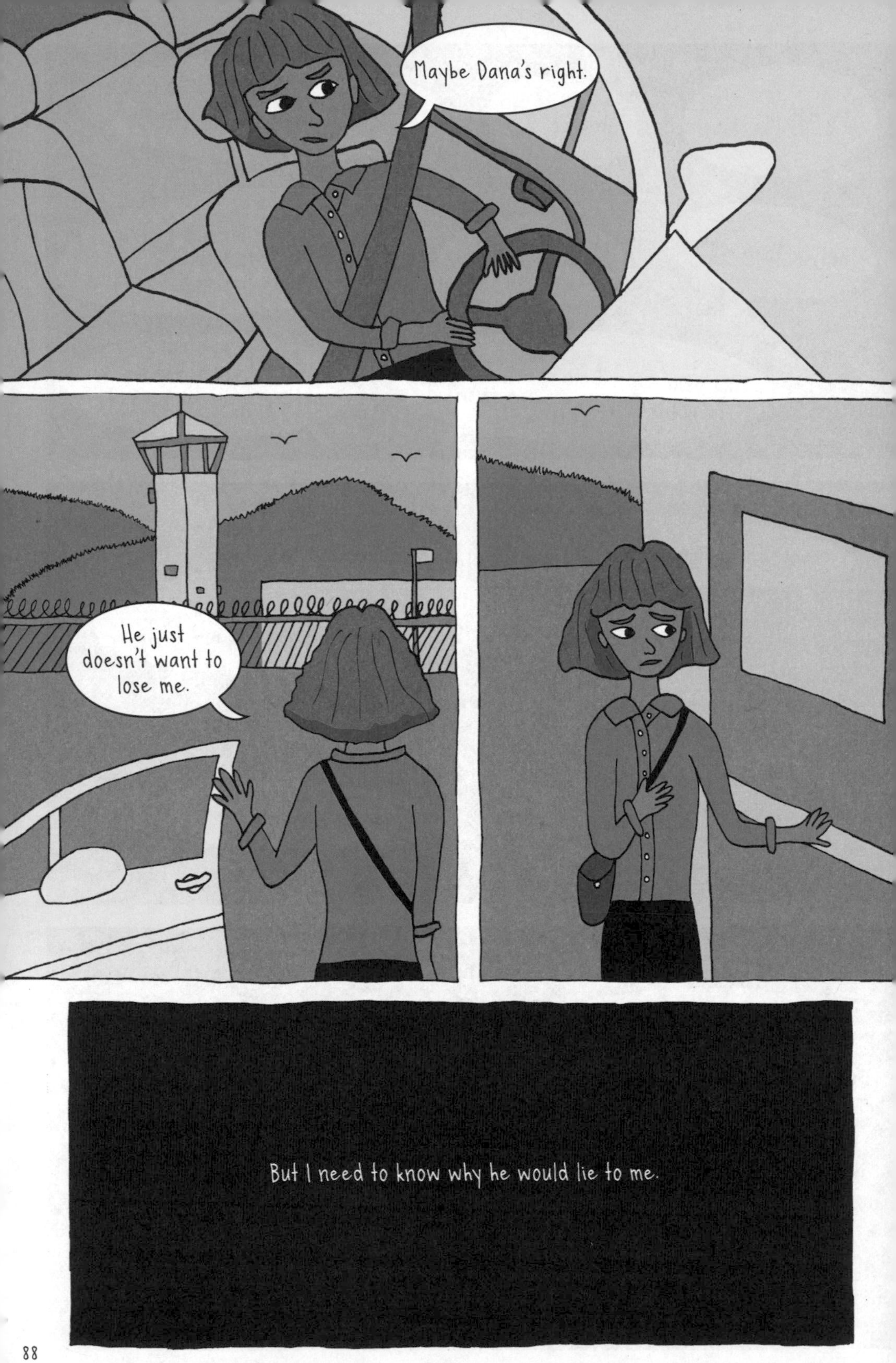

Maybe Dana's right.
He just doesn't want to lose me.
But I need to know why he would lie to me.

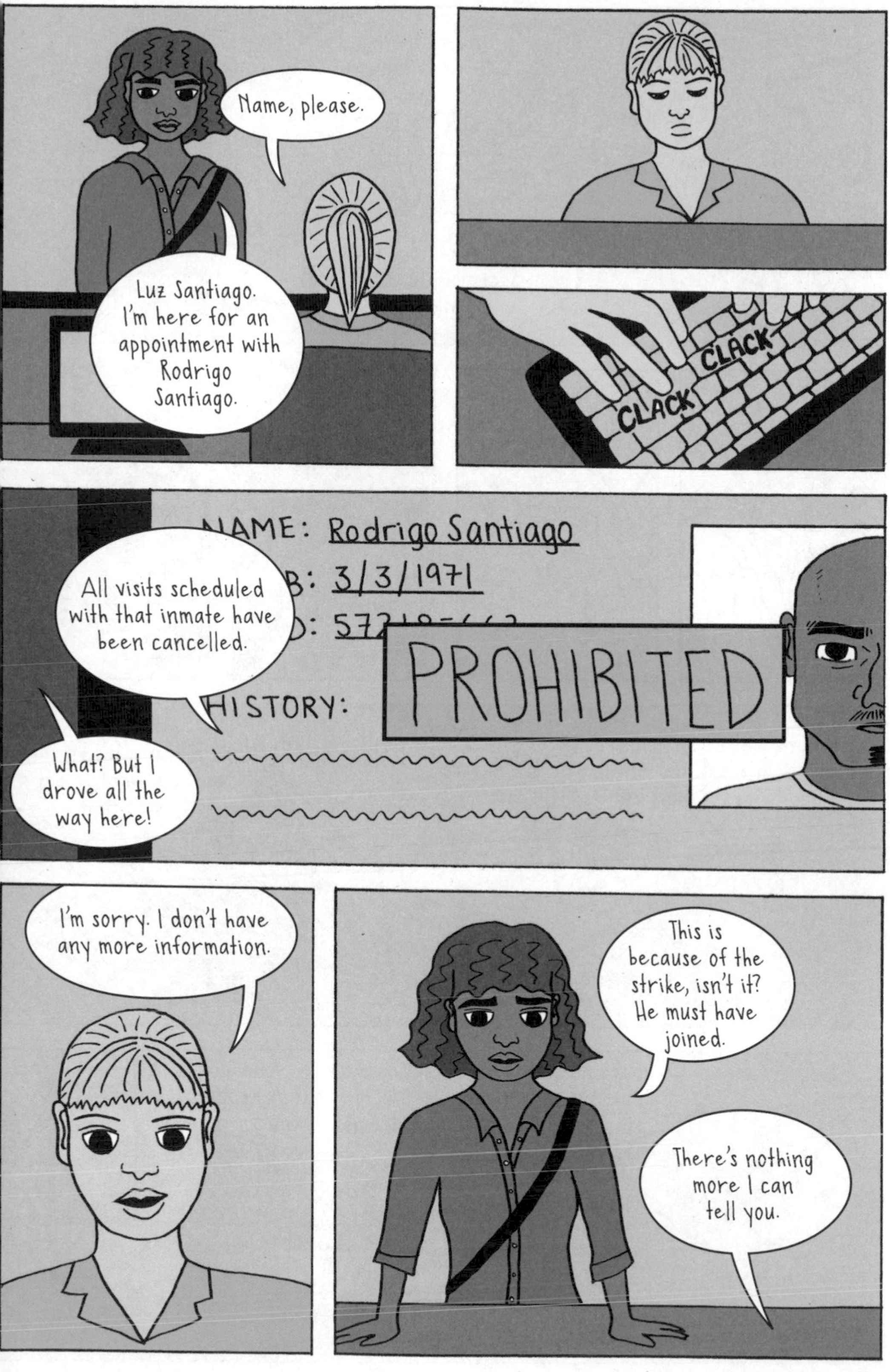

Name, please.
Luz Santiago. I'm here for an appointment with Rodrigo Santiago.
CLACK
CLACK
NAME: Rodrigo Santiago
3/3/1971
HISTORY:
PROHIBITED
All visits scheduled with that inmate have been cancelled.
What? But I drove all the way here!
I'm sorry. I don't have any more information.
This is because of the strike, isn't it? He must have joined.
There's nothing more I can tell you.

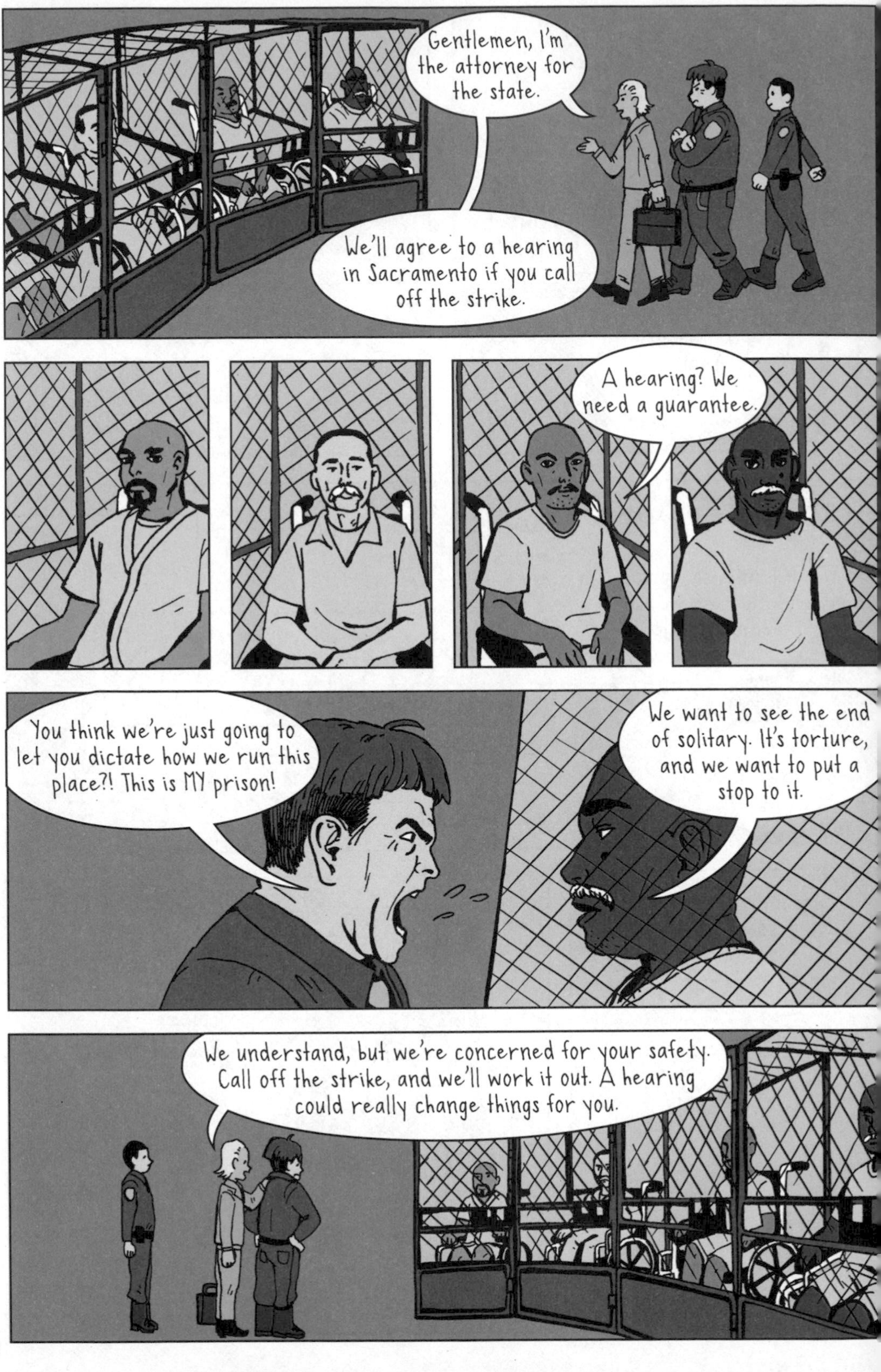
Gentlemen, I'm the attorney for the state.
We'll agree to a hearing in Sacramento if you call off the strike.
A hearing? We need a guarantee.
You think we're just going to let you dictate how we run this place?! This is MY prison!
We want to see the end of solitary. It's torture, and we want to put a stop to it.
We understand, but we're concerned for your safety. Call off the strike, and we'll work it out. A hearing could really change things for you.

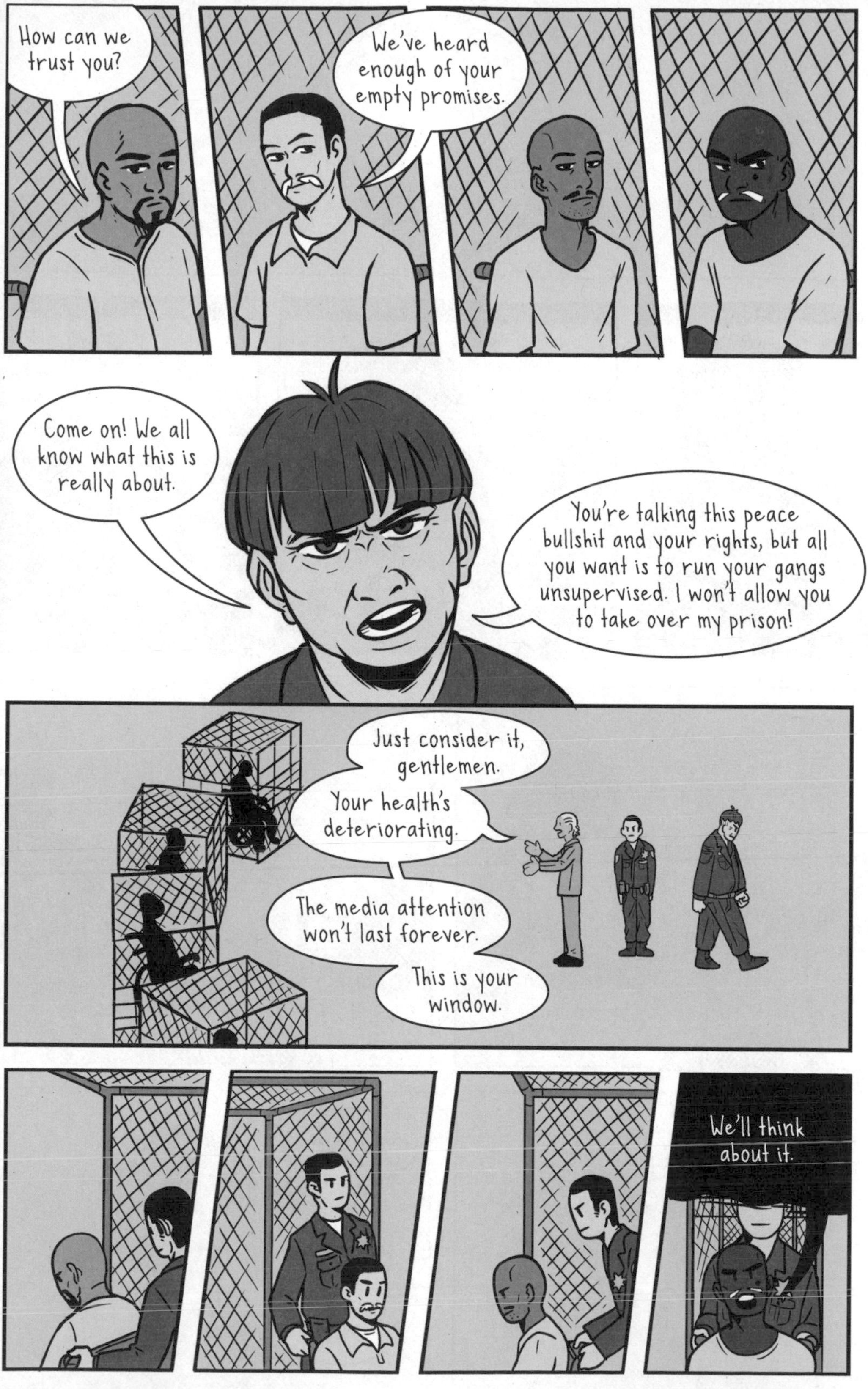
How can we trust you?
We've heard enough of your empty promises.
Come on! We all know what this is really about.
You're talking this peace bullshit and your rights, but all you want is to run your gangs unsupervised. I won't allow you to take over my prison!
Just consider it, gentlemen.
Your health's deteriorating.
The media attention won't last forever.
This is your window.
We'll think about it.

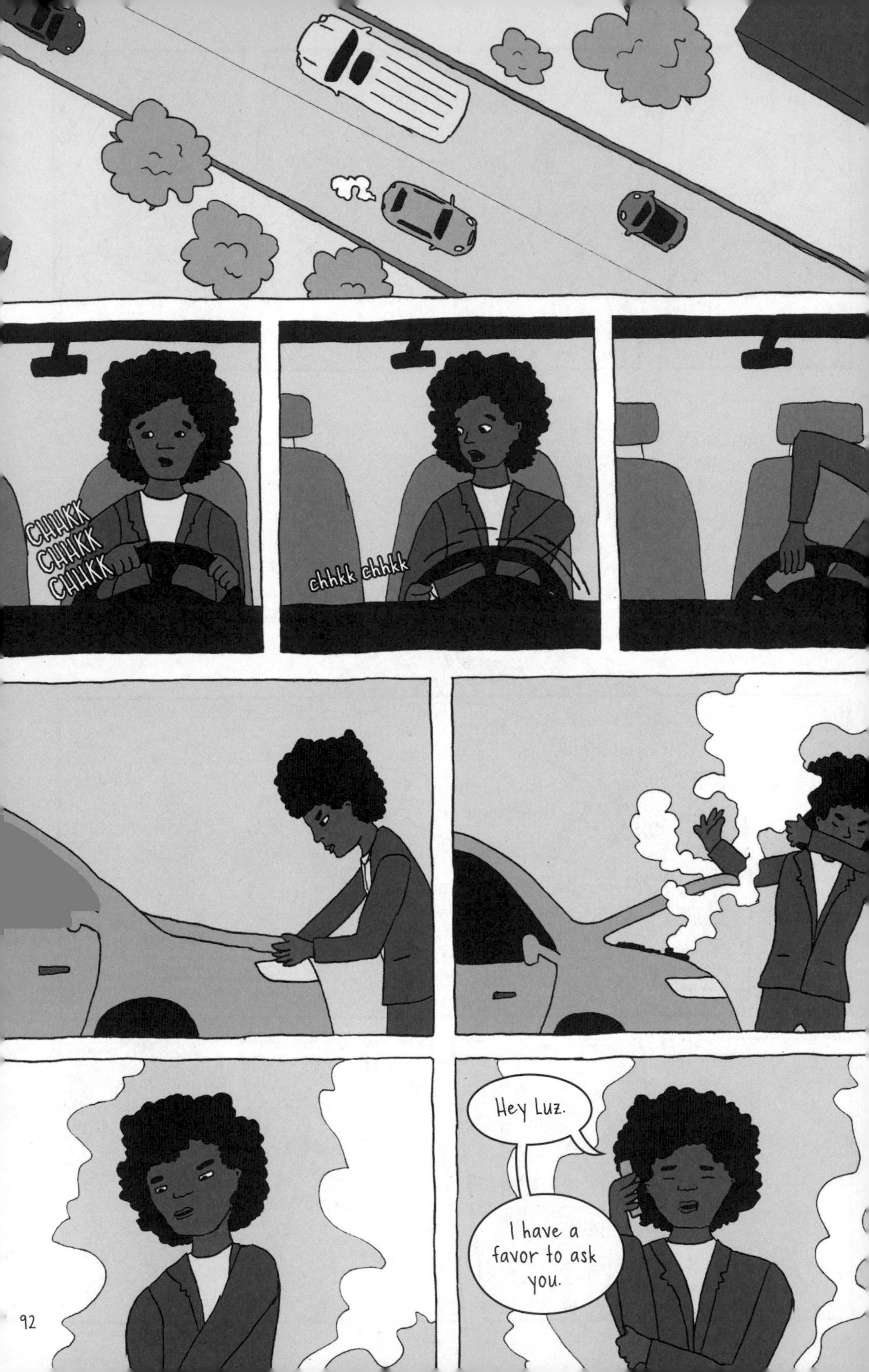
CHHKK
CHHKK
CHHKK
chhkk chhkk
Hey Luz.
I have a favor to ask you.

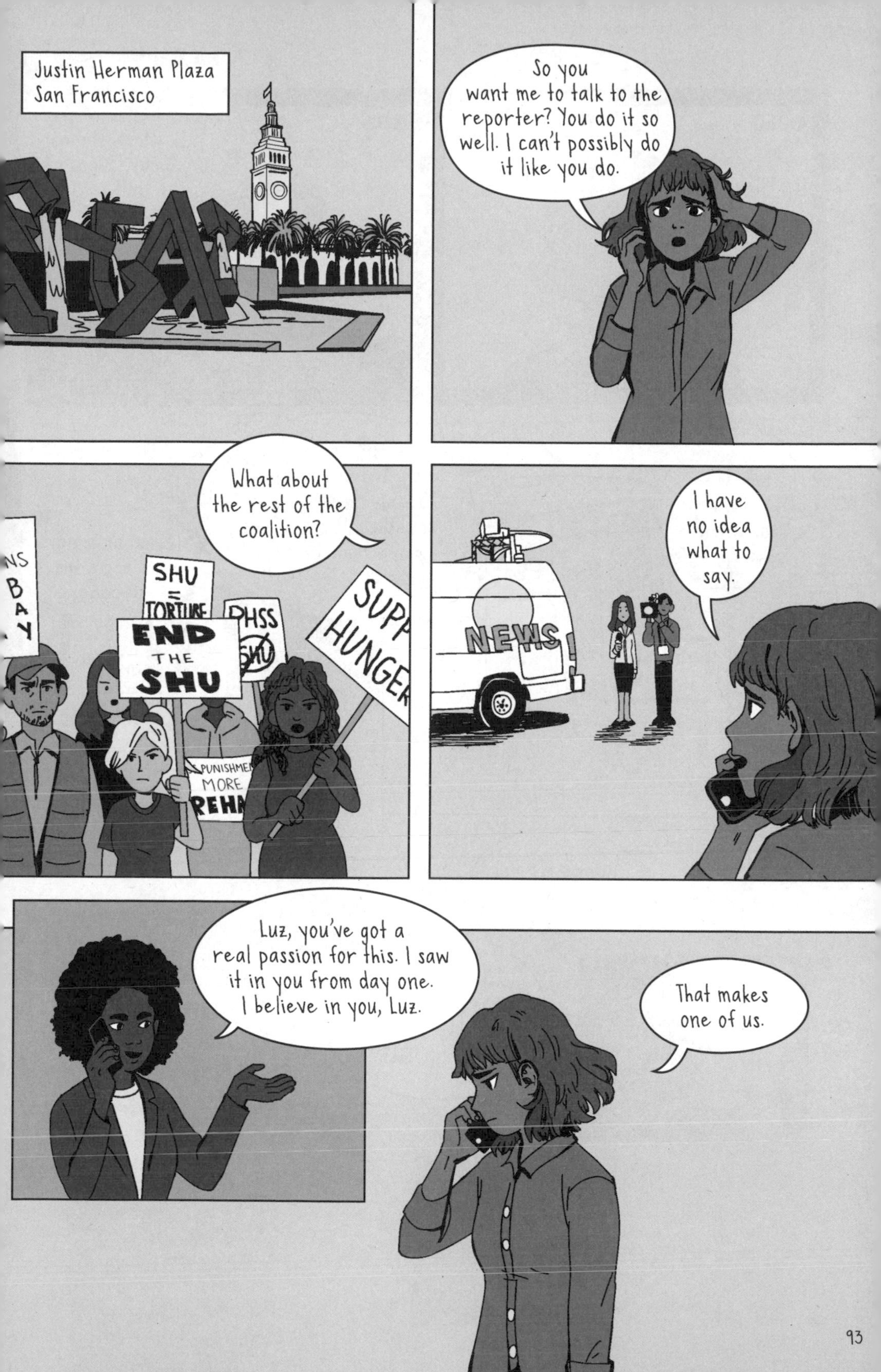
Justin Herman Plaza
San Francisco
So you want me to talk to the reporter? You do it so well. I can't possibly do it like you do.
What about the rest of the coalition?
SHU = TORTURE
END THE SHU
PHSS SHU
SUPP HUNGER
PUNISHMEN MORE REHA
NEWS
I have no idea what to say.
Luz, you've got a real passion for this. I saw it in you from day one. I believe in you, Luz.
That makes one of us.

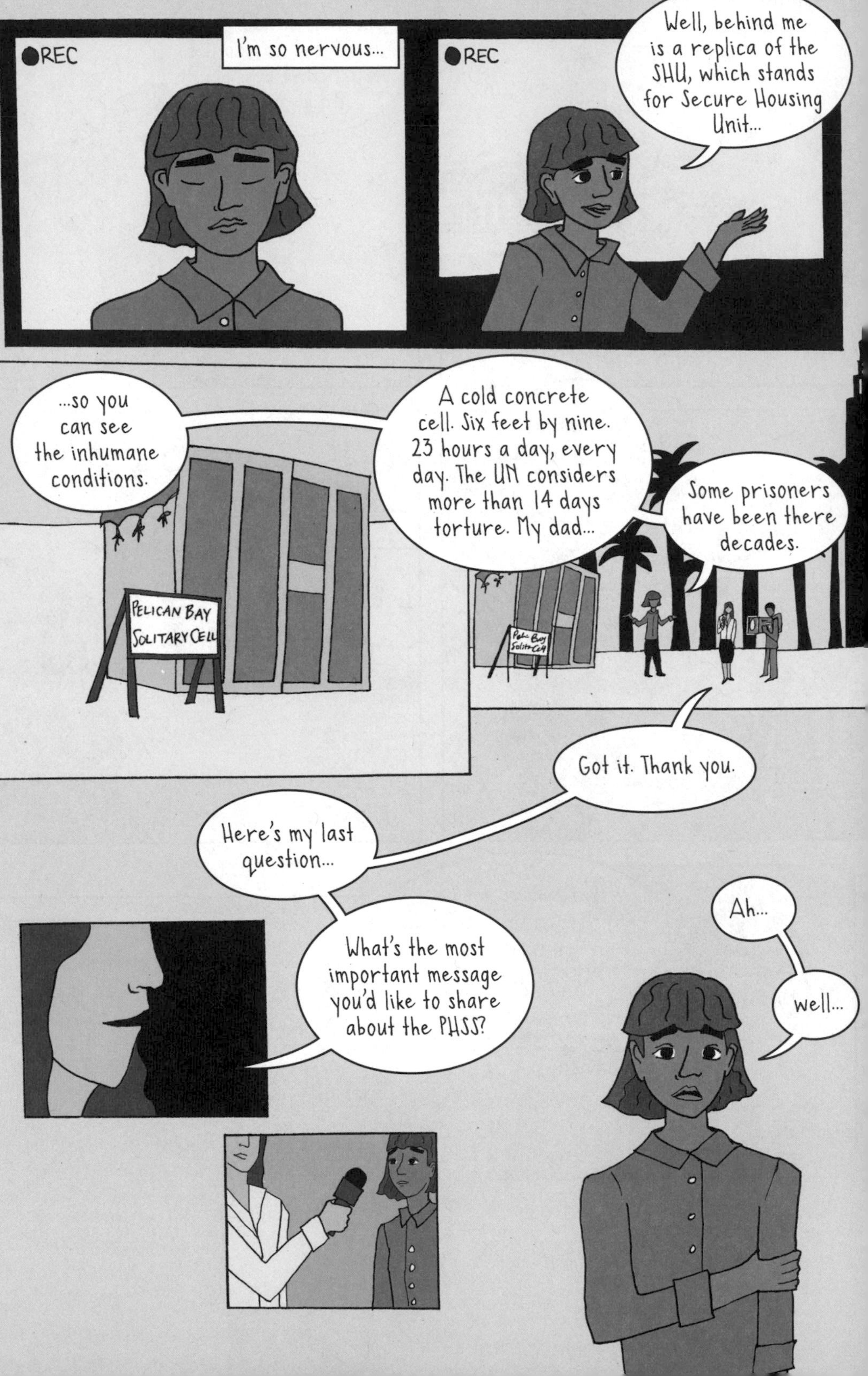
I'm so nervous...
REC
REC
Well, behind me is a replica of the SHU, which stands for Secure Housing Unit...
...so you can see the inhumane conditions.
A cold concrete cell. Six feet by nine. 23 hours a day, every day. The UN considers more than 14 days torture. My dad...
Some prisoners have been there decades.
PELICAN BAY SOLITARY CELL
Got it. Thank you.
Here's my last question...
What's the most important message you'd like to share about the PHSS?
Ah...
well...

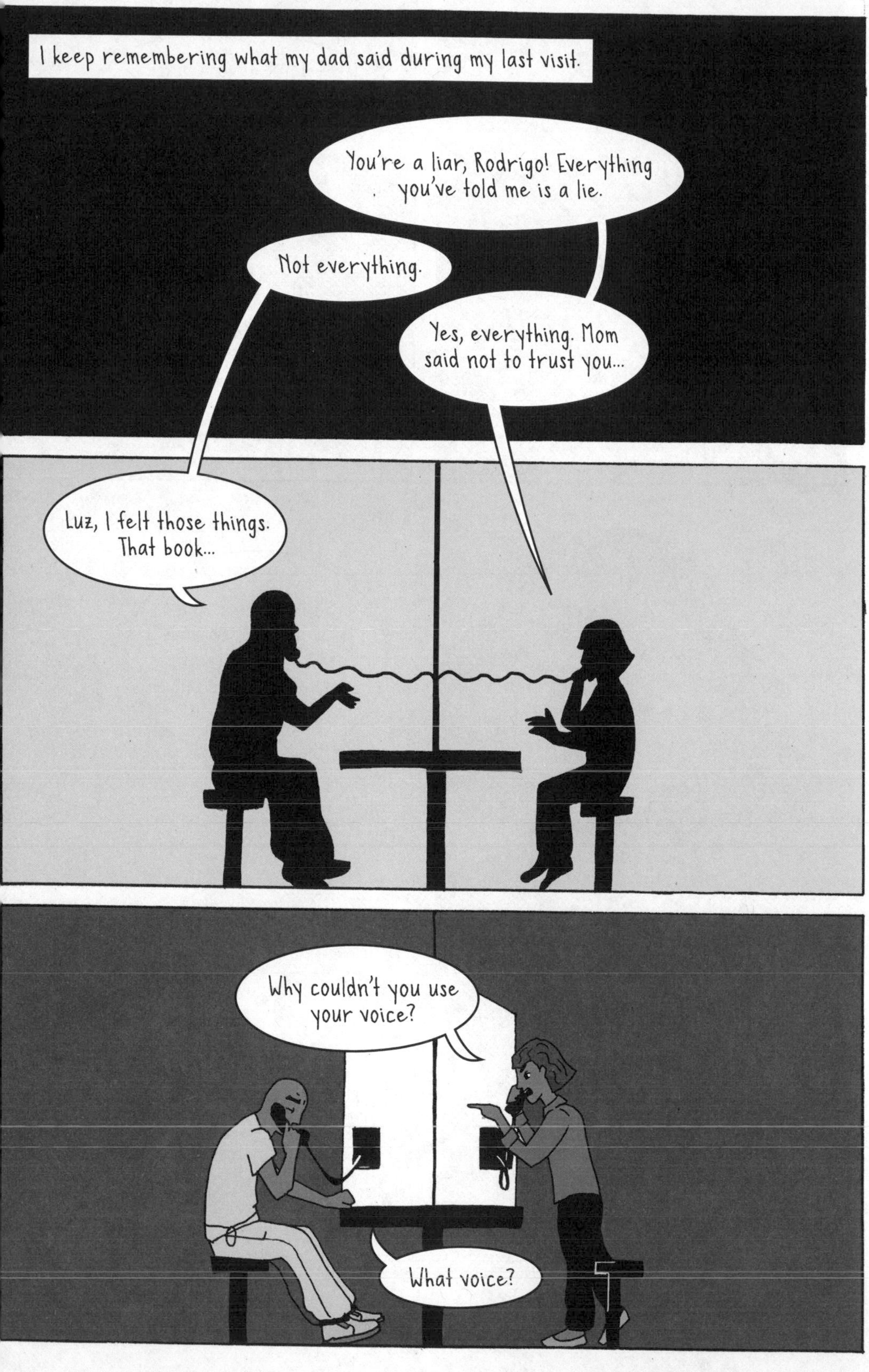
I keep remembering what my dad said during my last visit.
You're a liar, Rodrigo! Everything you've told me is a lie.
Not everything.
Yes, everything. Mom said not to trust you...
Luz, I felt those things. That book...
Why couldn't you use your voice?
What voice?

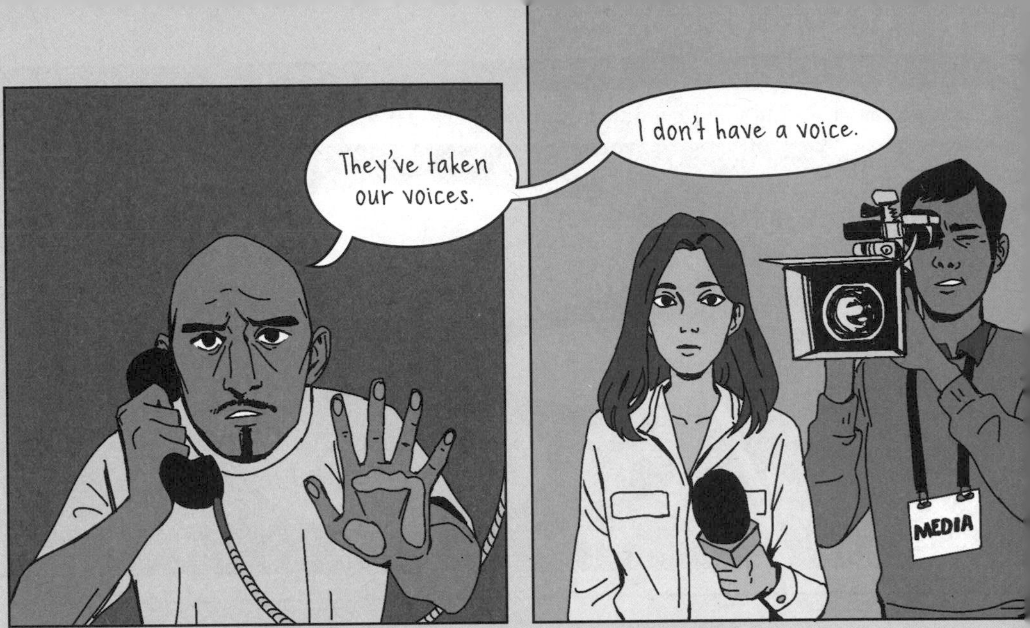
They've taken our voices.
I don't have a voice.
MEDIA

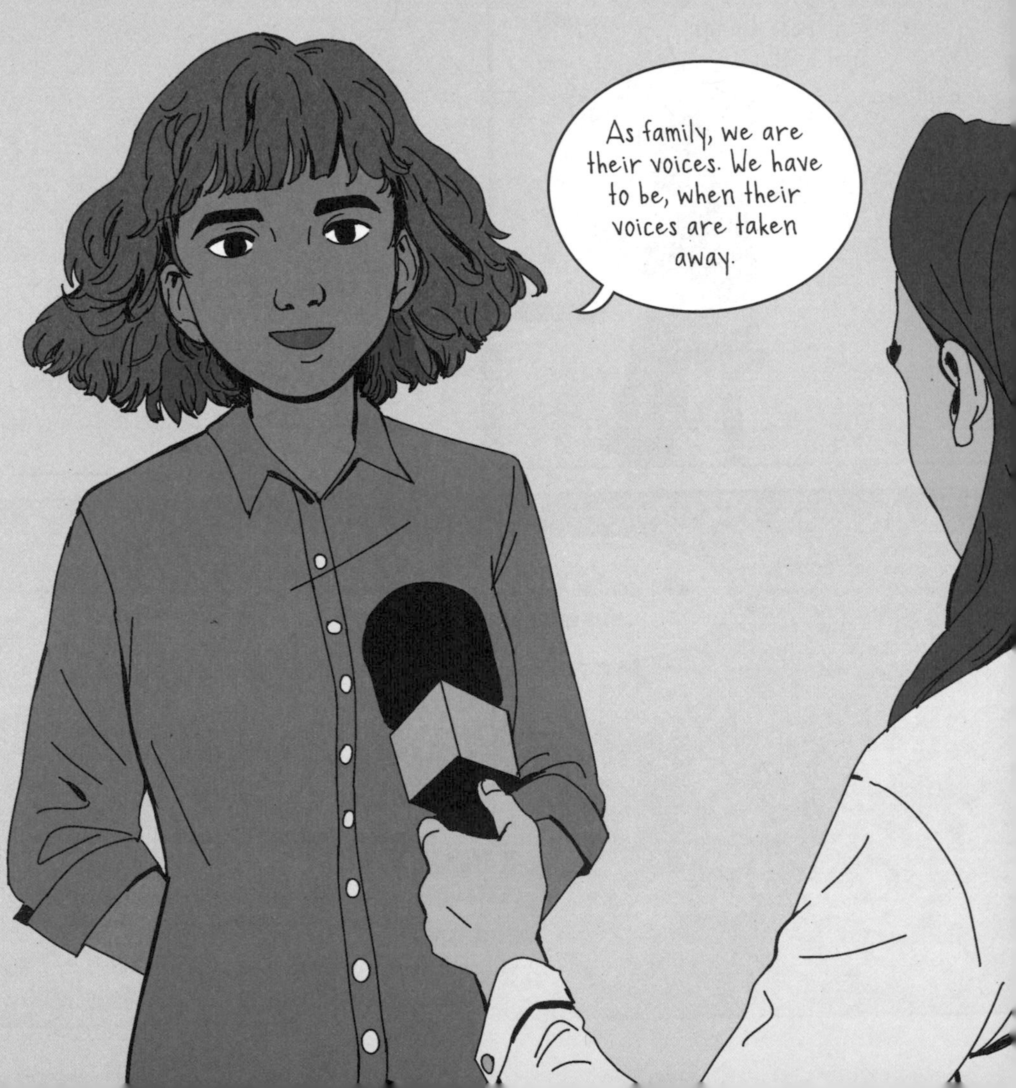
As family, we are their voices. We have to be, when their voices are taken away.

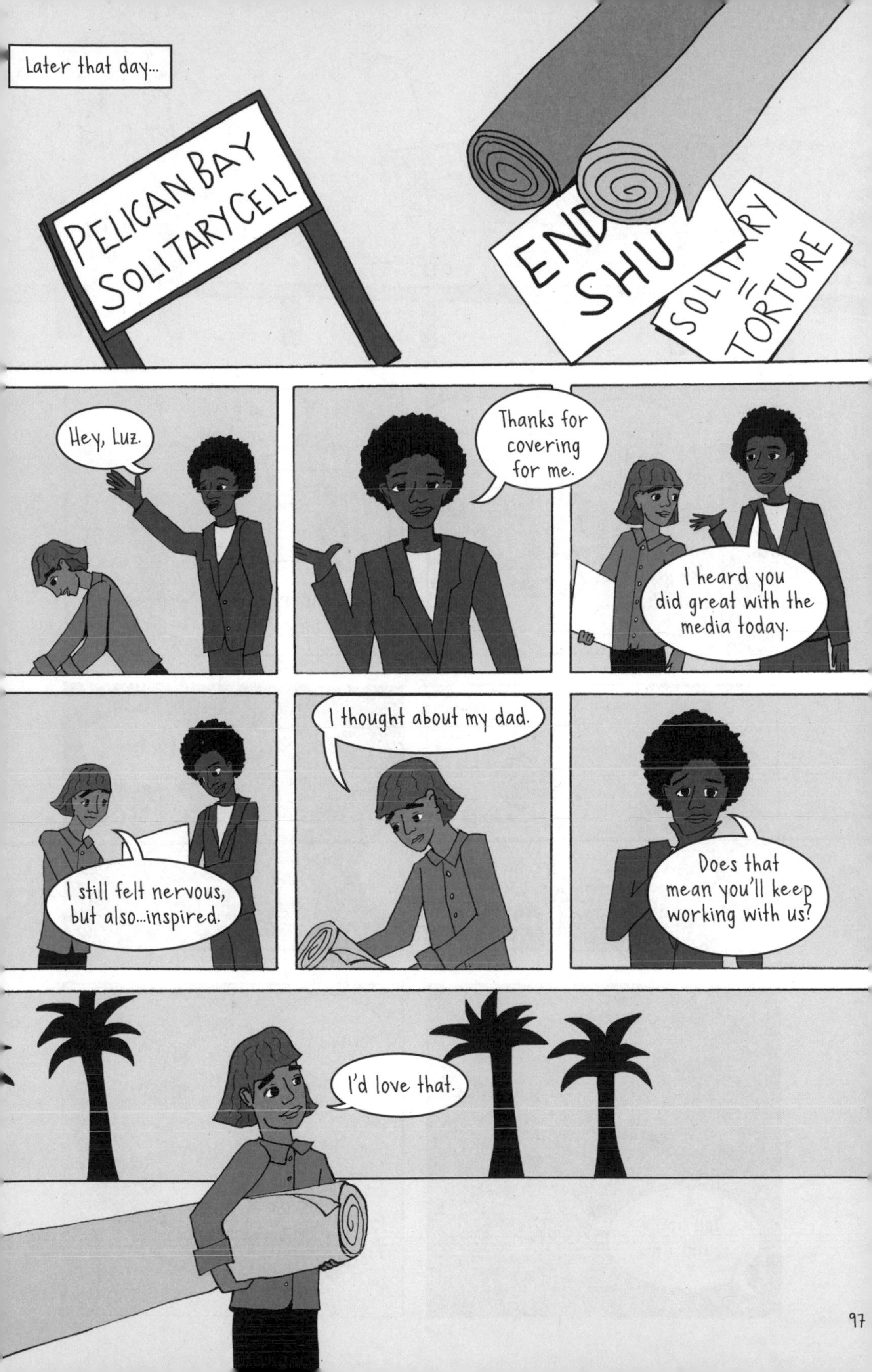
Later that day...
PELICAN BAY SOLITARY CELL
END SHU
SOLITARY = TORTURE
Hey, Luz.
Thanks for covering for me.
I heard you did great with the media today.
I still felt nervous, but also...inspired.
I thought about my dad.
Does that mean you'll keep working with us?
I'd love that.

Forty days... and forty... nights.
Move it.
No news for days.
I wonder what's going on out there.
Everything hurts.
Maybe you should take a break, kid.
I'm fine!
cough cough
You don't sound fine.
Lay off!

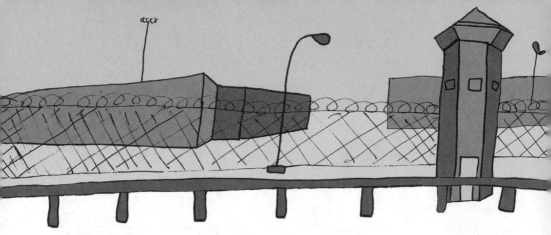

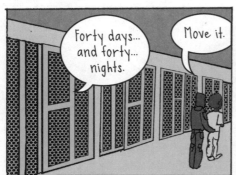

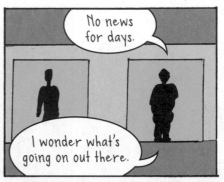

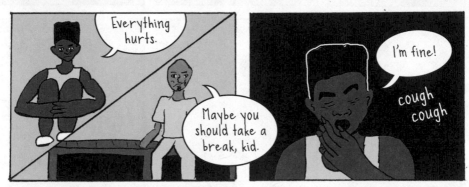

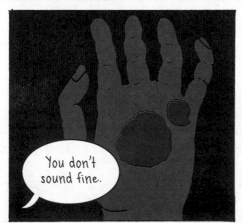

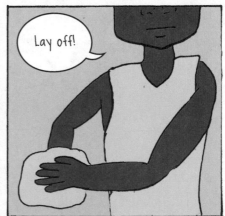

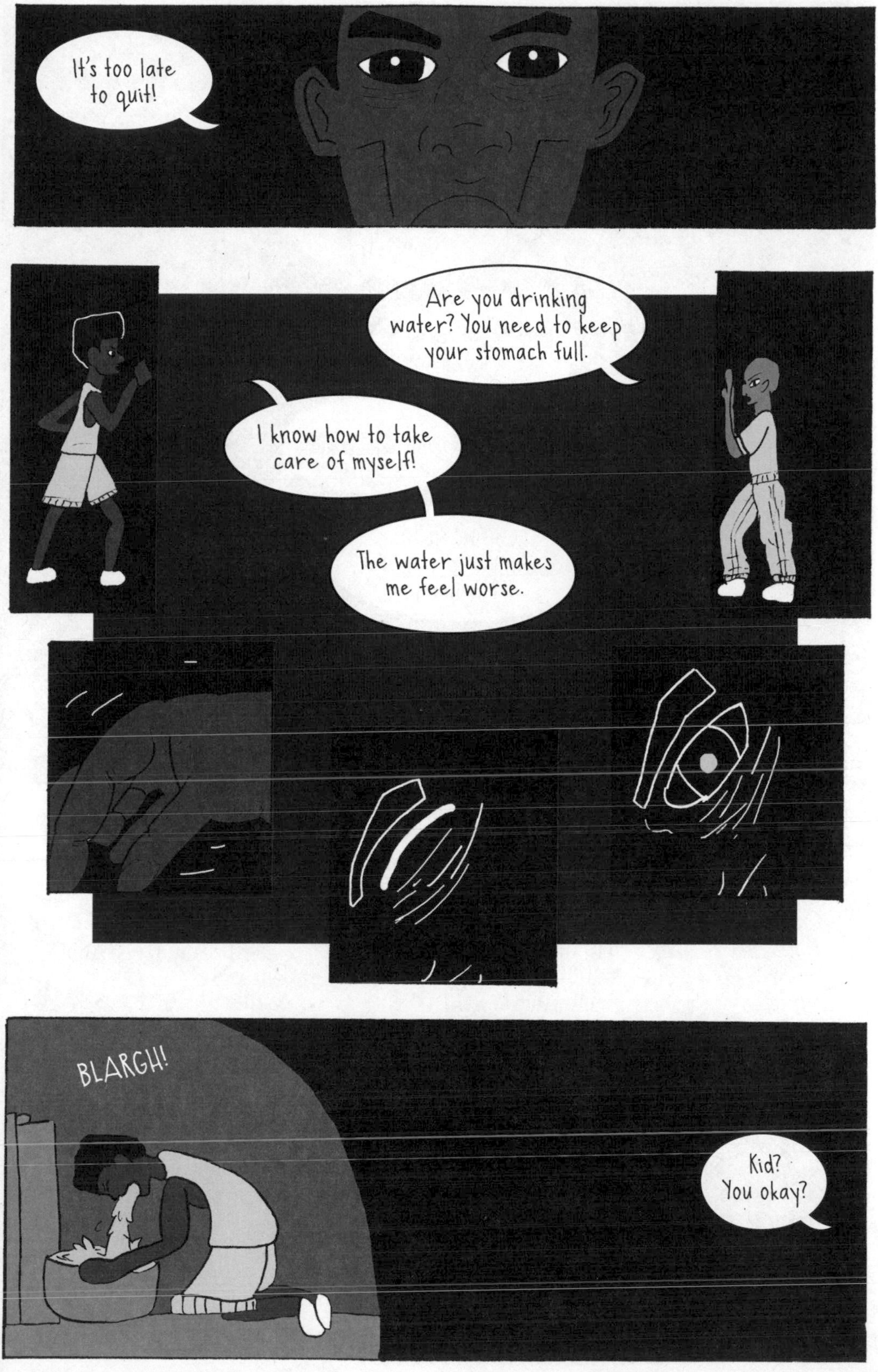
It's too late to quit!
Are you drinking water? You need to keep your stomach full.
I know how to take care of myself!
The water just makes me feel worse.
BLARGH!
Kid? You okay?

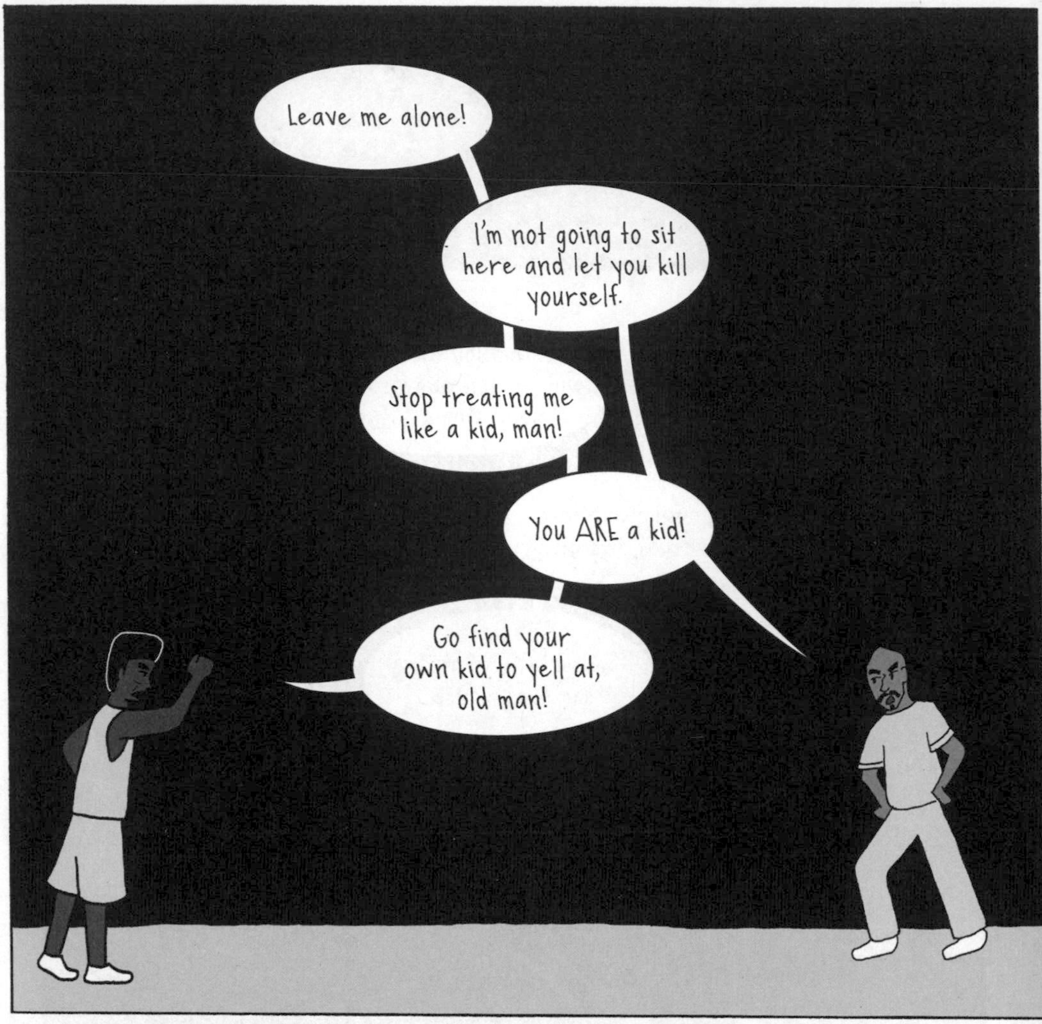
Leave me alone!
I'm not going to sit here and let you kill yourself.
Stop treating me like a kid, man!
You ARE a kid!
Go find your own kid to yell at, old man!

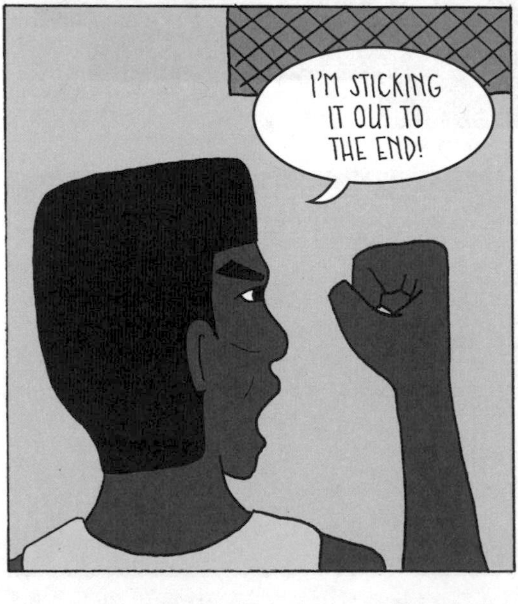
I'M STICKING IT OUT TO THE END!

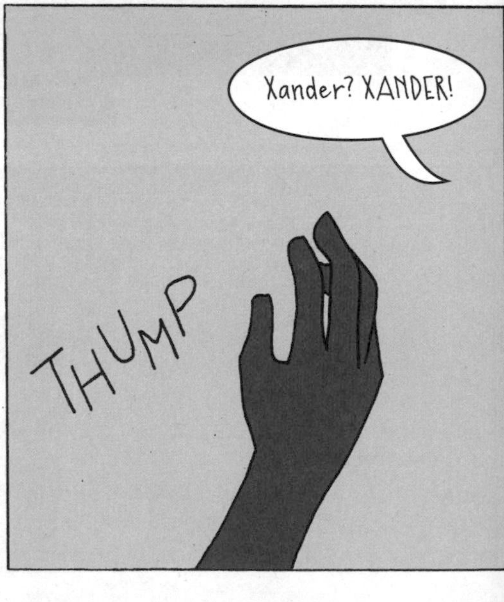
Xander? XANDER!
THUMP

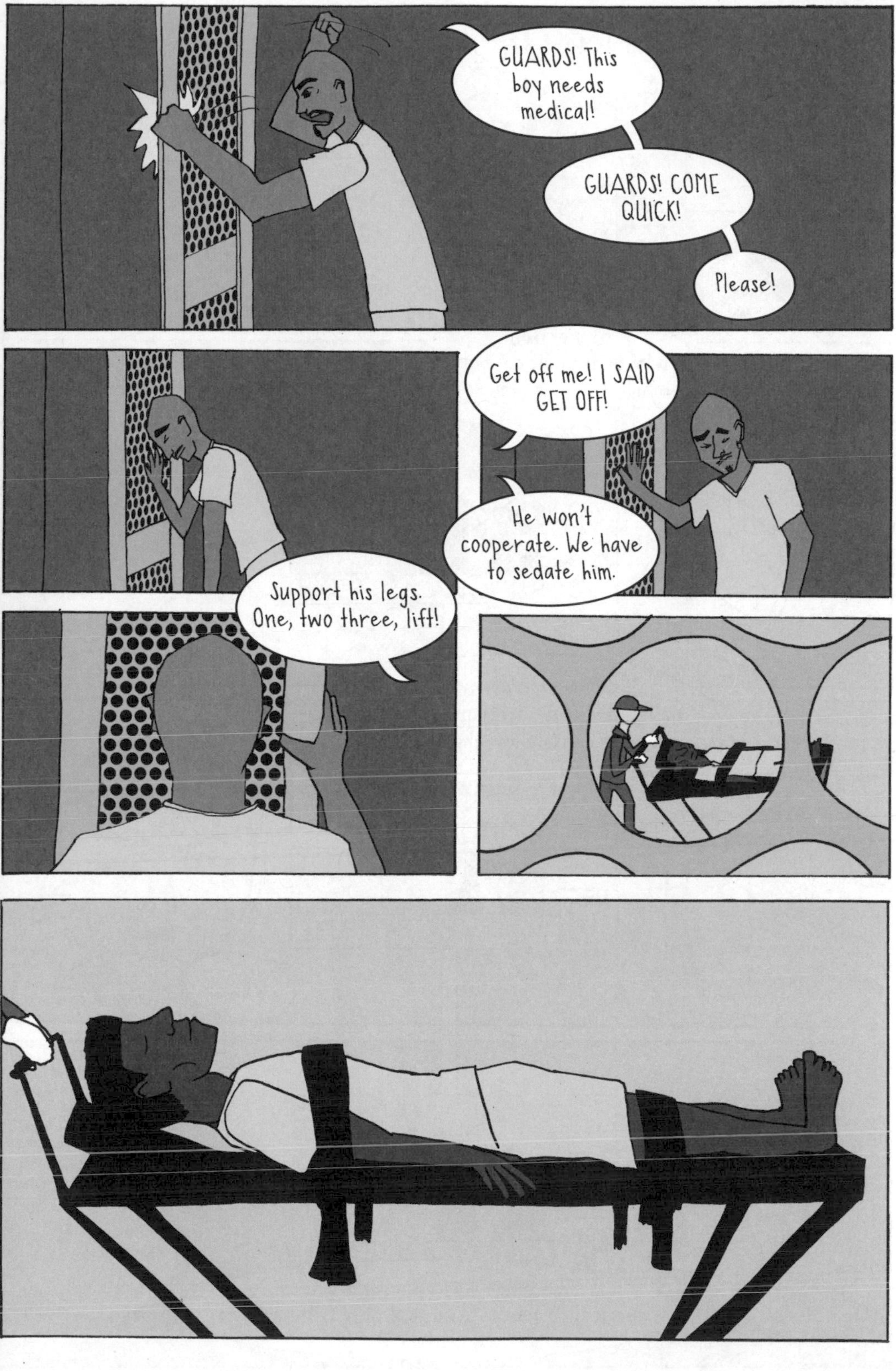
GUARDS! This boy needs medical!
GUARDS! COME QUICK!
Please!
Get off me! I SAID GET OFF!
He won't cooperate. We have to sedate him.
Support his legs. One, two three, lift!

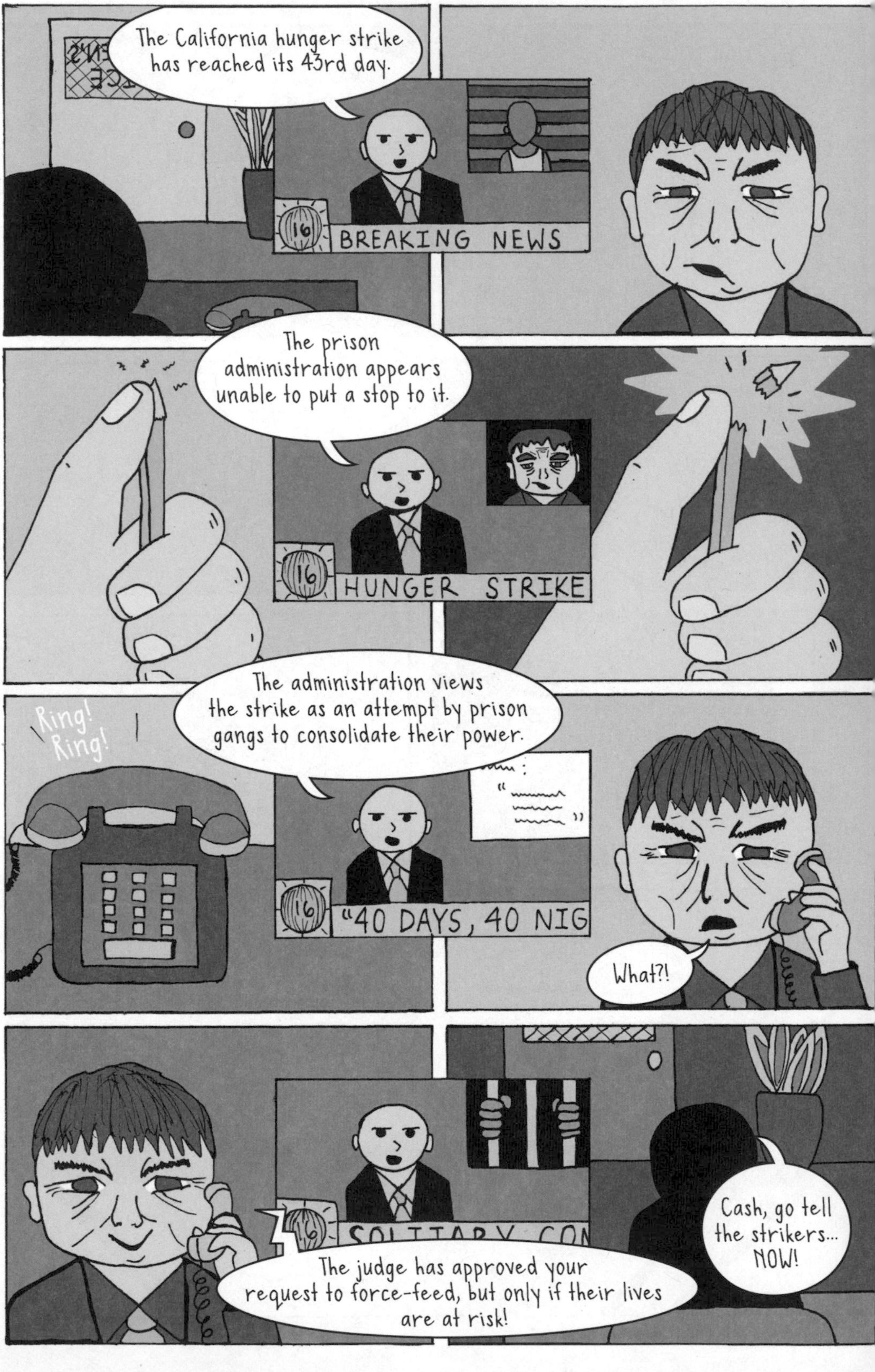
The California hunger strike has reached its 43rd day.
BREAKING NEWS
The prison administration appears unable to put a stop to it.
HUNGER STRIKE
The administration views the strike as an attempt by prison gangs to consolidate their power.
Ring! Ring!
"40 DAYS, 40 NIG
What?!
Cash, go tell the strikers... NOW!
The judge has approved your request to force-feed, but only if their lives are at risk!

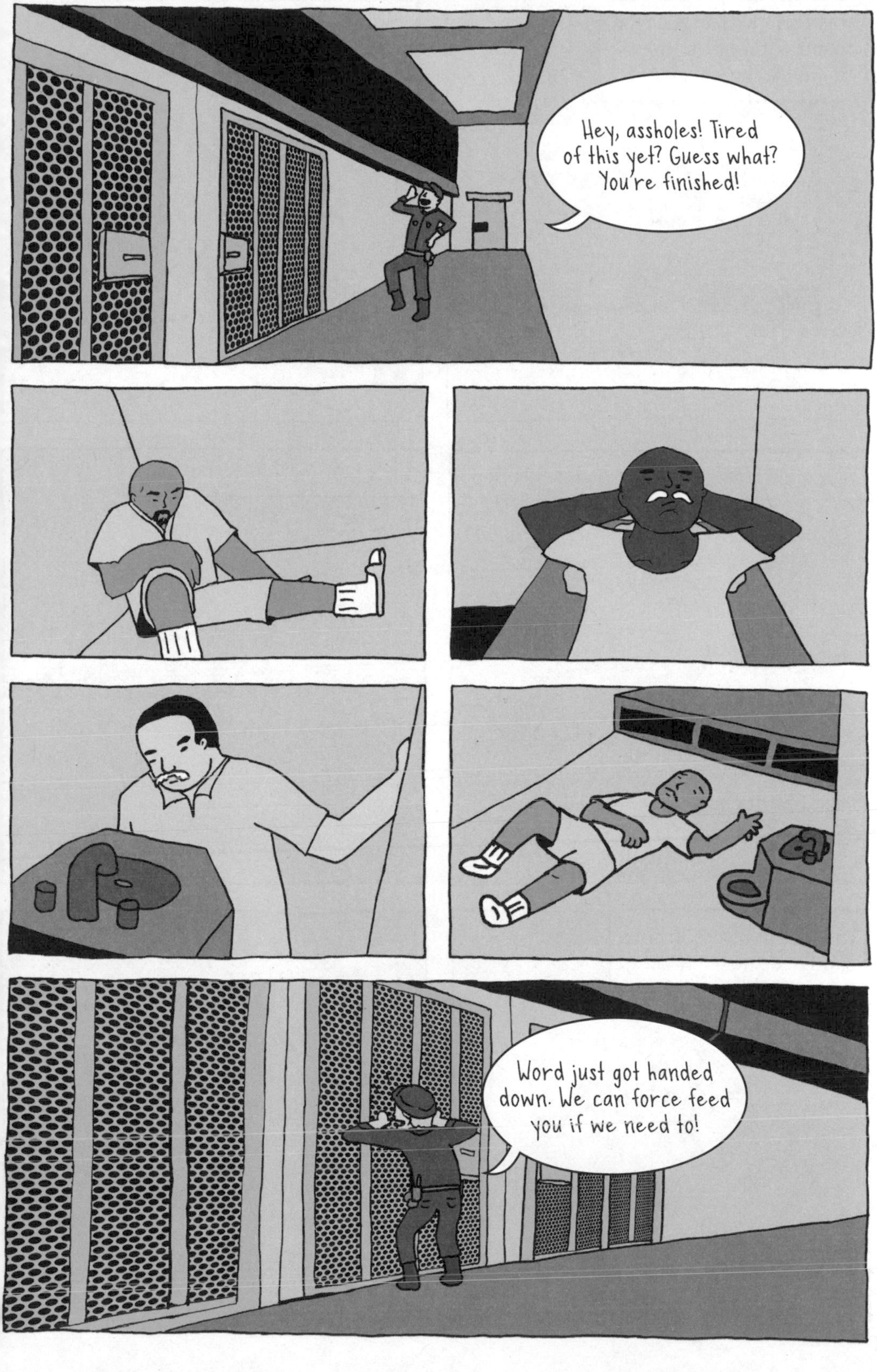
Hey, assholes! Tired of this yet? Guess what? You're finished!
Word just got handed down. We can force feed you if we need to!

It used to be that a day in solitary felt like a week, a month like half a year...

I haven't eaten in 52 days. But it feels like so much longer.

I'm running out of ways to distract myself.

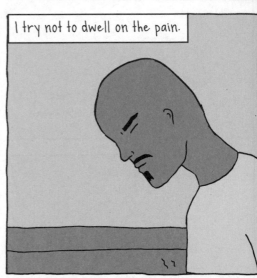

I try not to dwell on the pain.

When I get up, my heart starts racing in my chest.

Damn it! Are those ants?

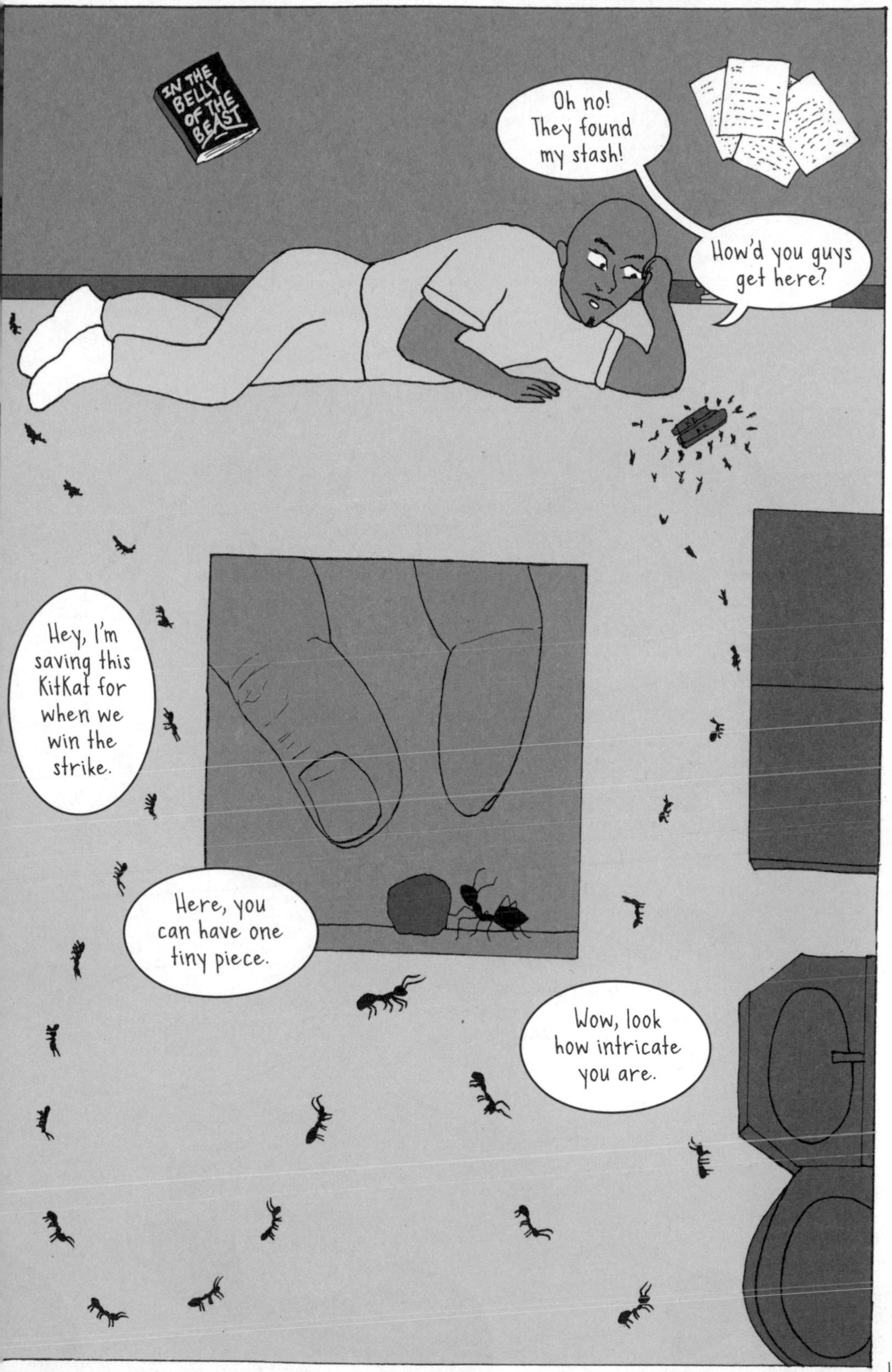
IN THE BELLY OF THE BEAST
Oh no! They found my stash!
How'd you guys get here?
Hey, I'm saving this KitKat for when we win the strike.
Here, you can have one tiny piece.
Wow, look how intricate you are.

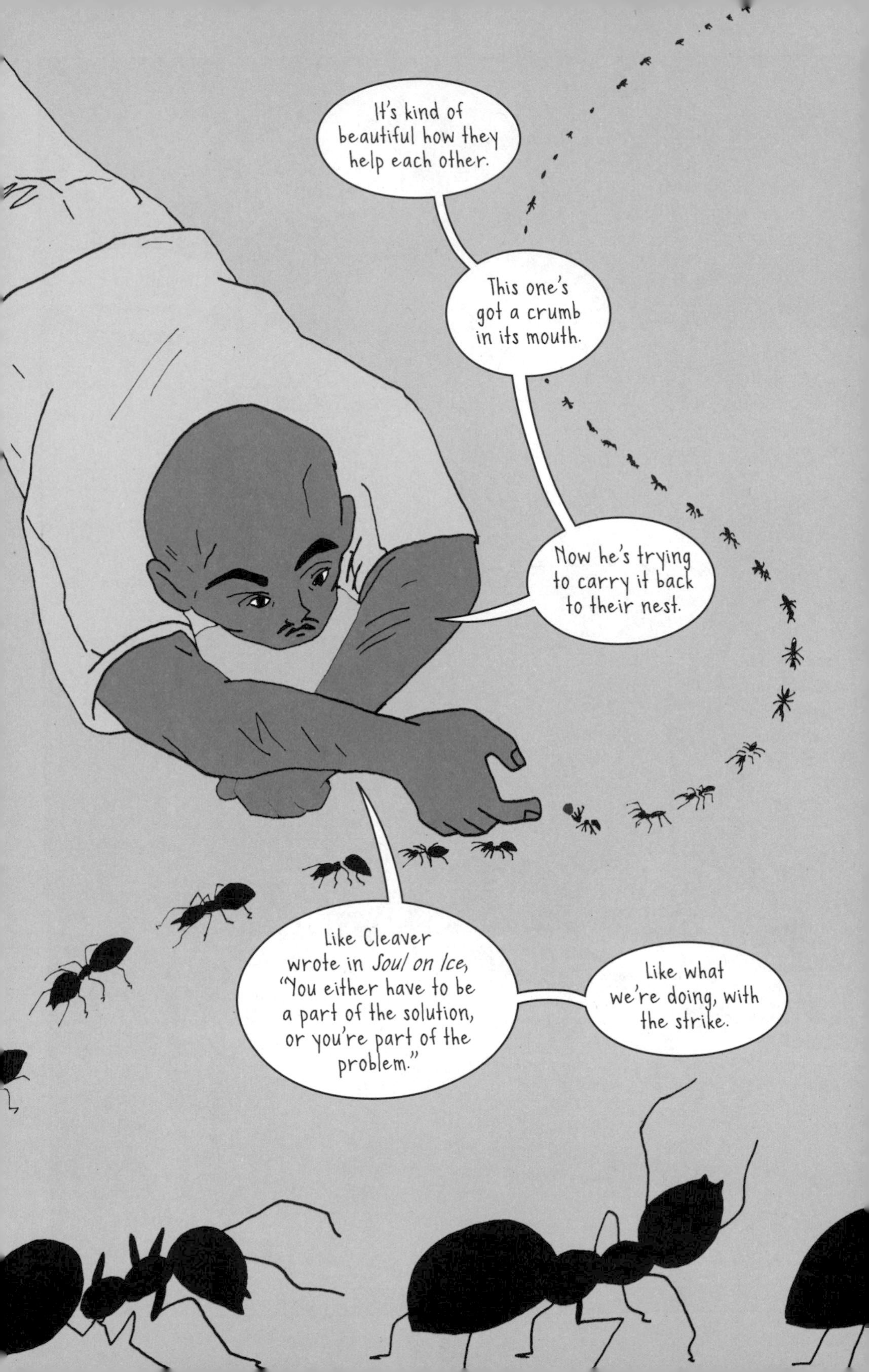
It's kind of beautiful how they help each other.
This one's got a crumb in its mouth.
Now he's trying to carry it back to their nest.
Like Cleaver wrote in *Soul on Ice*, "You either have to be a part of the solution, or you're part of the problem."
Like what we're doing, with the strike.

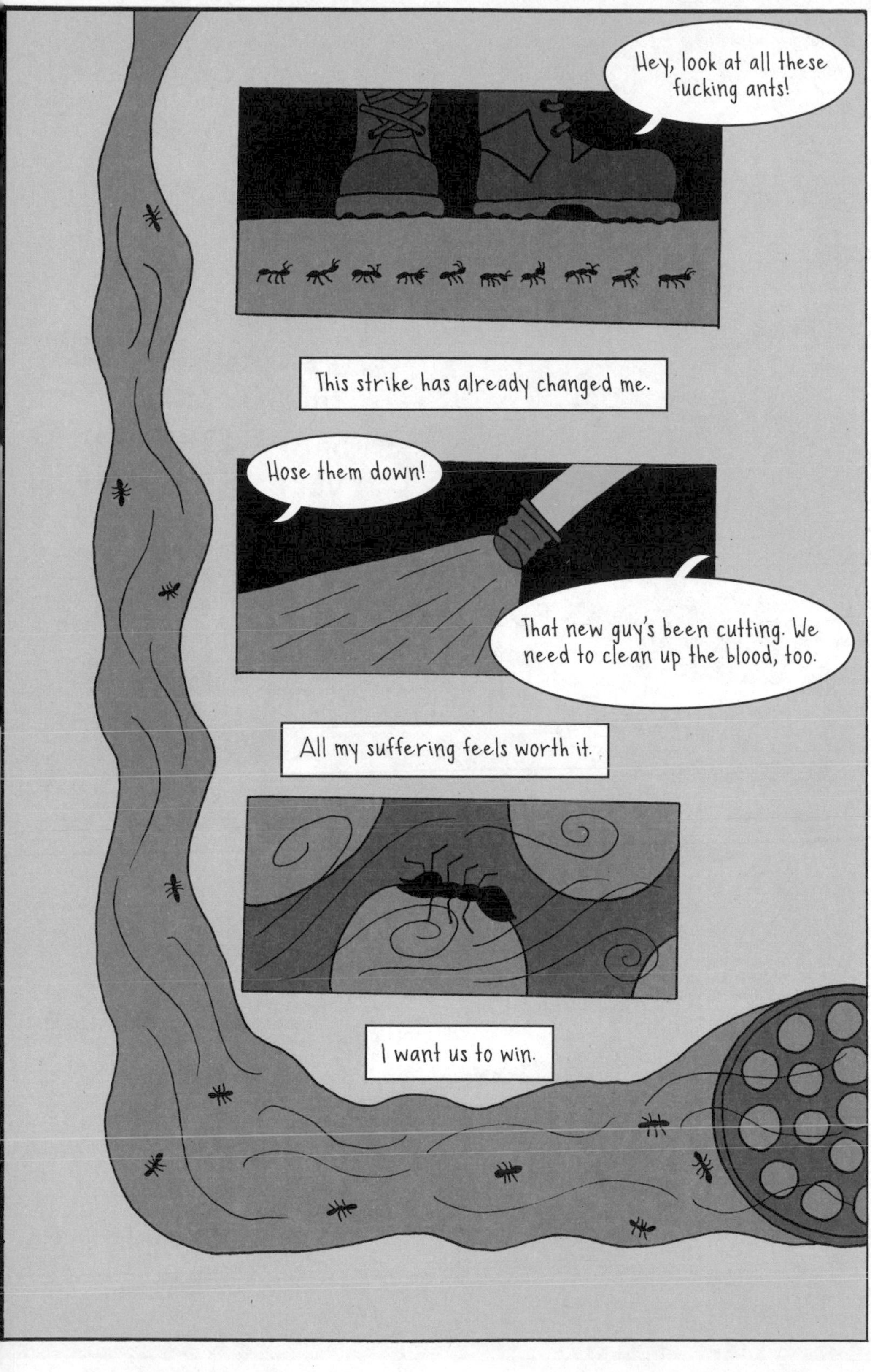
Hey, look at all these fucking ants!
This strike has already changed me.
Hose them down!
That new guy's been cutting. We need to clean up the blood, too.
All my suffering feels worth it.
I want us to win.

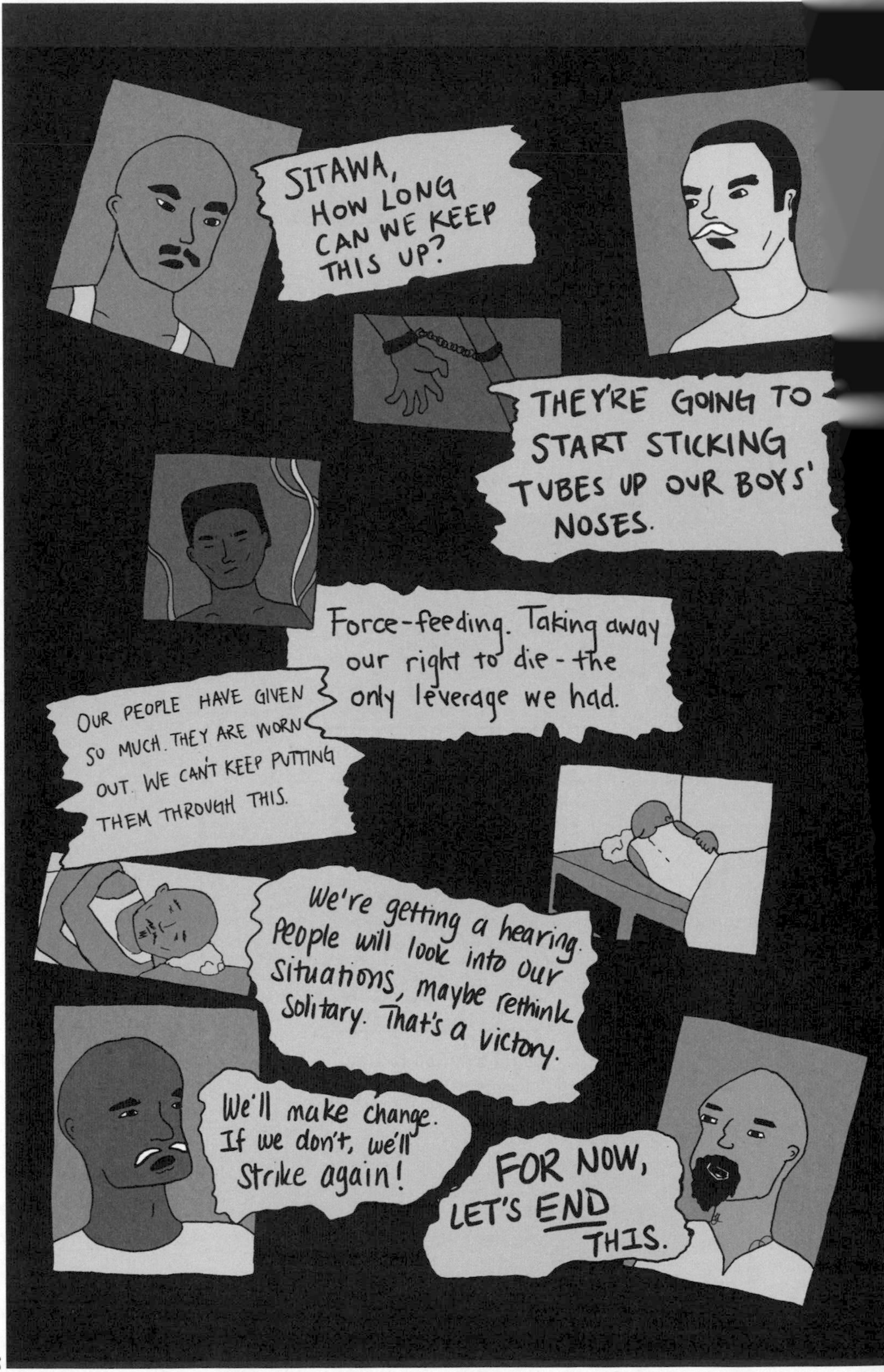
SITAWA, HOW LONG CAN WE KEEP THIS UP?
THEY'RE GOING TO START STICKING TUBES UP OUR BOYS' NOSES.
Force-feeding. Taking away our right to die - the only leverage we had.
OUR PEOPLE HAVE GIVEN SO MUCH. THEY ARE WORN OUT. WE CAN'T KEEP PUTTING THEM THROUGH THIS.
We're getting a hearing. People will look into our situations, maybe rethink solitary. That's a victory.
We'll make change. If we don't, we'll strike again!
FOR NOW, LET'S END THIS.

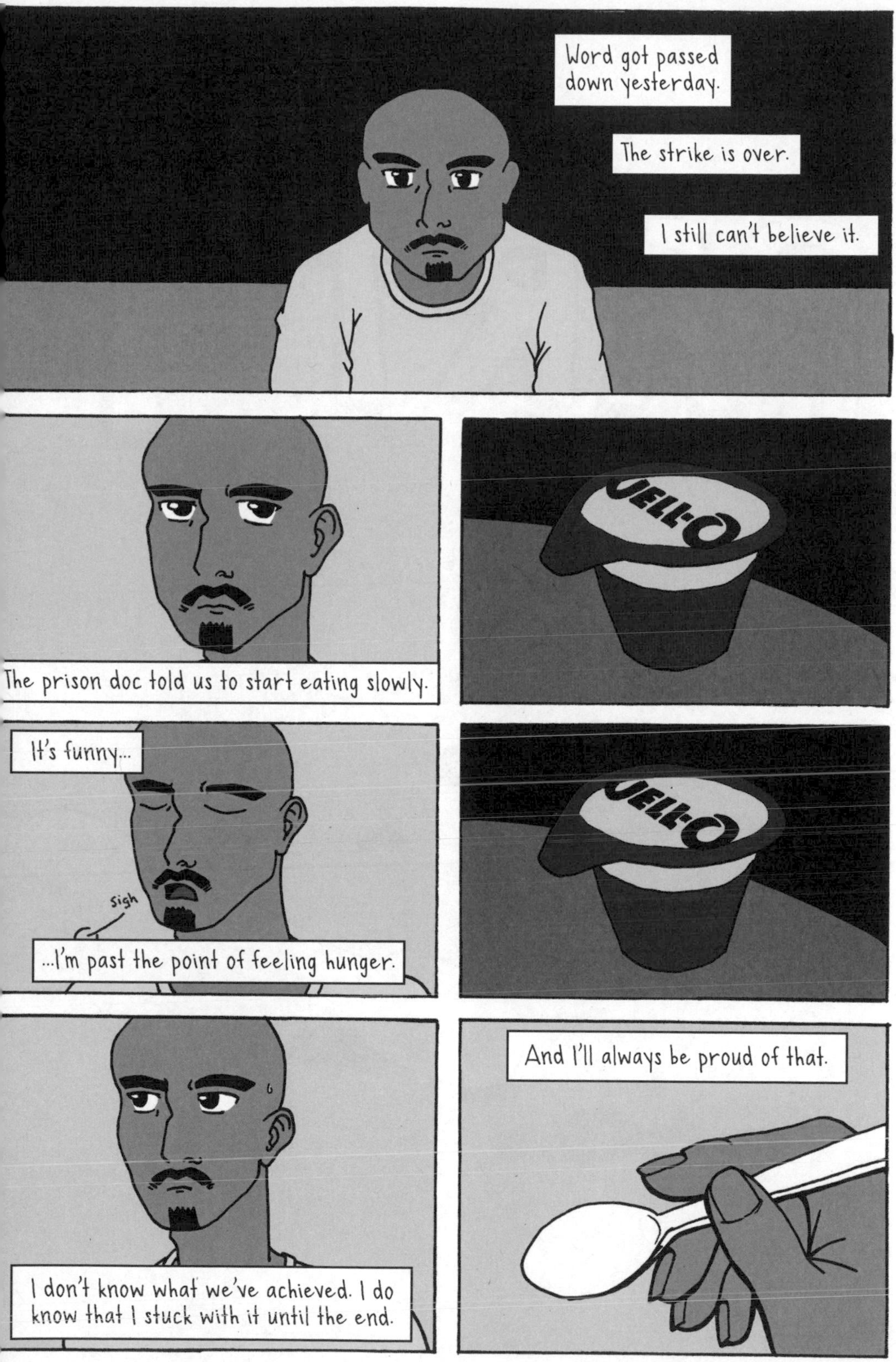

Word got passed down yesterday.
The strike is over.
I still can't believe it.
The prison doc told us to start eating slowly.
JELL-O
It's funny...
Sigh
...I'm past the point of feeling hunger.
JELL-O
I don't know what we've achieved. I do know that I stuck with it until the end.
And I'll always be proud of that.

PART 4

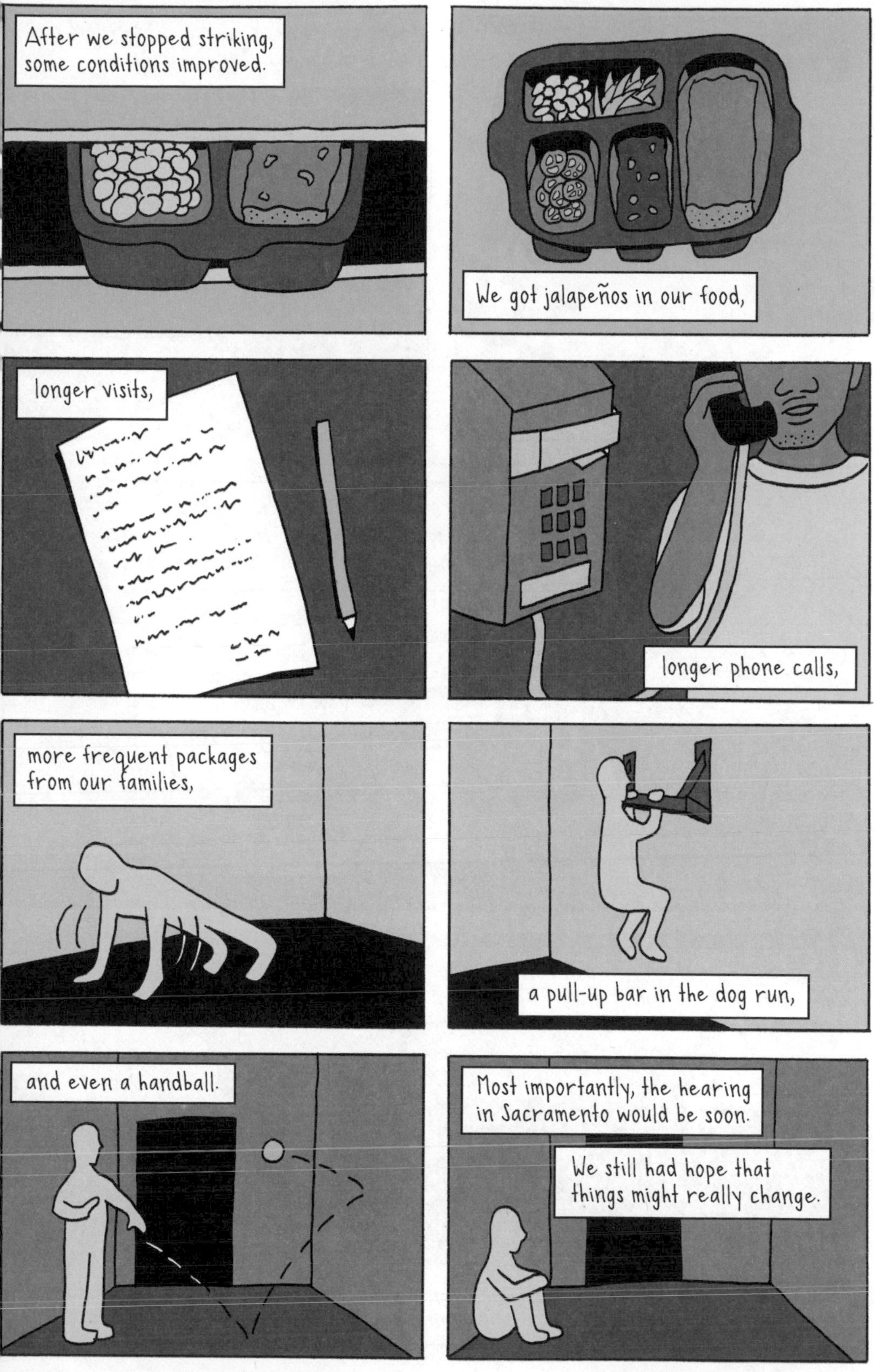
After we stopped striking, some conditions improved.
We got jalapeños in our food,
longer visits,
longer phone calls,
more frequent packages from our families,
a pull-up bar in the dog run,
and even a handball.
Most importantly, the hearing in Sacramento would be soon.
We still had hope that things might really change.

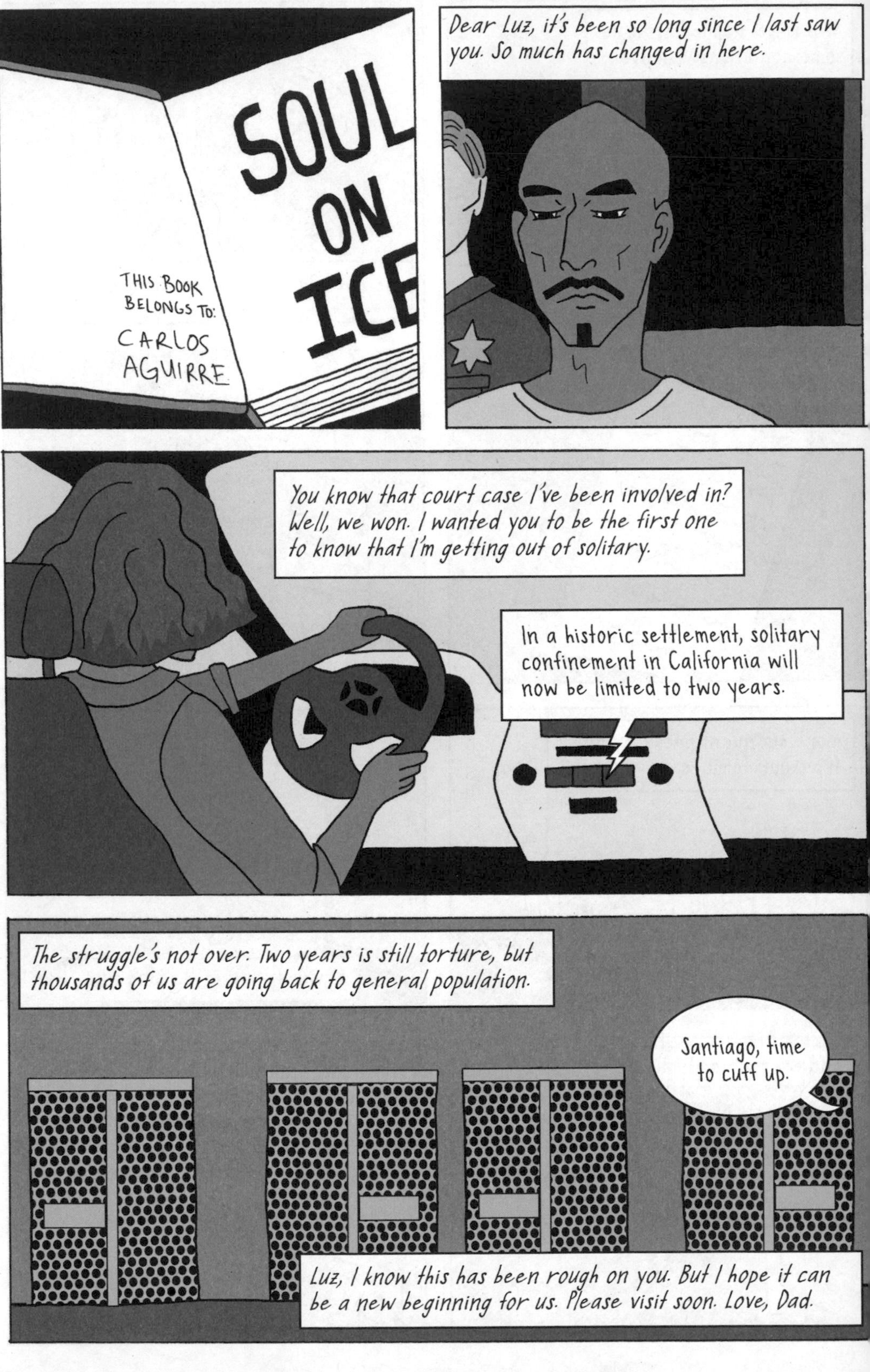
SOUL ON ICE
THIS BOOK BELONGS TO: CARLOS AGUIRRE
Dear Luz, it's been so long since I last saw you. So much has changed in here.
You know that court case I've been involved in? Well, we won. I wanted you to be the first one to know that I'm getting out of solitary.
In a historic settlement, solitary confinement in California will now be limited to two years.
The struggle's not over. Two years is still torture, but thousands of us are going back to general population.
Santiago, time to cuff up.
Luz, I know this has been rough on you. But I hope it can be a new beginning for us. Please visit soon. Love, Dad.

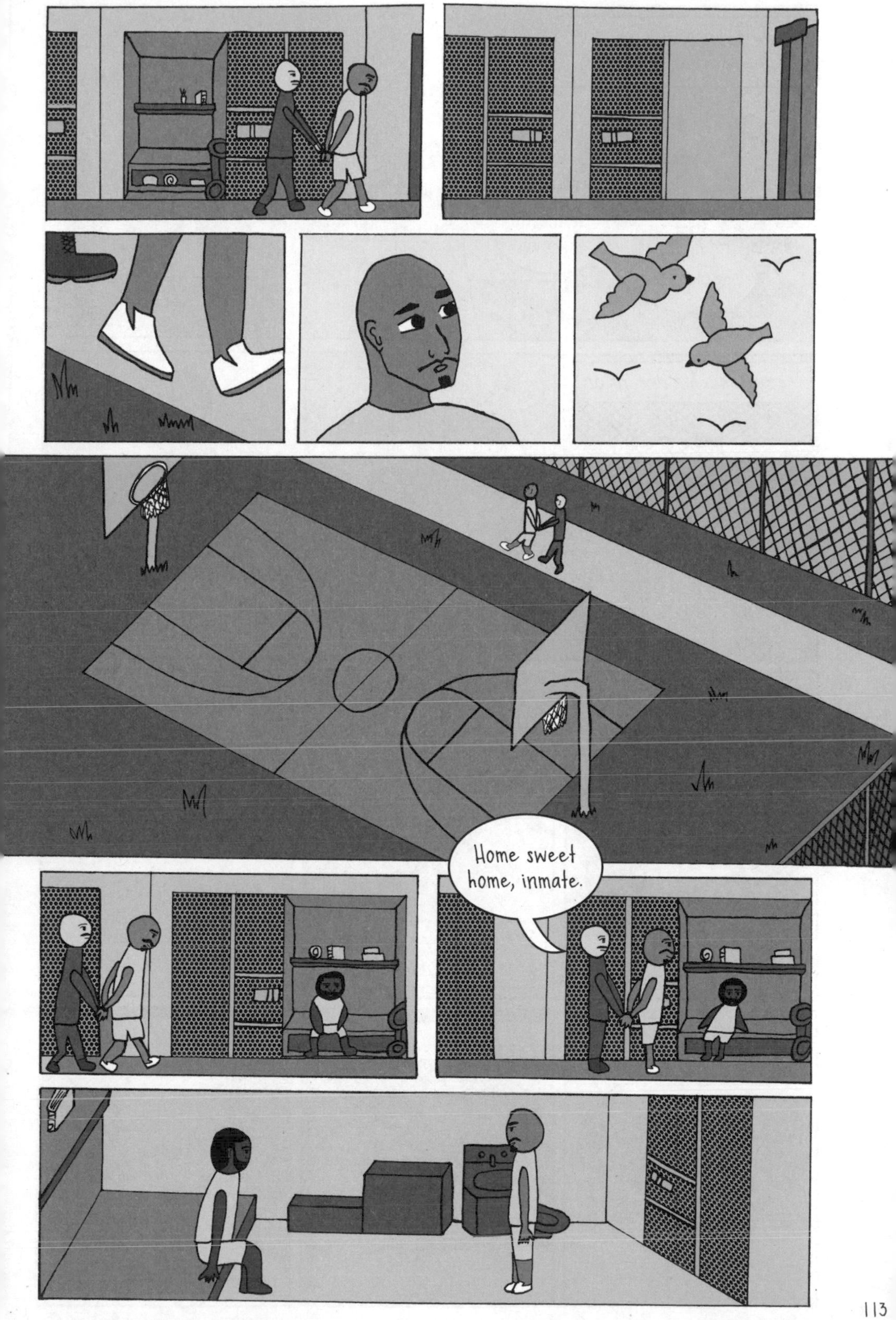
Home sweet home, inmate.

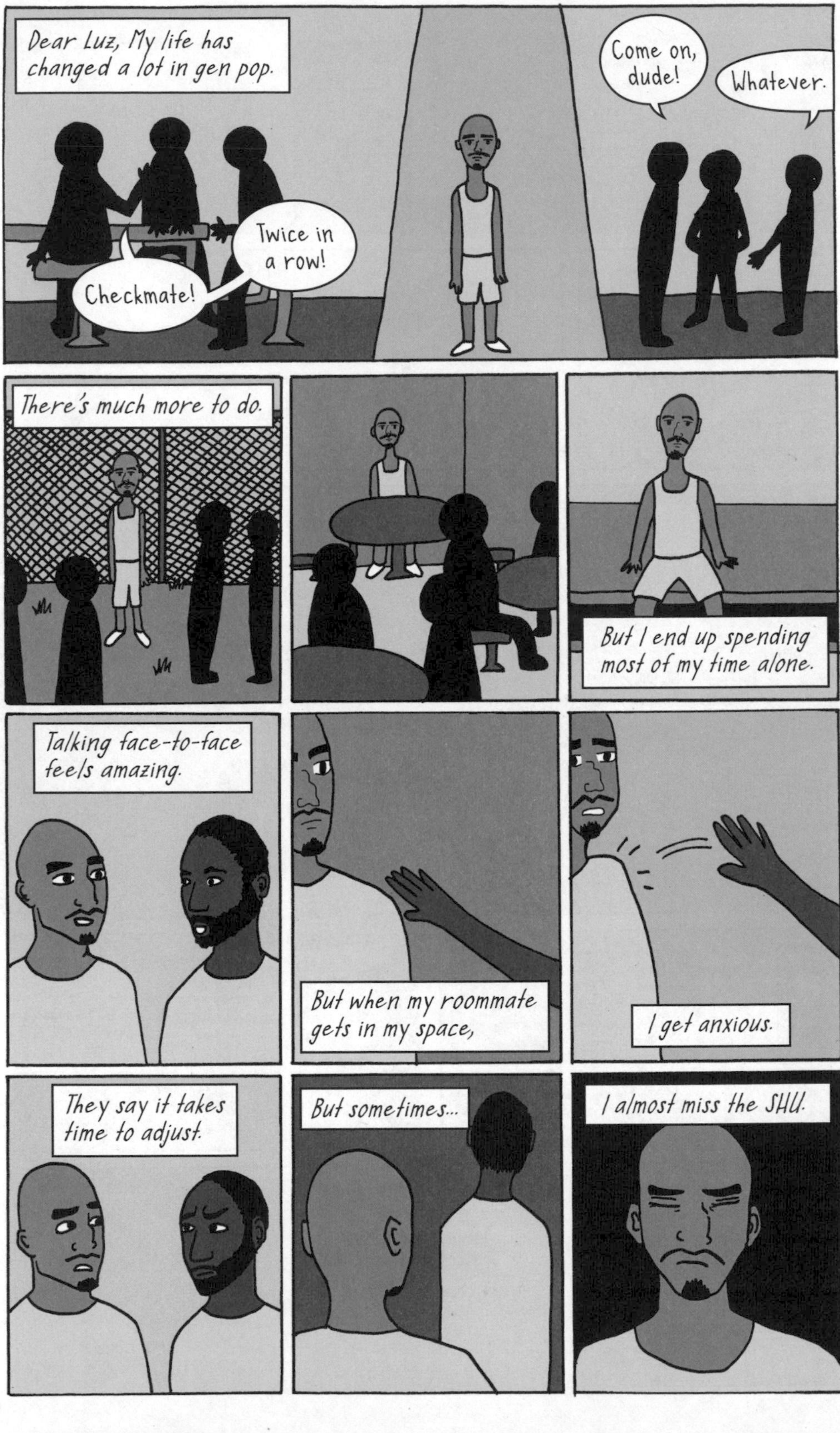
Dear Luz, My life has changed a lot in gen pop.
Checkmate!
Twice in a row!
Come on, dude!
Whatever.
There's much more to do.
But I end up spending most of my time alone.
Talking face-to-face feels amazing.
But when my roommate gets in my space,
I get anxious.
They say it takes time to adjust.
But sometimes...
I almost miss the SHU.

When I'm out on the yard, a lot of guys talk to me.

They all know about the hunger strike. Some of them even thank me.

It's an honor.

It's nice to know we made an impact.

But sometimes I can't help but think of Xander. They won't tell me what happened to him.

When he never came back from medical, I feared the worst.

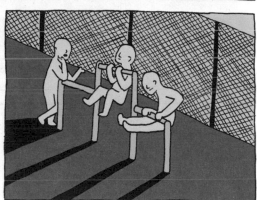

And I feel guilty.

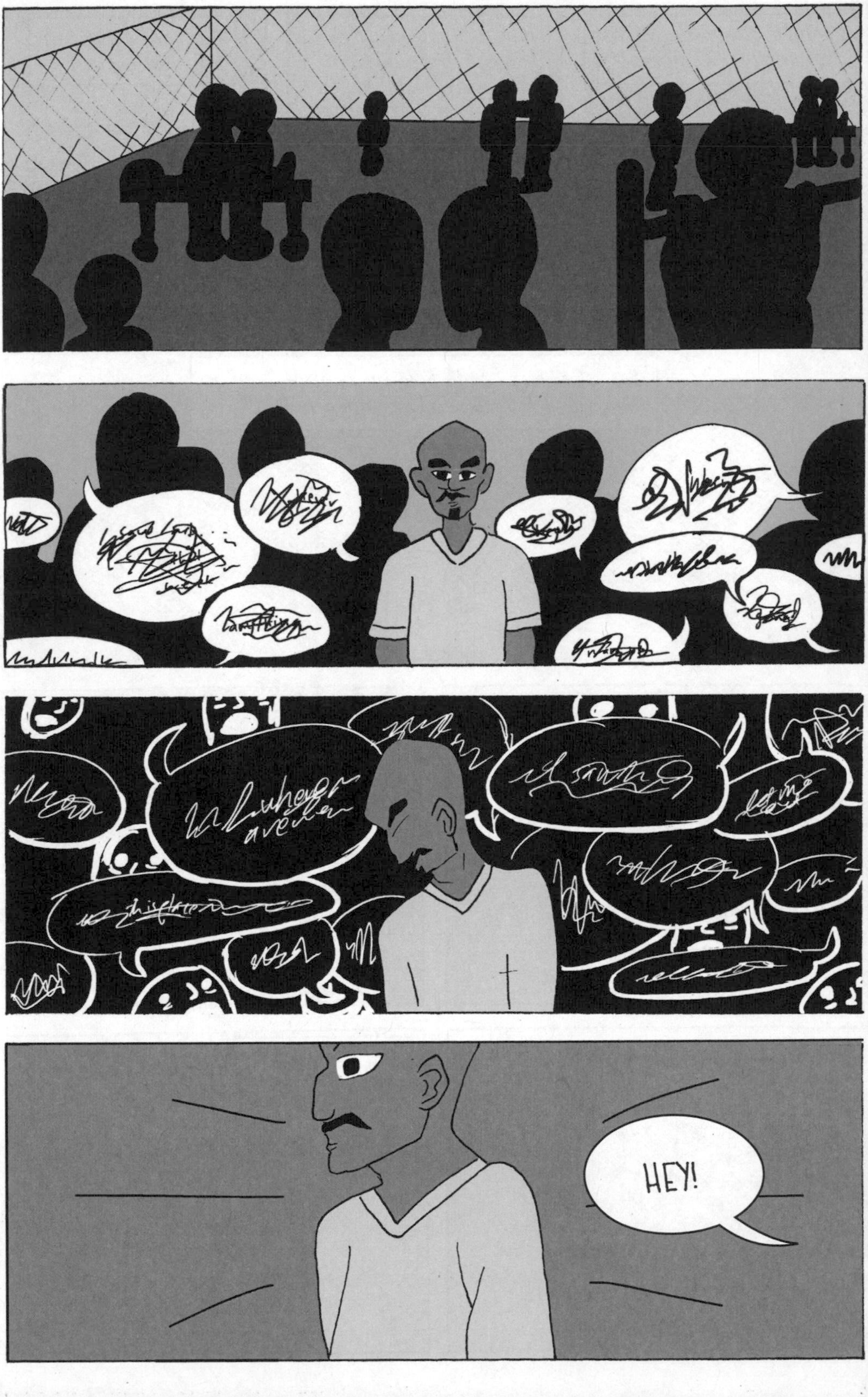
HEY!

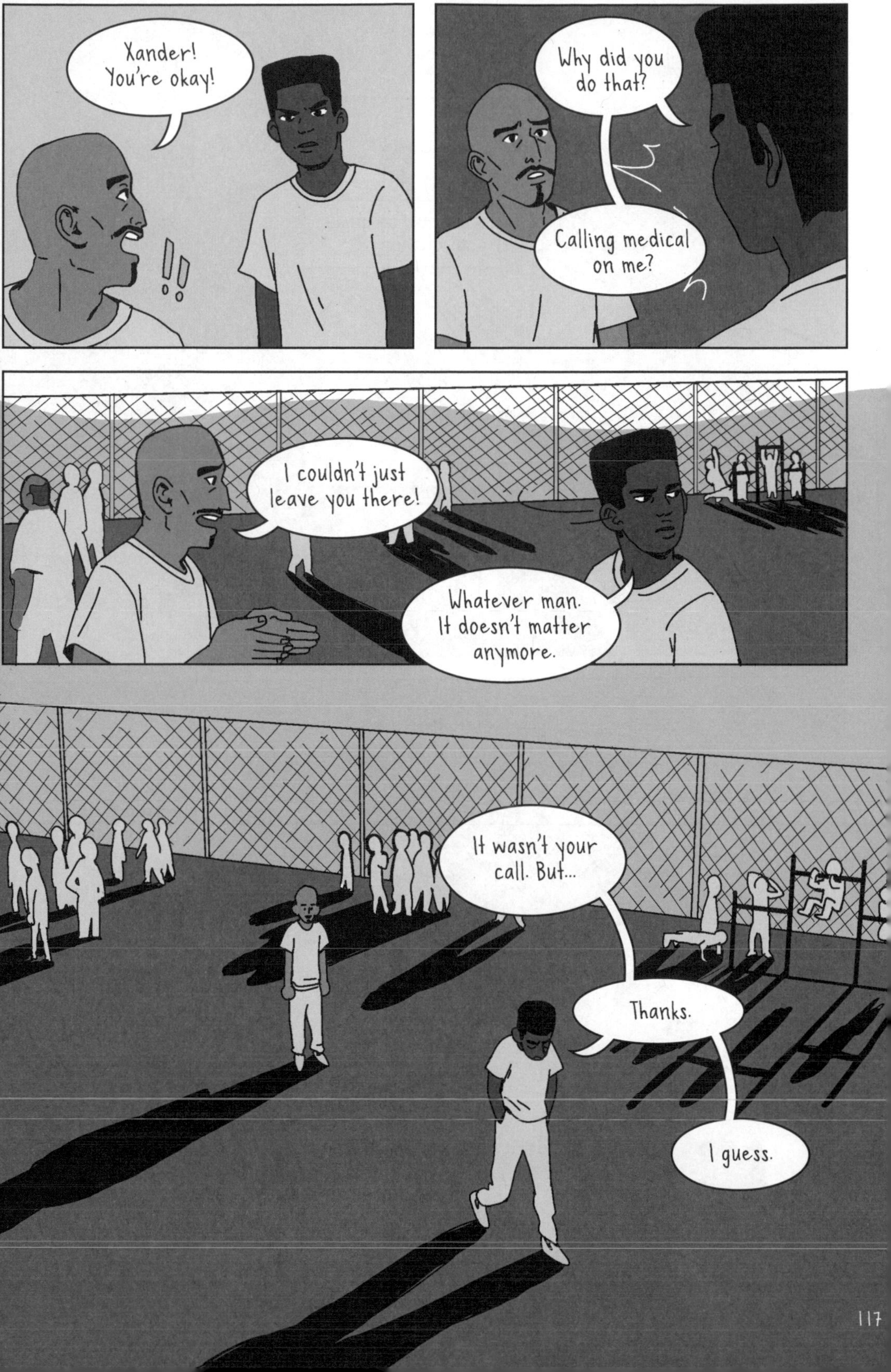
Xander! You're okay!
!!
Why did you do that?
Calling medical on me?
I couldn't just leave you there!
Whatever man. It doesn't matter anymore.
It wasn't your call. But...
Thanks.
I guess.

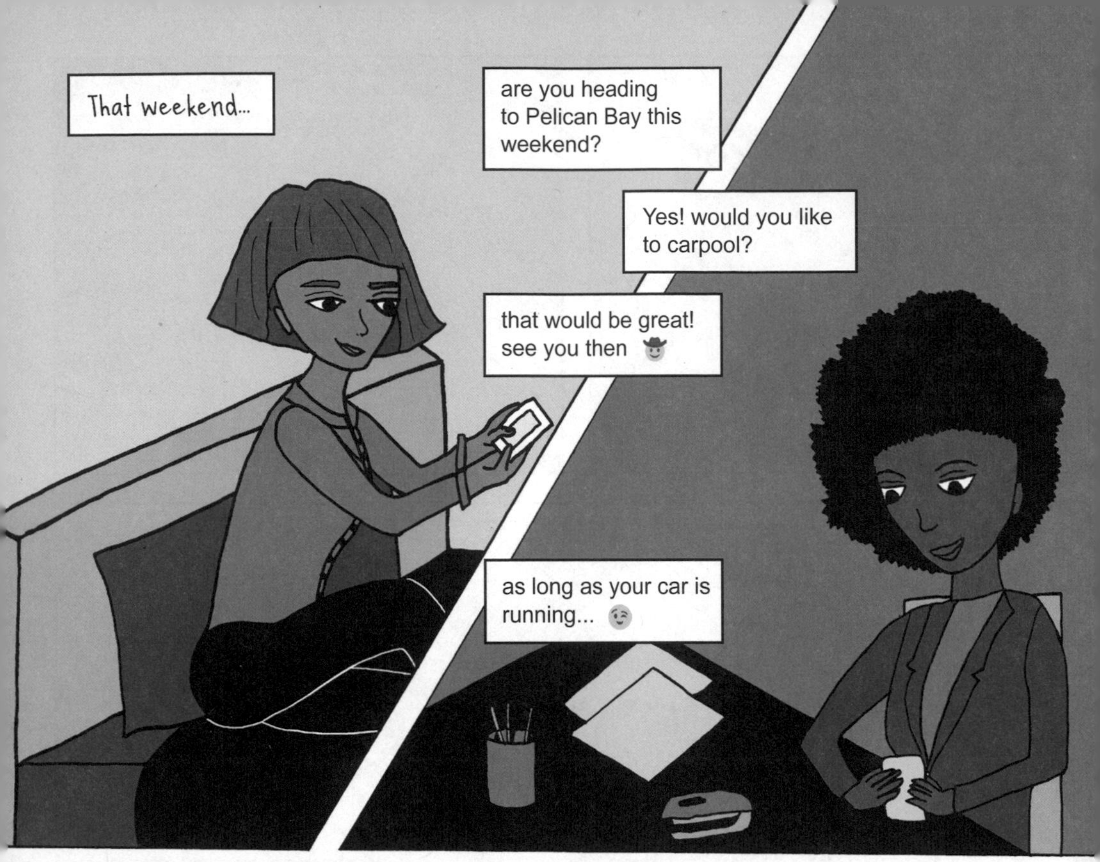
That weekend...
are you heading to Pelican Bay this weekend?
Yes! would you like to carpool?
that would be great! see you then
as long as your car is running...

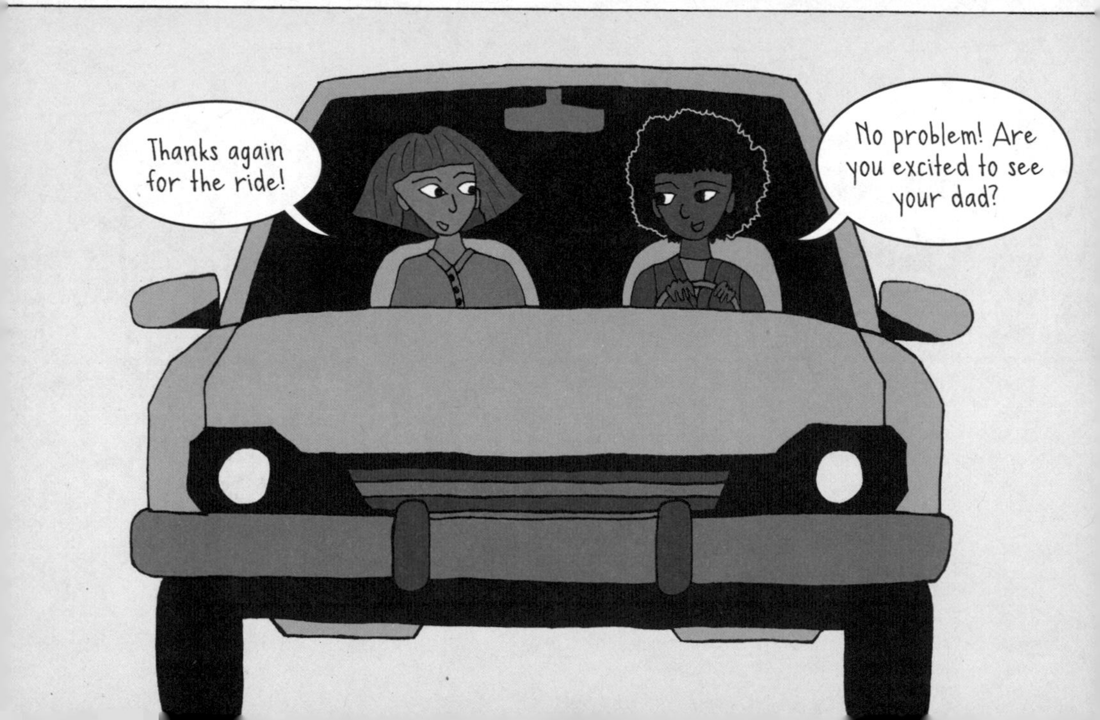
Thanks again for the ride!
No problem! Are you excited to see your dad?

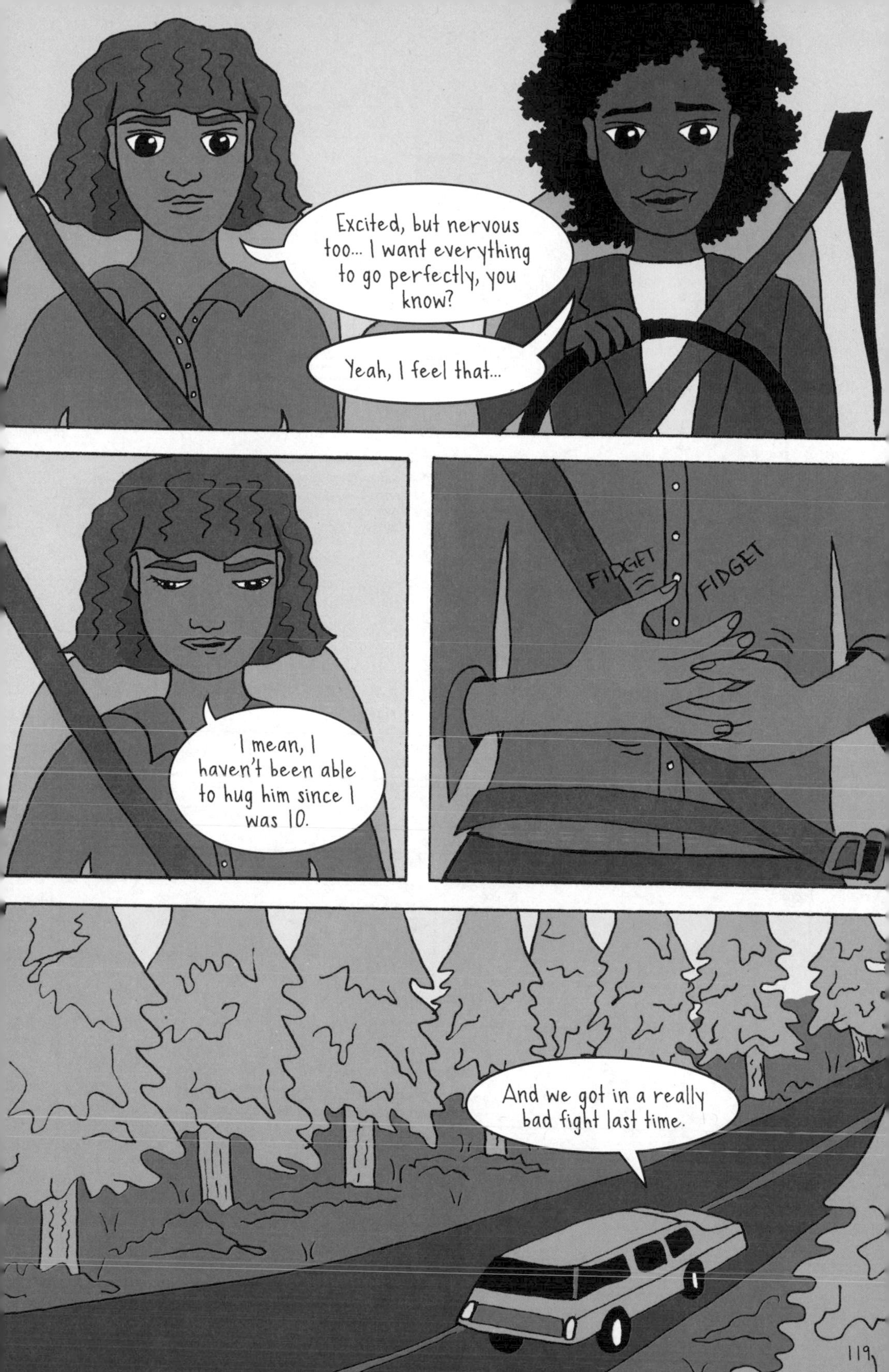
Excited, but nervous too... I want everything to go perfectly, you know?
Yeah, I feel that...
I mean, I haven't been able to hug him since I was 10.
FIDGET
FIDGET
And we got in a really bad fight last time.

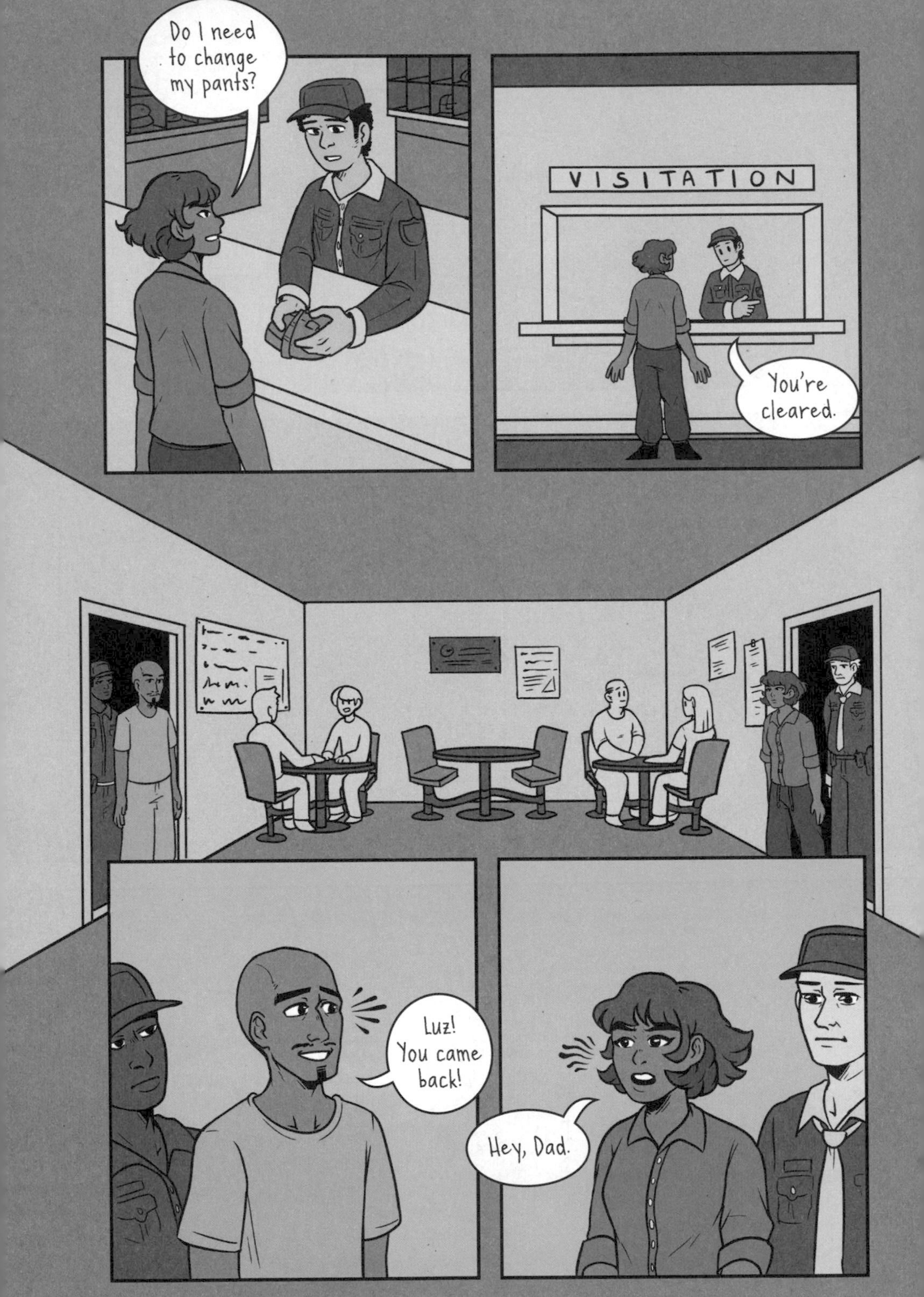
Do I need to change my pants?
VISITATION
You're cleared.
Luz! You came back!
Hey, Dad.

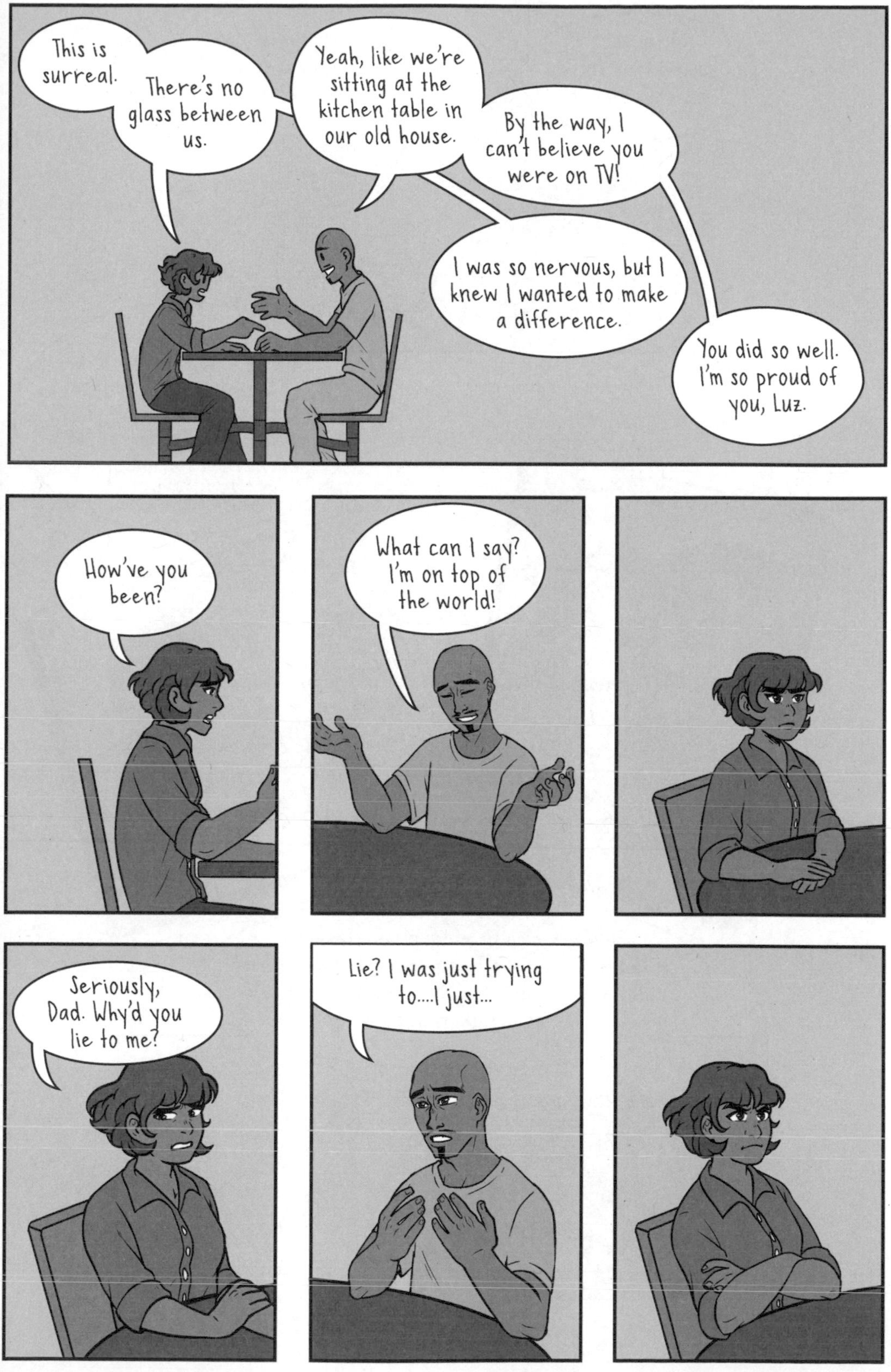
This is surreal.
There's no glass between us.
Yeah, like we're sitting at the kitchen table in our old house.
By the way, I can't believe you were on TV!
I was so nervous, but I knew I wanted to make a difference.
You did so well. I'm so proud of you, Luz.
How've you been?
What can I say? I'm on top of the world!
Seriously, Dad. Why'd you lie to me?
Lie? I was just trying to....I just...

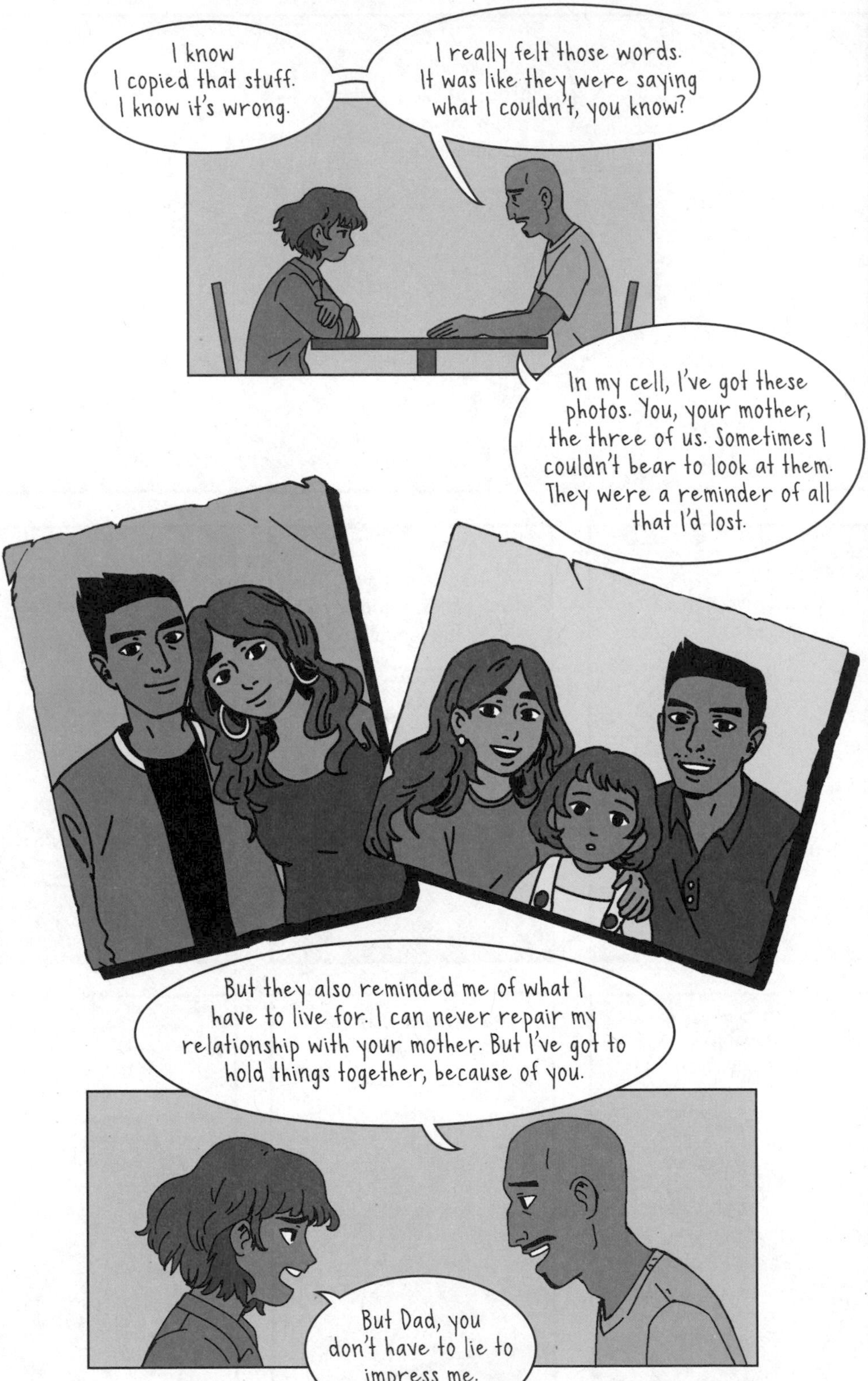
I know I copied that stuff. I know it's wrong.
I really felt those words. It was like they were saying what I couldn't, you know?
In my cell, I've got these photos. You, your mother, the three of us. Sometimes I couldn't bear to look at them. They were a reminder of all that I'd lost.
But they also reminded me of what I have to live for. I can never repair my relationship with your mother. But I've got to hold things together, because of you.
But Dad, you don't have to lie to impress me.

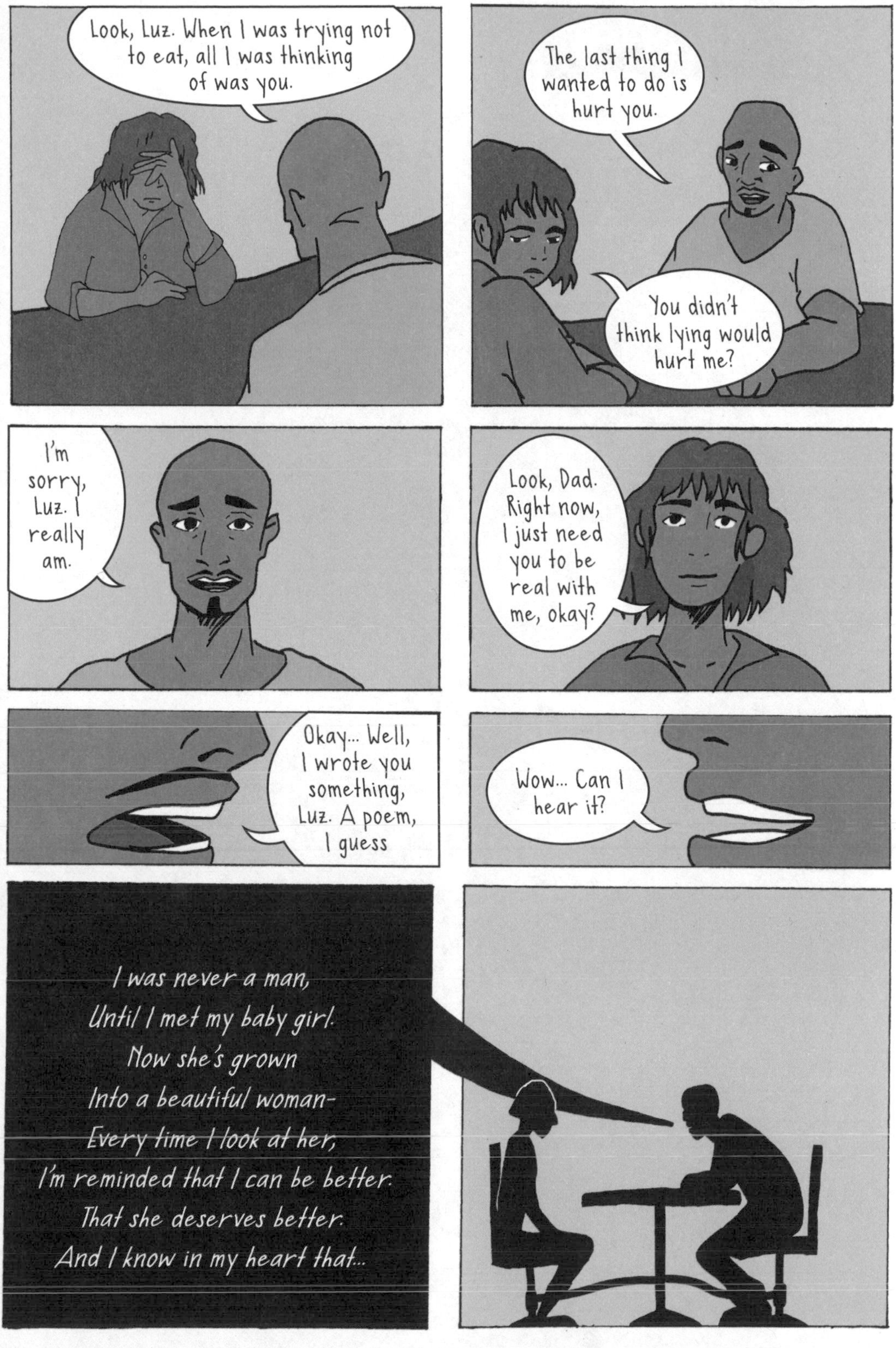
Look, Luz. When I was trying not to eat, all I was thinking of was you.
The last thing I wanted to do is hurt you.
You didn't think lying would hurt me?
I'm sorry, Luz. I really am.
Look, Dad. Right now, I just need you to be real with me, okay?
Okay... Well, I wrote you something, Luz. A poem, I guess
Wow... Can I hear it?
I was never a man,
Until I met my baby girl.
Now she's grown
Into a beautiful woman-
Every time I look at her,
I'm reminded that I can be better.
That she deserves better.
And I know in my heart that...

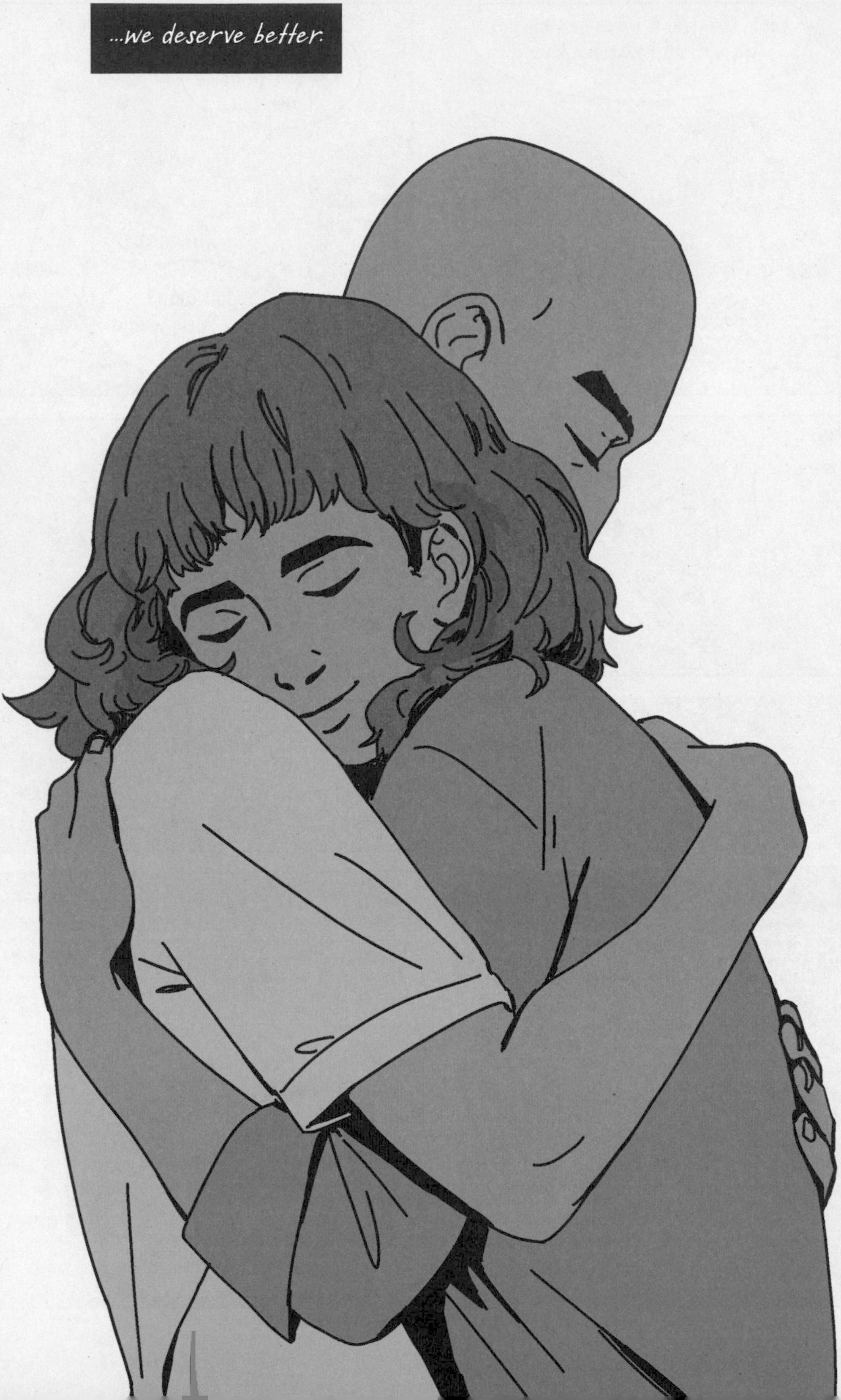
...we deserve better.

You've found your voice, Dad.

Luz, I was afraid you would stop caring about me.

I could never stop caring.

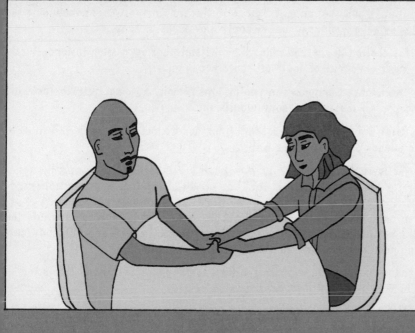

The End

Appendix A: Timeline of the California Prison Hunger Strikes

1989 - Pelican Bay State Prison opens.

2006 - Four alleged gang leaders (Todd Ashker, Arturo Castellanos, Antonio Guillen, Sitawa Jamaa) are placed side-by-side in the same solitary pod at Pelican Bay State Prison.

2011 - Ashker, Castellanos, Guillen, and Jamaa form the Short Corridor Collective alliance.

July 1-20, 2011 - The Short Corridor Collective initiates a hunger strike to bring attention to the torturous conditions of solitary confinement. At its peak, more than 6,500 prisoners refuse their meals.

September 26 - October 16, 2011 - The second mass hunger strike begins. After three days, it reaches a peak of 4,252 prisoners in eight California state prisons.

November 2011 - The UN Committee Against Torture notes that full isolation for twenty-two to twenty-three hours a day in super-maximum security prisons is unacceptable and bans the use of solitary confinement for longer than fifteen days.

2012 - The Short Corridor Collective writes and publishes a letter calling for the end of hostility between racial groups in prison.

June 2013 - The Short Corridor Collective sends letters to activist groups and family members, listing their grievances and announcing the strike. Word spreads throughout the state.

July 8, 2013 - Over thirty thousand prisoners join the largest prisoners' hunger strike in US history.

July 11, 2013 - More than twelve thousand prisoners remain striking.

August 6, 2013 - Jeffrey Beard, then head of the California Department of Corrections and Rehabilitation (CDCR), publishes an op-ed piece in the *Los Angeles Times* denouncing the strike as a ploy by gang leaders to assert control over the prisons.

August 19, 2013 - Judge Thelton Henderson rules that the state has permission to force-feed prisoners at "near-term risk of death or acute bodily injury."

September 4, 2013 - One hundred prisoners in two prisons remain on hunger strike. Forty of them have been on a hunger strike continuously since July 8.

September 5, 2013 - After fifty-nine days, the Short Corridor Collective suspends the strike. All remaining hunger strikers resume eating.

September 1, 2015 - The lawsuit *Todd Ashker vs. Governor of the State of California*, filed by the Center for Constitutional Rights (CCR) on behalf of ten Pelican Bay prisoners, comes to a historic settlement. It results in the termination of indefinite solitary confinement in California, and thousands of people are released from solitary into the mainline. (CDCR has not totally honored the terms of the settlement and CCR continues to exert legal pressure to ensure its continued implementation).

October 2017 - Colorado prison system becomes the first to announce that it will stop using solitary confinement beyond fifteen days.

By 2020, dozens of states around the country have grassroots campaigns against solitary confinement, inspired in part by the Pelican Bay hunger strikes.

Appendix B: Solitary by the Numbers

HOW MANY PRISONERS ARE IN SOLITARY CONFINEMENT?

ENTIRE UNITED KINGDOM

50

ENTIRE UNITED STATES

80,000

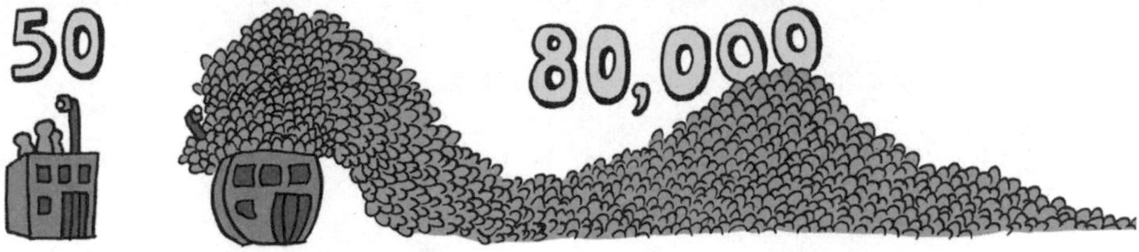

HOW BIG IS THE CELL?

SIZE OF AN AVERAGE PARKING SPACE

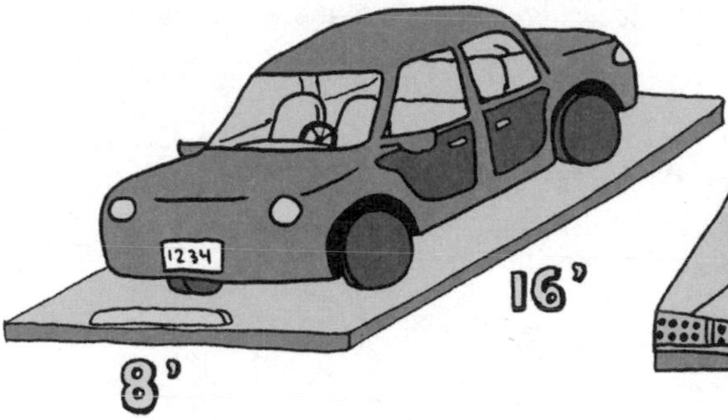
1234
16'
8'

SIZE OF A CELL IN THE SHU

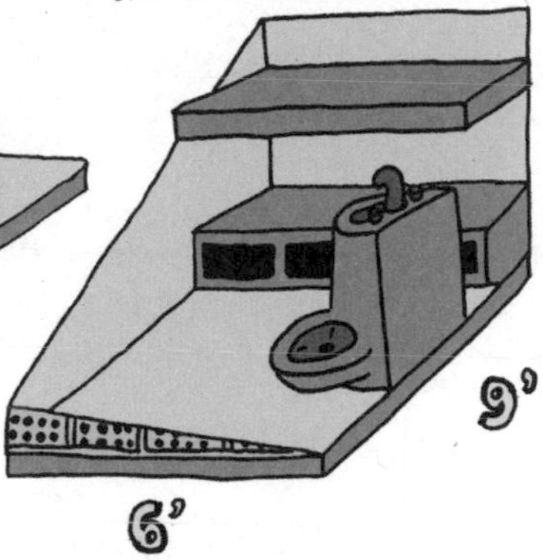
9'
6'

WHAT'S MISSING?

>0% IMPROVEMENT IN PRISON SAFETY AND DISCIPLINE THROUGH USE OF SOLITARY

>0% DECREASE IN PRISON VIOLENCE THROUGH USE OF SOLITARY

>0% OF PEOPLE SENTENCED TO SOLITARY BY A JUDGE OR JURY

HOW LONG DO YOU STAY?

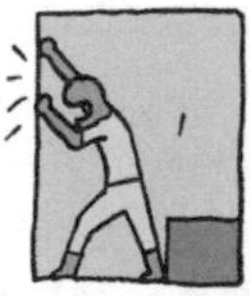

1 NIGHT

MADE COLORADO'S CORRECTIONS DIRECTOR DECIDE TO TRY TO END THE USE OF SOLITARY.

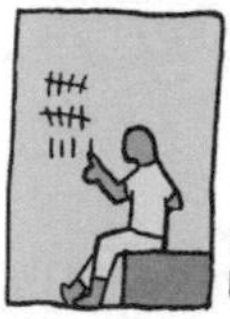

14 DAYS

IS THE MAXIMUM TIME TO PUT SOMEONE IN SOLITARY, ACCORDING TO THE UNITED NATIONS.

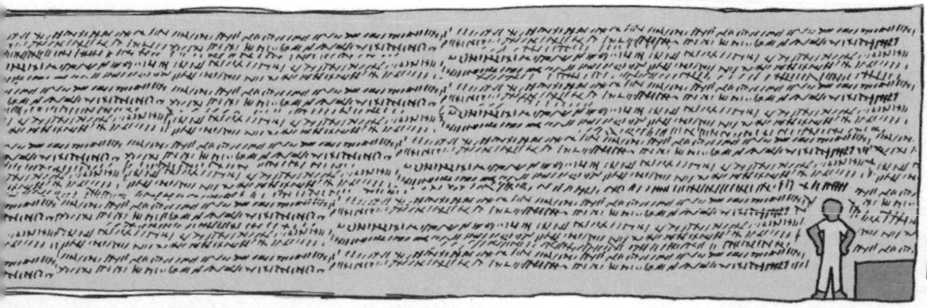

44 YEARS

IS THE LONGEST TIME A PRISONER IN THE U.S. HAS SPENT IN SOLITARY.

Appendix C:
Interview with Charles Carbone

Charles Carbone is a human rights attorney based in San Francisco. He was on a team of lawyers that sued the California Department of Corrections and Rehabilitation (CDCR) on the constitutionality of its solitary confinement policies. Over the last twenty years, his work has helped free hundreds of prisoners. On November 23, 2018, he visited the SGNP class.

SGNP: So, after the hunger strike ended, the prisoners were promised a legislative hearing in Sacramento. What came of that?

Charles Carbone: Well, the department made some small changes, but the prisoners, their families, and the lawyers were not satisfied.

S: So then the class-action suit became the focus, correct? And you were one of the lawyers on the team?

C: Right, an amazing group of lawyers came together, and the department settled in 2016. This was a historic settlement. It ended the use of indefinite solitary confinement in California and limited anyone's time in the SHU to two years maximum. Over three thousand prisoners have gotten out of solitary. Well, more than that now.

S: Do you believe the hunger strike led to this historic legal victory?

C: Undoubtedly, yes. The strike, the family involvement, the skill of the lawyers, the obvious wrongnesss of the treatment . . . all of that led to the Department seeing the writing on the wall. They knew it would be ugly for them in court. We were going to show the world the horrors of solitary confinement, and the press would be very bad. So, they settled.

S: And with the settlement there were certain terms, right? They had to allow the lawyers to monitor the implementation of the new policies?

C: Yes, the monitoring was supposed to last two years, but just a few months ago the judge extended the monitoring for one more year, maybe two.

S: On what basis?

C: Continuous, gross violations of the settlement terms and the Constitution.

S: What violations did the judge see?

C: The biggest one is that they're still illegally using confidential informants.

S: That's what prisoners call snitching on each other, right?

C: Right. Snitching is not a legitimate way to get evidence to validate prisoners as gang members.

S: Because prisoners lie about other prisoners? In order to get favor with the department and benefit themselves?

C: Yes. And the department is still using that evidence, not to keep people in solitary anymore, but to keep people in prison. The parole board uses old, unreliable evidence to deny people release.

S: So a prisoner like our character, Rodrigo, even though he got out of the SHU, the same evidence that got him in there could be used to stop him from getting released?

C: Yes. We're trying to fix it. A lot of things have changed for the better though. Men are rejecting the gangs in larger numbers. As a lawyer, I go inside prisons on a weekly basis. I've seen more men rejecting gangs in the last two years than I did in the last eighteen years.

S: Why do you think that is?

C: Because now they have more options. Before they thought they were going to die in the SHU. Now there's a way to get out. They can spend more time with their families, pursue a trade, get self-help. They have other priorities than the gang life.

S: What do you want for these men and women? What do you think they deserve?

C: I think they deserve fundamental fairness, options, access to education. Ultimately, the goal is to bring them home. I believe less people in prison is good for society. It leads to stronger communities and less crime. But first, we need to give them ways to prepare for that, to show they're ready to come home. Interview conducted on 3/4/2019

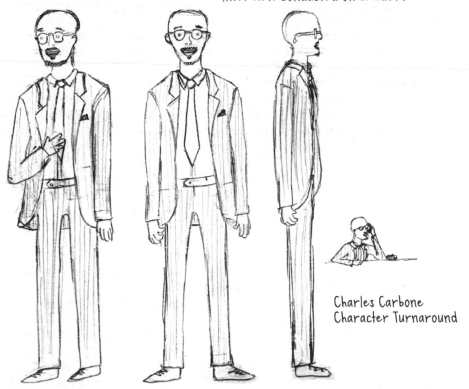

Charles Carbone
Character Turnaround

Appendix D: The Campaign to End Solitary

Compiled with the assistance of Solitary Watch

In most democratic countries, the use of long-term solitary confinement is rare.

Until forty years ago, this was true in the United States as well. With the rise of mass incarceration, beginning in the 1980s, prisons increasingly used isolation to control or punish growing incarcerated populations, until solitary became an everyday practice across the country. By the year 2000, there were at least one hundred thousand people in solitary confinement on an average day in US prisons and jails.

In the 21st century, even as resistance to mass incarceration began to grow, solitary confinement remained all but invisible until only a decade ago, when a small number of advocates, journalists, and mental health professionals began calling attention to what they considered an underreported domestic human rights issue.

In 2011, the United Nations Special Rapporteur on Torture, Juan Mendez, advanced their cause by declaring long-term solitary confinement a form of cruel and degrading treatment that often rose to the level of torture. He recommended banning solitary altogether for vulnerable populations such as children and people with mental illness, and limiting it to fourteen days for all others. The UN would later adopt these guideline as part of its Standard Minimum Rules for the Treatment of Prisoners, known as the Mandela Rules.

That same year marked the first of three hunger strikes against solitary in California; the third, in 2013, involved more than thirty thousand people and helped place solitary confinement in the national consciousness. Media coverage and advocacy work around solitary increased, and in 2016, president Barack Obama denounced long-term solitary as "an affront to our common humanity" and took the first steps toward limiting its use in the federal prison system.

Since the election of Donald Trump, solitary confinement reforms at the federal level have ground to a halt. But in states across the country, where the majority of the prison population is held, resistance to solitary is growing--and is beginning to produce real change. Through legislation, lawsuits, and policy reforms, many states have made incremental reductions in their use of solitary. One state--Colorado--has all but eliminated long-term solitary confinement.

In 2018, leading advocacy groups including the ACLU National Prison Project, National Religious Campaign Against Torture, Center for Children's Law and Policy, and Solitary Watch came together to launch Unlock the Box, a national campaign aimed at ending long-term solitary confinement and bringing the United States in compliance with the Mandela Rules within ten years. It now supports and coordinates campaigns in a dozen states, most of them led by formerly incarcerated people who have experienced solitary confinement and people with loved ones in solitary.

What You Can Do to Help End Solitary Confinement

While the tide is turning on solitary confinement in the United States, there is still a long way to go.

To date, reforms have reduced the total number of people in solitary on an average day by perhaps 20 percent, from at least one hundred thousand to about eighty thousand (sixty thousand in federal and state prisons and twenty thousand more in local jails, with an unknown number in immigration and juvenile detention). An informed and involved public is needed to bring an end to the torture of solitary confinement--and there are many things you can do to help.

Learn more about solitary confinement. Subscribe to articles and updates from Solitary Watch at solitarywatch.com, and check out the FAQ for a comprehensive introduction to solitary facts and figures. For more in-depth information, visit the Solitary Confinement Resource Center, a searchable database of advocacy tools, articles, personal accounts, multimedia, court cases, and more, at scrc.solitarywatch.org.

Read personal accounts written by people in solitary in the book *Hell Is a Very Small Place: Voices from Solitary Confinement*, available in bookstores and online. More books, as well as films and videos, about solitary confinement can be found at scrc.solitarywatch.org.

Experience for a few minutes what it might feel like to be in a solitary confinement cell by downloading "6 x 9," a virtual reality created by the *Guardian* and available free at the App Store, Google Play, and Gear VR.

Correspond with someone in solitary confinement through Lifelines to Solitary, a pen pal program run by Solitary Watch. To learn about the program, visit solitarywatch.org/lifelines.

Join a campaign to end solitary in your state, or connect with one to find out what actions you can take on your own. Visit Unlock the Box at unlocktheboxcampaign.org to learn about some active campaigns. For a list of national and state organizations working against solitary, visit scrc.solitarywatch.org and click on Advocacy Groups. Check out your state ACLU affiliate, since many have made solitary a priority issue. If you are part of a faith community, visit the National Religious Campaign Against Torture at nrcat.org.

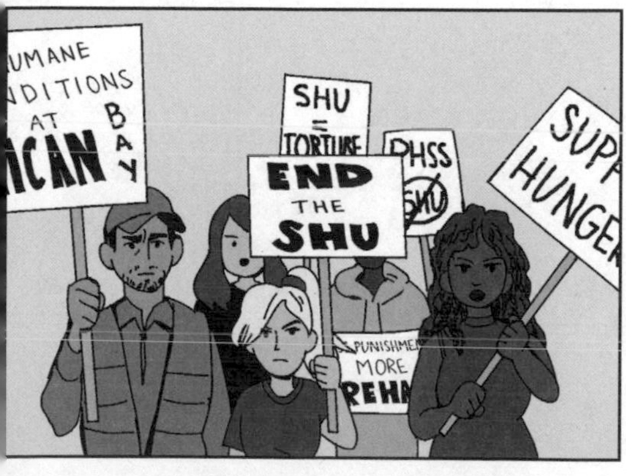
UMANE
DITIONS
AT
ICAN
BAY
SHU
=
TORTURE
END
THE
SHU
PHSS
SHU
PUNISHME
MORE
REHA
SUPP
HUNGER

All of the proceeds from this graphic novel will be donated to solitarywatch.org.

Remember the courage of the hunger strikers, the suffering of people who live in solitary, and the common humanity we all share.

Student Essay

On Collaboration

One of the most important lessons our class learned from the 2013 prison hunger strike is the necessity of collaboration. Only through the union of the Short Corridor Collective and the setting aside of gang rivalries across the state penal system were prisoners all over California able to rally behind one purpose and effect change.

With *Flying Kites*, our primary goal was to figure out how our voices could be used to amplify the voices of those suffering from the inhumane conditions of solitary confinement. We decided the best way to do this was creating composite characters, or fictional characters based on more than one nonfictional individual. The challenge of creating composite characters was something the SGNP had never tried before. However, we met the challenge head-on because we believed that through composite characters like Rodrigo, Bobby, and Xander, especially, we could better convey the wide range of narratives and experiences of solitary confinement that we witnessed in our research. The creation of these characters demanded intentionality and care with the lived experiences we were borrowing from.

To co-write a graphic novel about a hunger strike that was itself rooted in collaboration was to be aware of the necessities behind a collective movement. As a collaborative work, *Flying Kites* would not exist as it does if a single one of us had not joined this journey twenty weeks ago. From planning, to thumbnailing, to penciling, to inking, to coloring, and to editing multiple drafts, each of us had a hand in everything. To produce the graphic novel, every single person had to learn to trust, to be present, and to listen to each other.

Although the graphic novel itself is over and the 2013 prison hunger strike ended with various successes and failures, solitary confinement is still a widely used form of punishment in the United States. We hope that all of the efforts in this graphic novel, but more importantly in the hunger strike itself, remind you that the fight against solitary is far from over. We hope that the voices of those in solitary continue to rise above the walls that trap them.

We hope that their kites fly on.

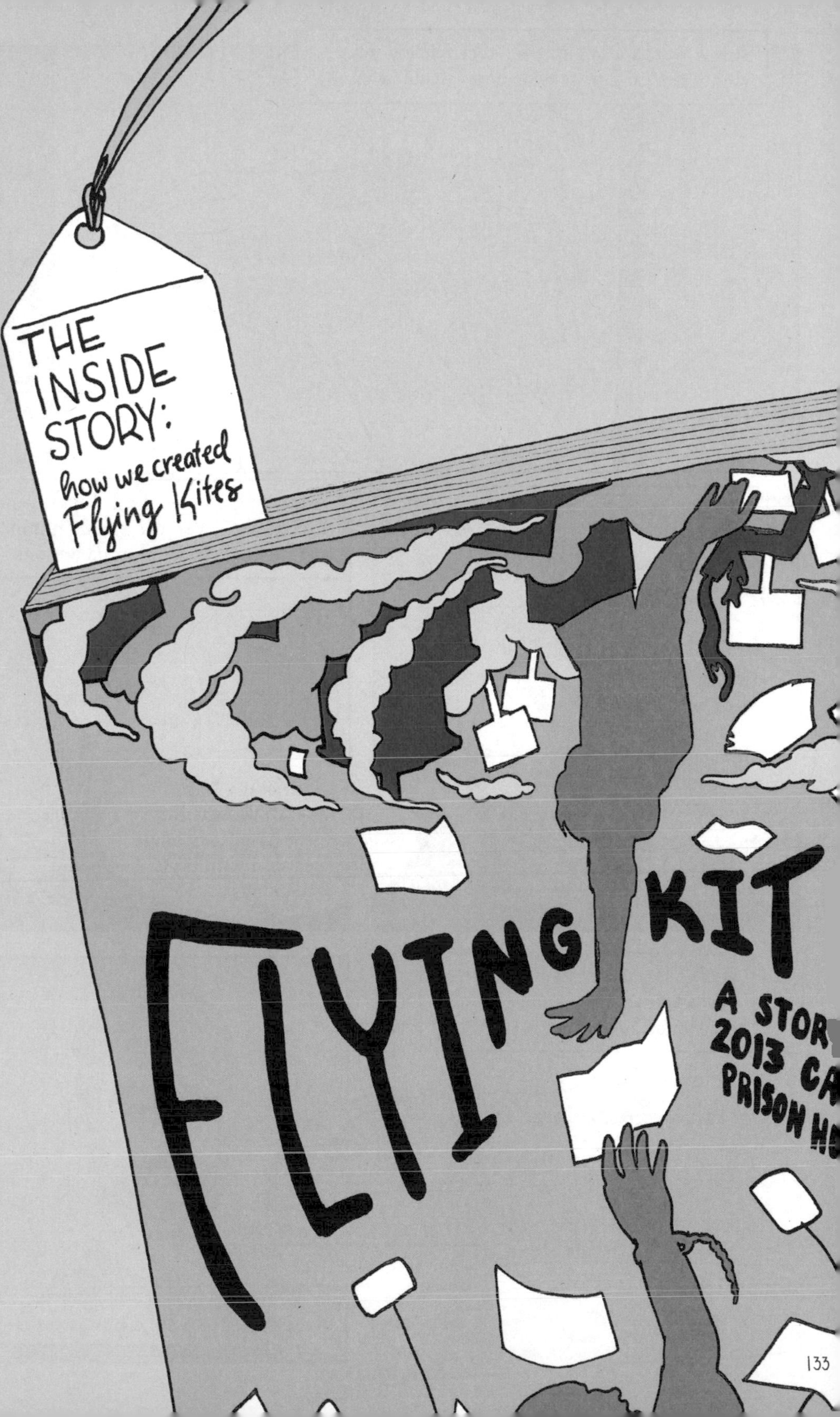
THE INSIDE STORY:
how we created Flying Kites
FLYING KIT
A STOR
2013 CA
PRISON H

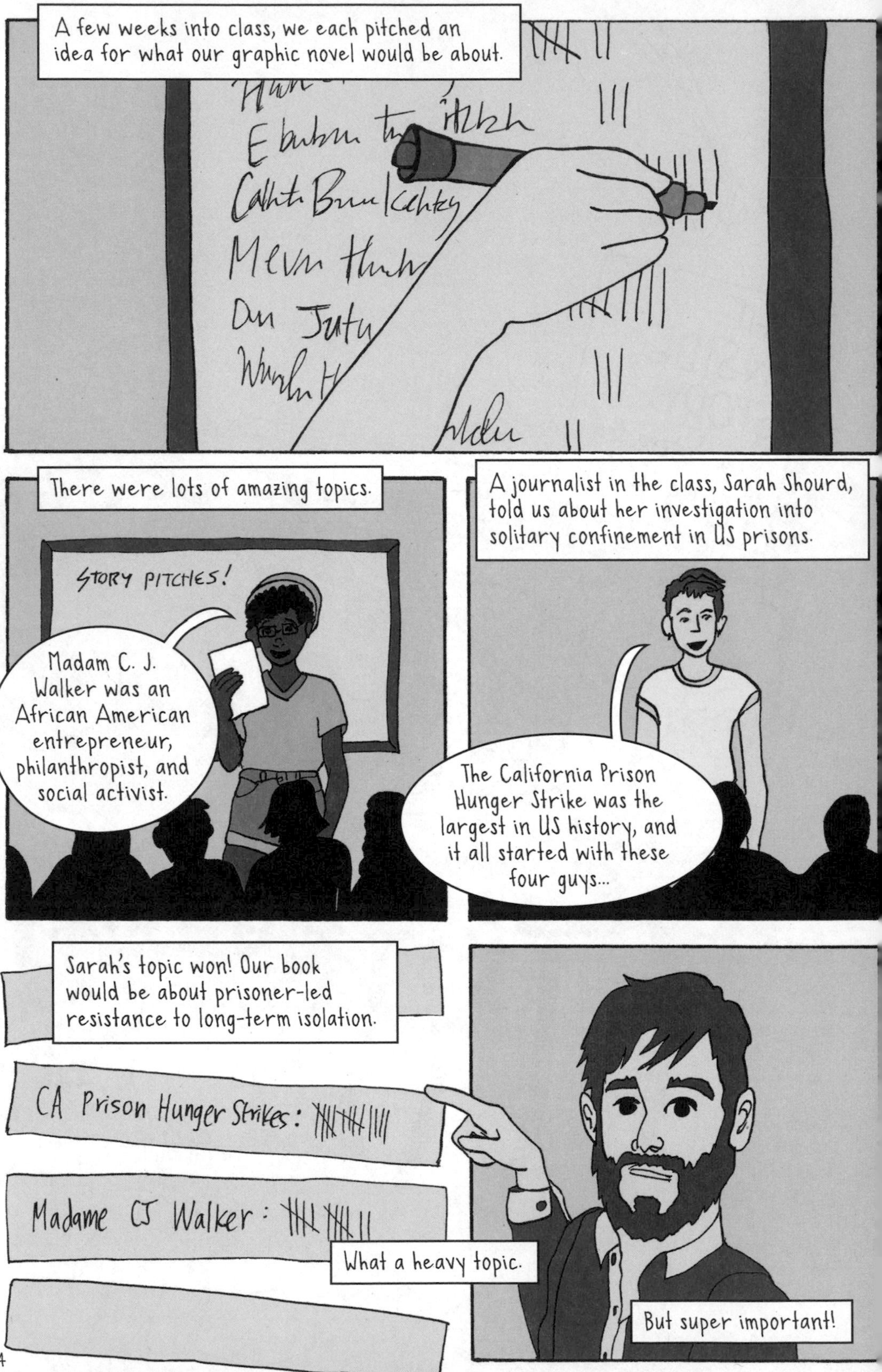
A few weeks into class, we each pitched an idea for what our graphic novel would be about.
There were lots of amazing topics.
STORY PITCHES!
Madam C. J. Walker was an African American entrepreneur, philanthropist, and social activist.
A journalist in the class, Sarah Shourd, told us about her investigation into solitary confinement in US prisons.
The California Prison Hunger Strike was the largest in US history, and it all started with these four guys...
Sarah's topic won! Our book would be about prisoner-led resistance to long-term isolation.
CA Prison Hunger Strikes:
Madame CJ Walker:
What a heavy topic.
But super important!

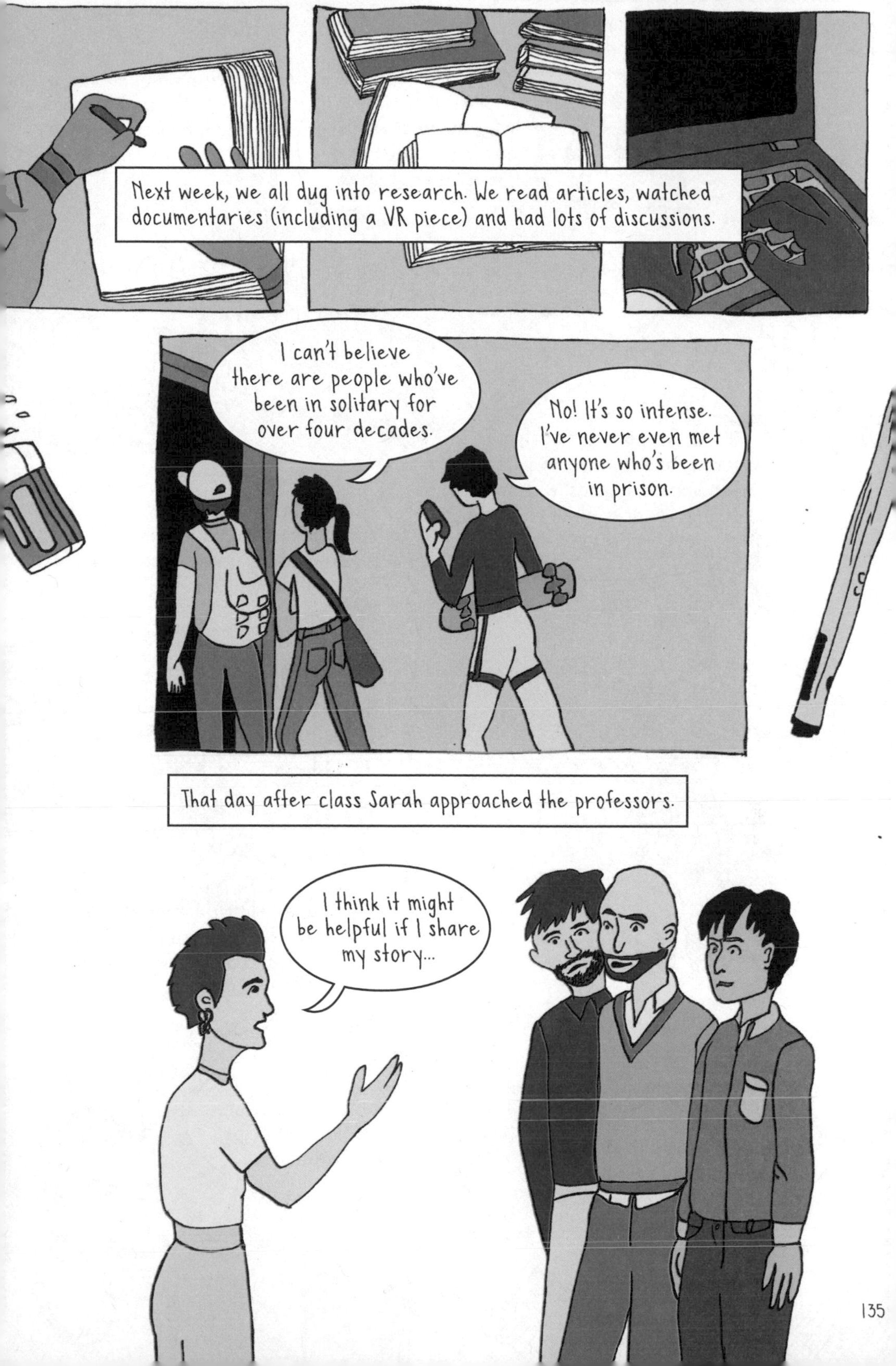
Next week, we all dug into research. We read articles, watched documentaries (including a VR piece) and had lots of discussions.
I can't believe there are people who've been in solitary for over four decades.
No! It's so intense. I've never even met anyone who's been in prison.
That day after class Sarah approached the professors.
I think it might be helpful if I share my story...

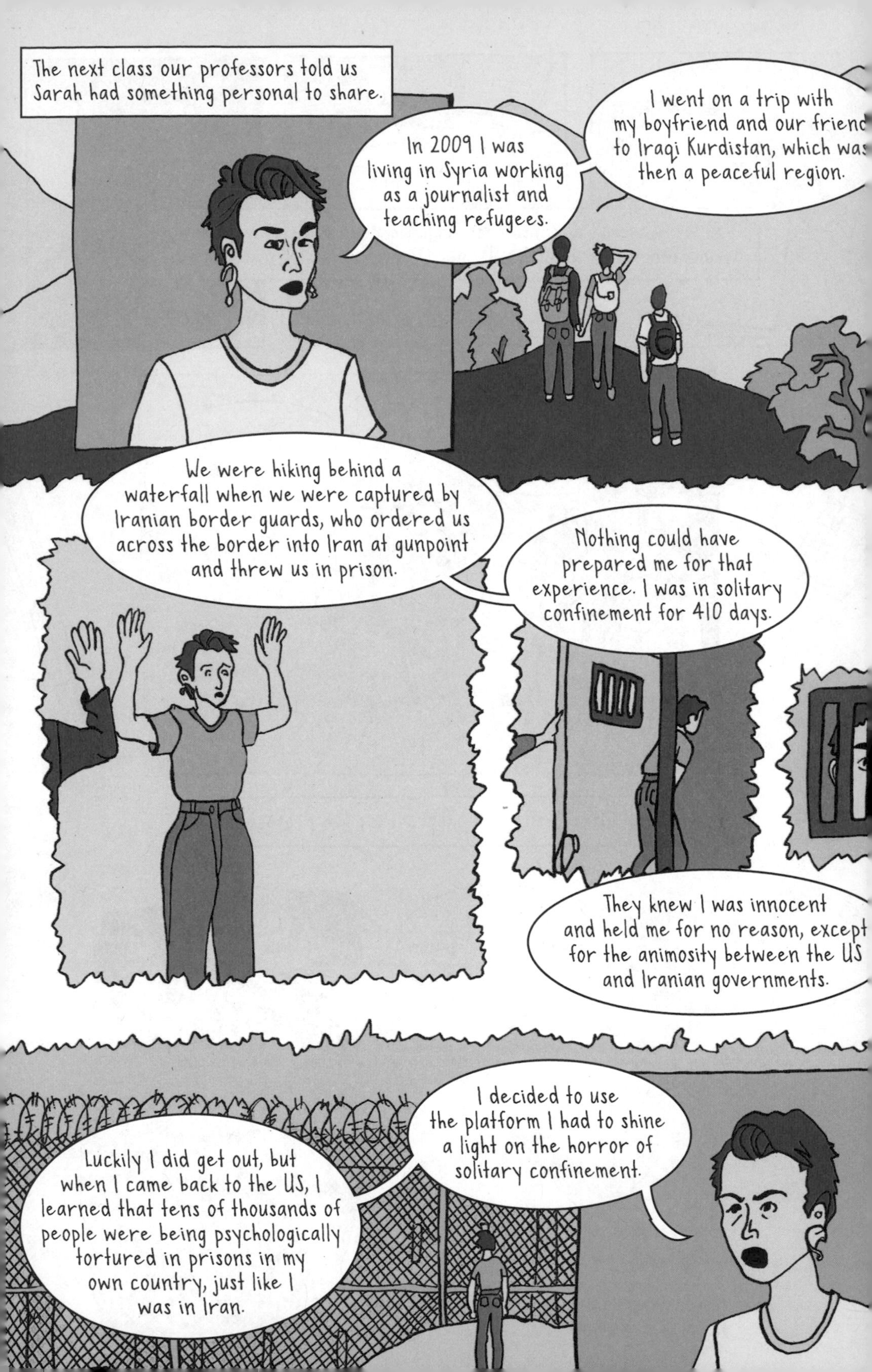
The next class our professors told us Sarah had something personal to share.
In 2009 I was living in Syria working as a journalist and teaching refugees.
I went on a trip with my boyfriend and our friend to Iraqi Kurdistan, which was then a peaceful region.
We were hiking behind a waterfall when we were captured by Iranian border guards, who ordered us across the border into Iran at gunpoint and threw us in prison.
Nothing could have prepared me for that experience. I was in solitary confinement for 410 days.
They knew I was innocent and held me for no reason, except for the animosity between the US and Iranian governments.
Luckily I did get out, but when I came back to the US, I learned that tens of thousands of people were being psychologically tortured in prisons in my own country, just like I was in Iran.
I decided to use the platform I had to shine a light on the horror of solitary confinement.

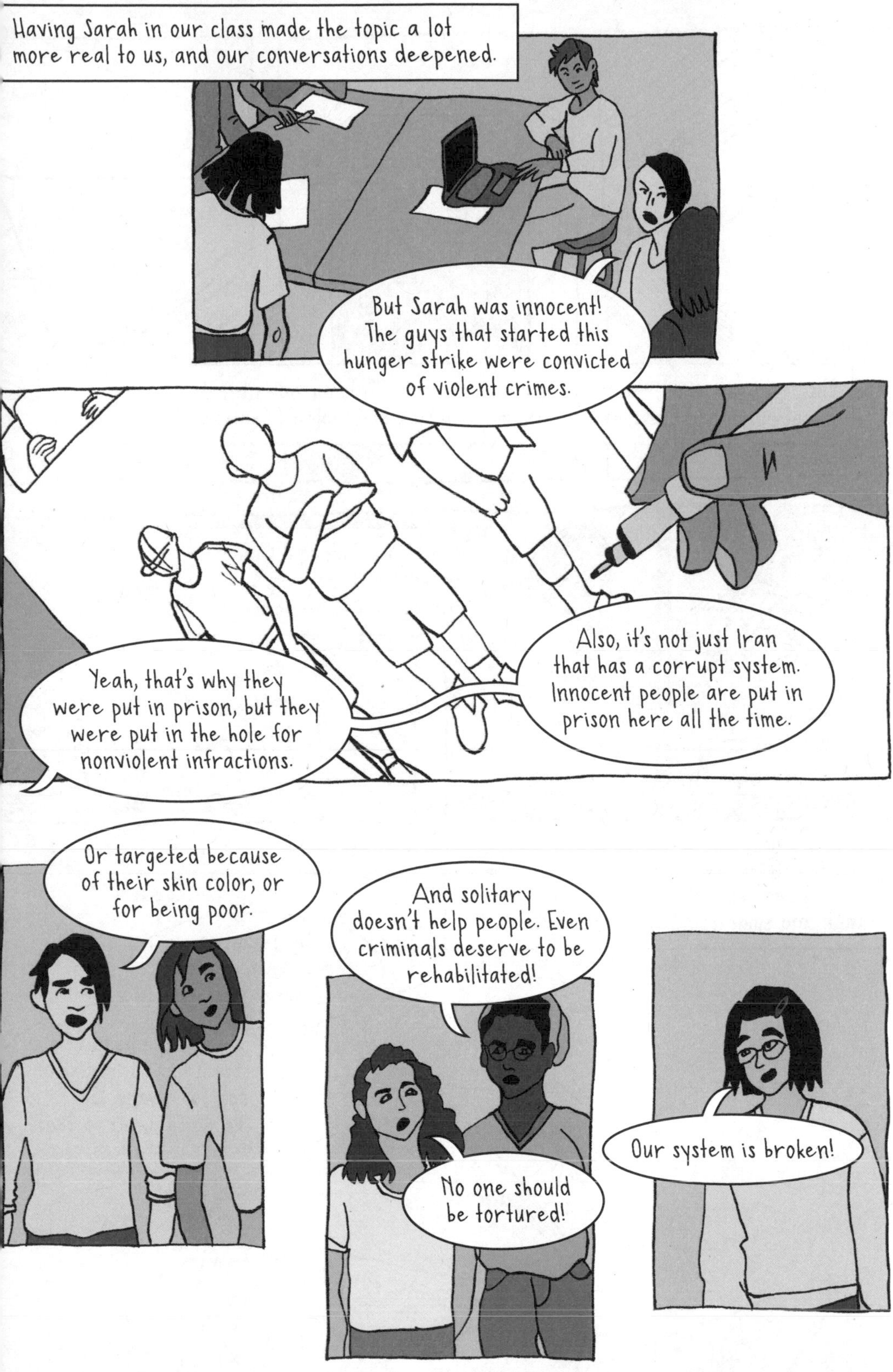
Having Sarah in our class made the topic a lot more real to us, and our conversations deepened.
But Sarah was innocent! The guys that started this hunger strike were convicted of violent crimes.
Yeah, that's why they were put in prison, but they were put in the hole for nonviolent infractions.
Also, it's not just Iran that has a corrupt system. Innocent people are put in prison here all the time.
Or targeted because of their skin color, or for being poor.
And solitary doesn't help people. Even criminals deserve to be rehabilitated!
No one should be tortured!
Our system is broken!

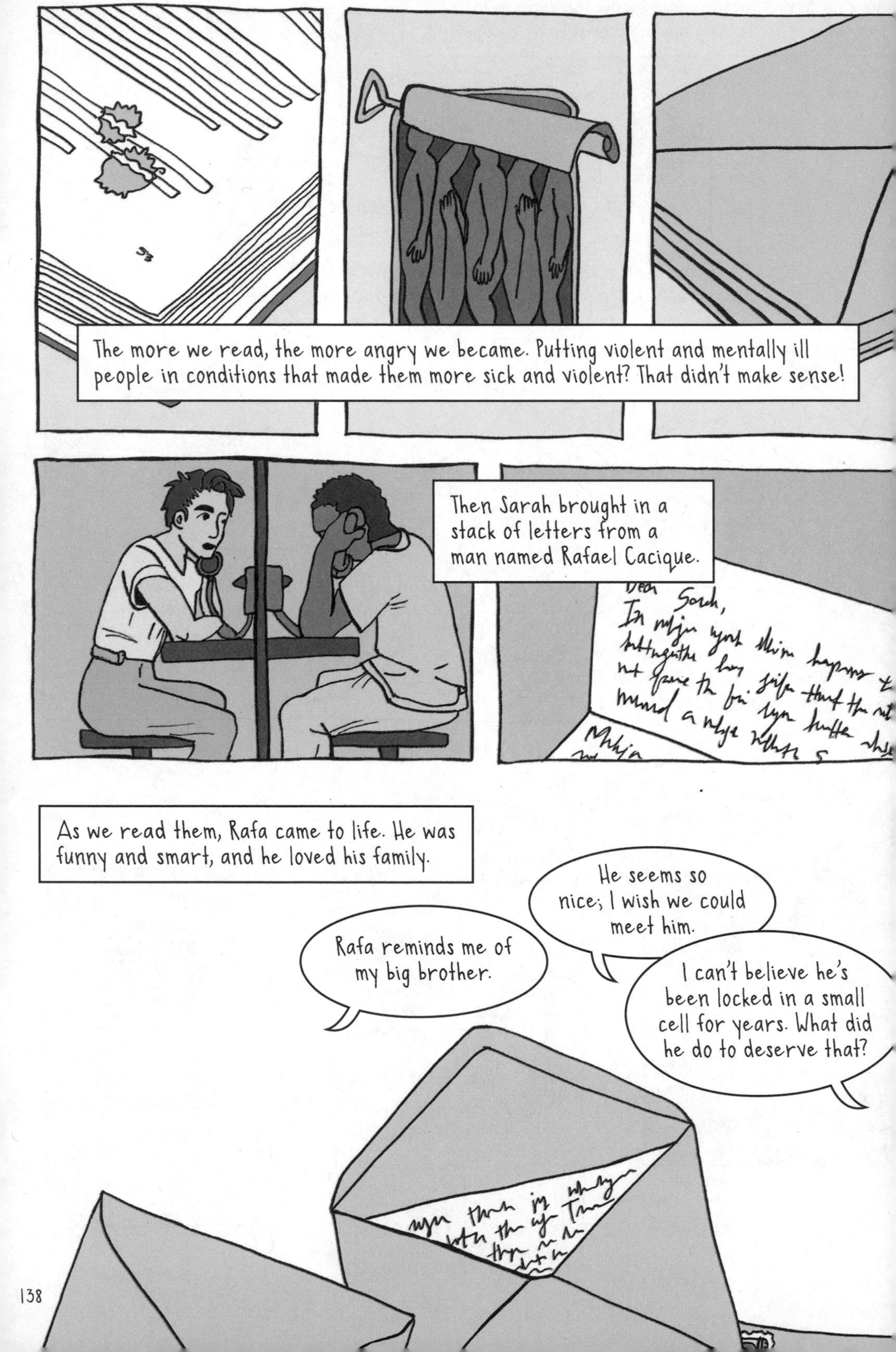

The more we read, the more angry we became. Putting violent and mentally ill people in conditions that made them more sick and violent? That didn't make sense!
Then Sarah brought in a stack of letters from a man named Rafael Cacique.
As we read them, Rafa came to life. He was funny and smart, and he loved his family.
Rafa reminds me of my big brother.
He seems so nice; I wish we could meet him.
I can't believe he's been locked in a small cell for years. What did he do to deserve that?

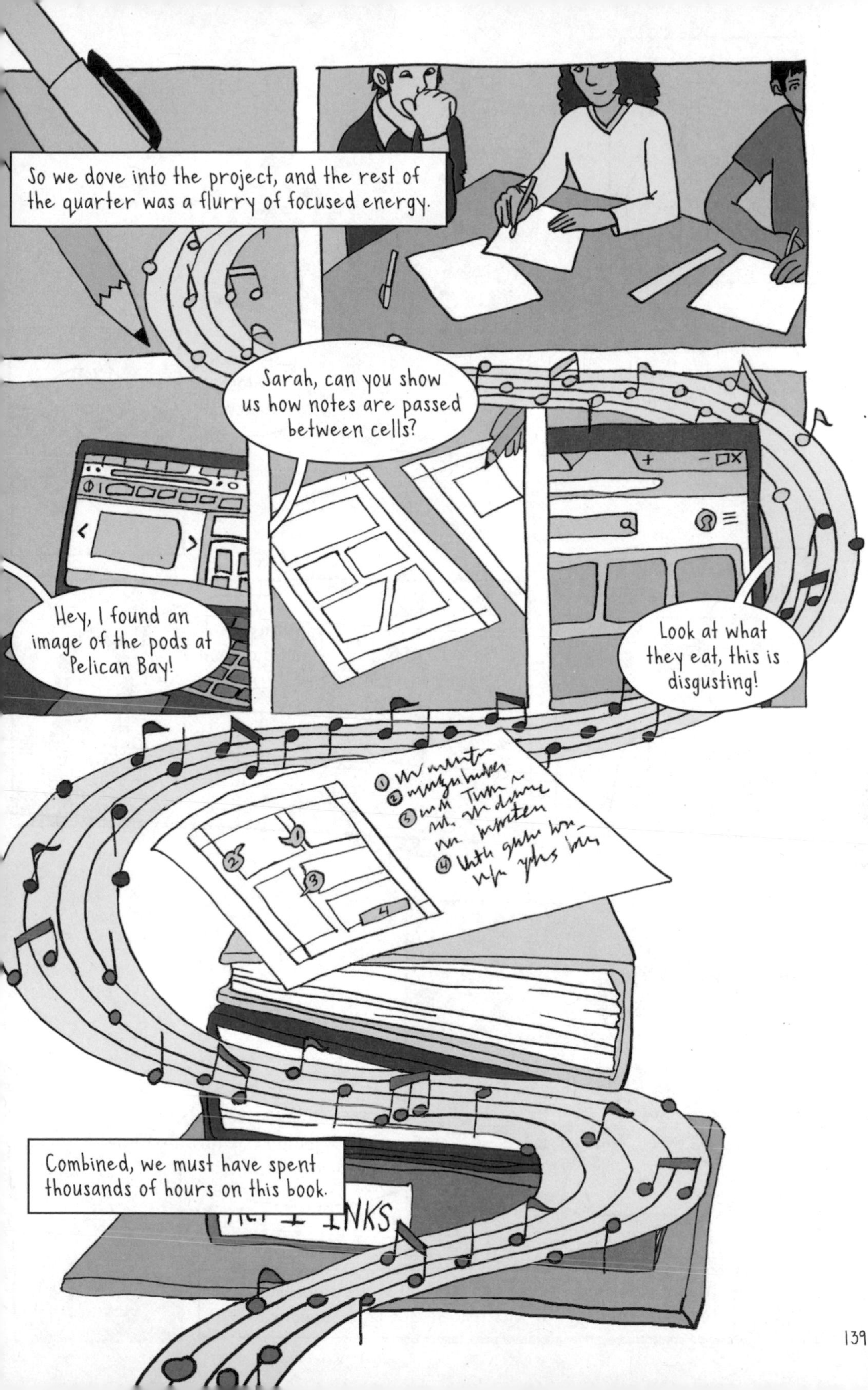
So we dove into the project, and the rest of the quarter was a flurry of focused energy.
Sarah, can you show us how notes are passed between cells?
Hey, I found an image of the pods at Pelican Bay!
Look at what they eat, this is disgusting!
Combined, we must have spent thousands of hours on this book.

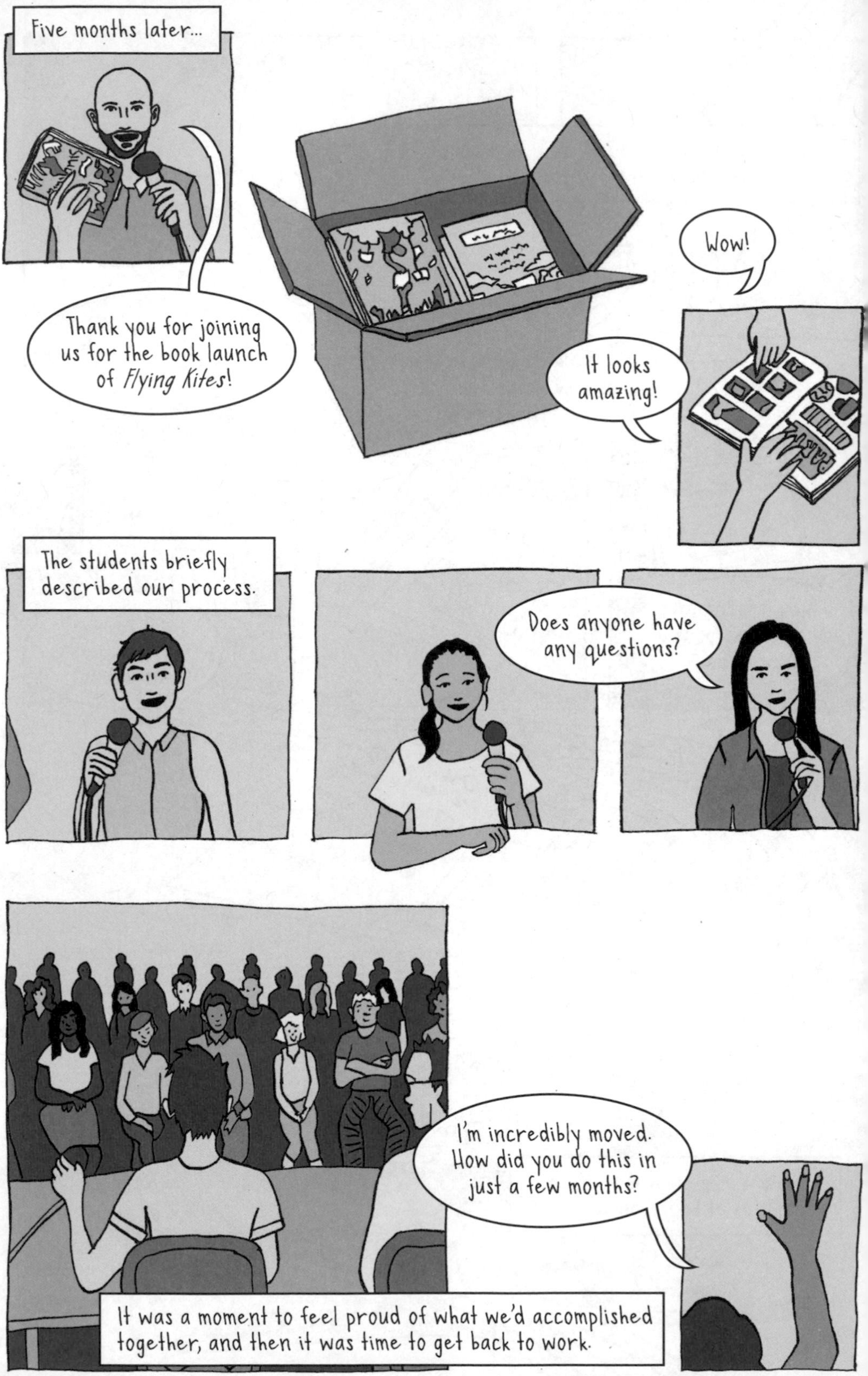
Five months later...
Thank you for joining us for the book launch of *Flying Kites*!
It looks amazing!
Wow!
The students briefly described our process.
Does anyone have any questions?
I'm incredibly moved. How did you do this in just a few months?
It was a moment to feel proud of what we'd accomplished together, and then it was time to get back to work.

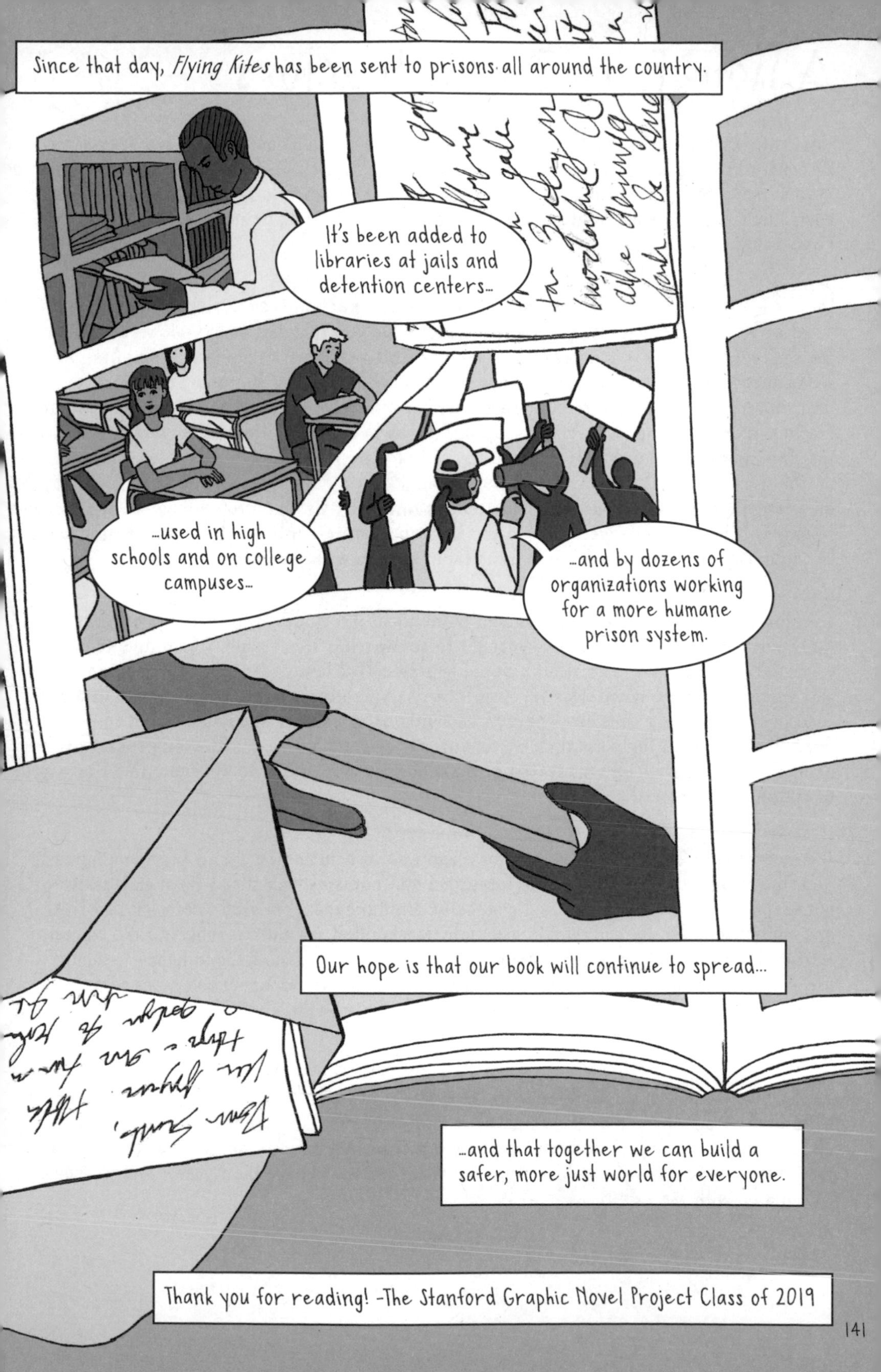
Since that day, *Flying Kites* has been sent to prisons all around the country.
It's been added to libraries at jails and detention centers...
...used in high schools and on college campuses...
...and by dozens of organizations working for a more humane prison system.
Our hope is that our book will continue to spread...
...and that together we can build a safer, more just world for everyone.
Thank you for reading! -The Stanford Graphic Novel Project Class of 2019

A Note From The Instructors

This is the eighth iteration of the Graphic Novel Project. All of our books have been motivated by concerns of social justice but—with the possible exception of *From Busan to San Francisco* --none more so than this volume, *Flying Kites*. We were drawn to this story because it is compelling, but also because it speaks so exactly to our guiding principles, which you can read below.

For each book, we try to push the project in a new direction from a storytelling or technical point of view. We've gone long. We've gone short. We've expanded colors. We've enriched the experience of the endnotes and appendices. We've drawn in landscape orientation. We've introduced a very valuable comprehensive editing stage. This year, our storytelling innovation involves the use of composite characters. We've long had to invent dialogue and certain scenes, but here we challenged ourselves to create fictional characters who evoke the real, honest, and accurate experience of being in prison and having a loved one in prison. Partially, we sought a coherent emotional arc, a narrative thread to follow through an event that involved thousands of prisoners and activists. Our main purpose, however, was to protect the real lives we compiled for these composite portraits. Individual prisoners can be, and have been, punished for sharing their stories with the outside world.

To tell a story is to witness it. We are so thankful to the students for the incredible depth of their research and the care they brought to getting this story right. Again and again, we were faced with hard facts about a penal practice that is widespread, capricious, and cruel. The students braced themselves through hours of video footage of people driven insane by time in the SHU. They read first-person accounts of prisoners who had been in solitary for decades. They did visual research on violent, racist gang members. At every turn of this process, we as instructors marveled at the students' dedication to engaging this story in its depth and its complexity.

This twenty-week, two-term project has always been a sustained sprint from beginning to end. This year was no different. We discussed and painstakingly sifted through the story pitches; developed style guides and character turnarounds; created two color palettes, one for prison, one for out; wrote a script; thumbnailed the entire book; inked; colored; lettered; edited; rethumbnailed; reinked; re-edited; and so on. We are happy to again use a student-generated font for the book's text, including the essay you're reading now. Also we were thrilled that--in the midst of all this work--the students produced their own minicomics, images of which are on page 133.

This book was an enormous job, but--we believe--a labor of love. The students had to work hard and consistently. They had to hit crucial deadlines while managing a full load of college classes. At every step of the way they delivered, with grace. We are incredibly proud of their work. They threw themselves into the making of this book--their book--and we couldn't be happier with the result.

About the Stanford Graphic Novel Project:

Since its inception, the Stanford Graphic Novel Project has adhered to a few central tenets:

1) that the telling of a human story is a deeply necessary enterprise, one worthy of study and creative devotion; 2) that sourcing stories from the real world increases their capacity to do good, seek justice, and bring about change; and finally, 3) that through collaboration, a story can become richer, more inspired, and more layered with human experience.

This twenty-week, two-course project is designed to teach nonfiction research, visual storytelling, and long-form narrative structure to undergraduates through the collaborative creation of a graphic novel. Early in the course, students propose real-life stories as possible subjects to adapt. After plotting the storyline and producing sample illustrations, the class discusses the merits of each proposal before selecting one to tell as a group. We then work through the rough outlines of the story, begin thumbnailing scenes (for more on how a page is created, see pages 136-137), compositing characters, and researching backgrounds. In recent years we have introduced student-generated fonts and mini-comics.

Our new technical process this year is the use of 3D modeling. Using SketchUp, students created a correctly proportioned solitary confinement cell. This model saved time when drawing from a bird's-eye or other perspective, and it also helped the artists keep the layout of the cell consistent. Even more important the model was a constant reality check on how small 6'x9' is to spend a life in.

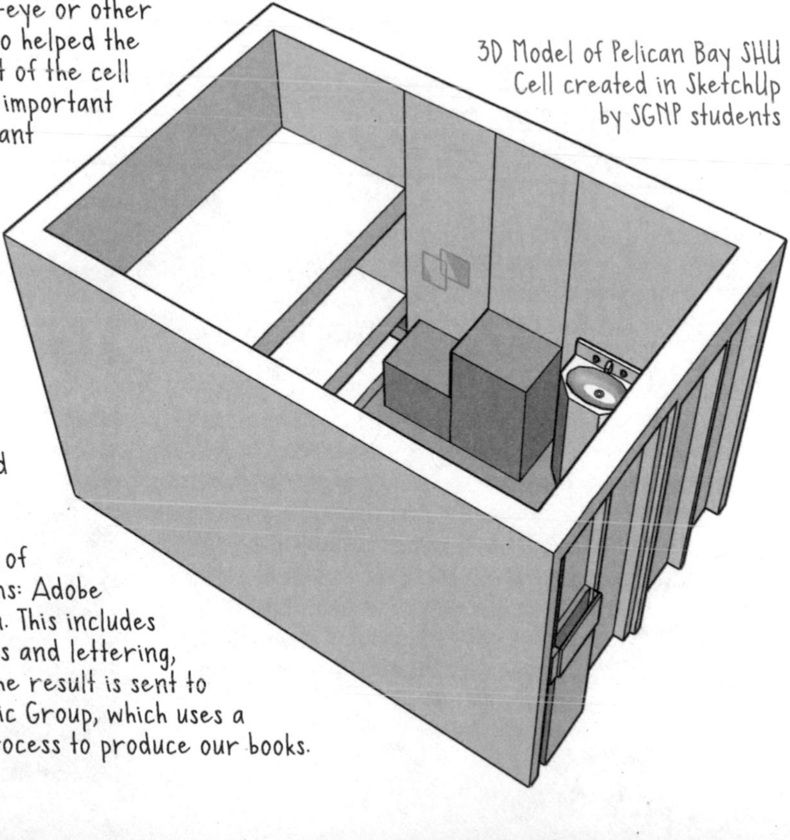

3D Model of Pelican Bay SHU Cell created in SketchUp by SGNP students

After the modeling, we ink, which is done by hand on Bristol board or electronically. The Bristol is then scanned and the remainder of the work is done through a combination of two computer programs: Adobe Photoshop and InDesign. This includes cleaning, word balloons and lettering, coloring, and layout. The result is sent to our printer, The Prolific Group, which uses a traditional printing process to produce our books.

The Making of a Page

(A1S01b) Scene 1b - (V)(4 pages): Luz daily routine. Text from Dana invite to party, initially writes "no" but deletes and rewrites "see you there." Has to leave party early because she's waking up early to visit dad, friend sympathetic, Luz feigns that she has come to terms with it, Luz leaves party, reveals that she is sadder about dad than she let on to friend.

Students first draft a rough script for the entire graphic novel, planning the page counts per scene.

Scene: Luz sad
Verso / Recto
1. See you later then Have a safe drive home
2. Thanks. See you.
3. Oh, dad...
hands in pocket
darkest (but not spot black)
bright
dark color

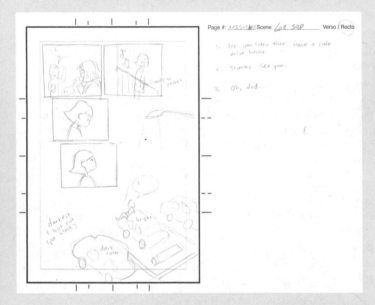

Scenes are then assigned to be thumbnailed. At this time the layout of the page, content of each panel, and basic dialogue are sketched out.

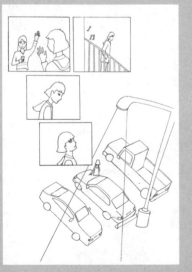

The pages are penciled and inked, adapting the directions on the thumbnail...

...And then scanned into Photoshop for thresholding, cleaning, and blackspotting.

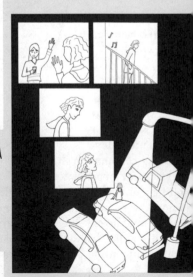

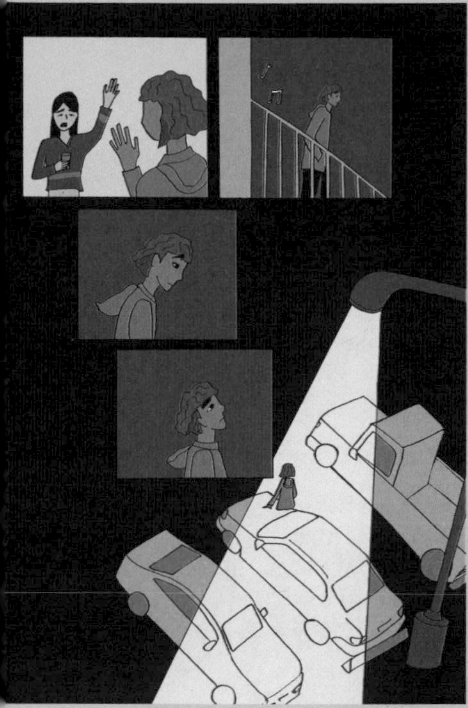

Inked pages are colored in Photoshop using a limited color palette chosen by the class...

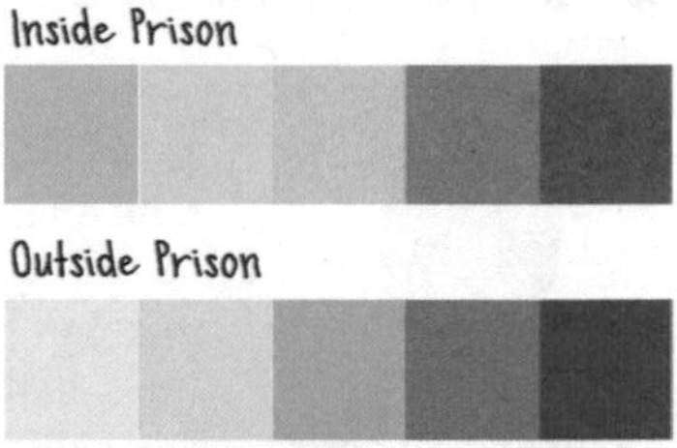
Inside Prison
Outside Prison

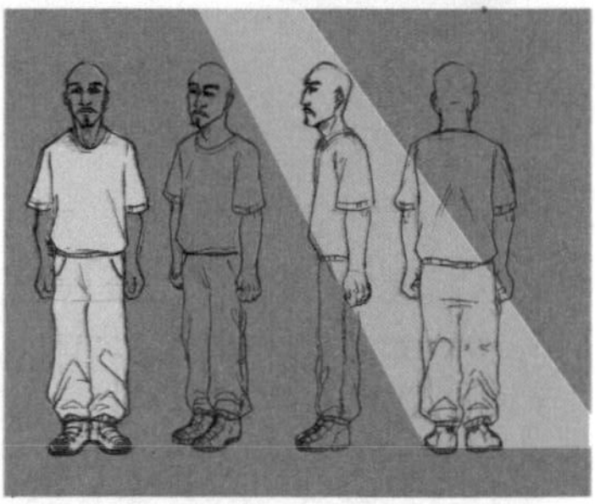

...And then subjected to a round of visual and color edits before finally being lettered in InDesign using a font created by the students!

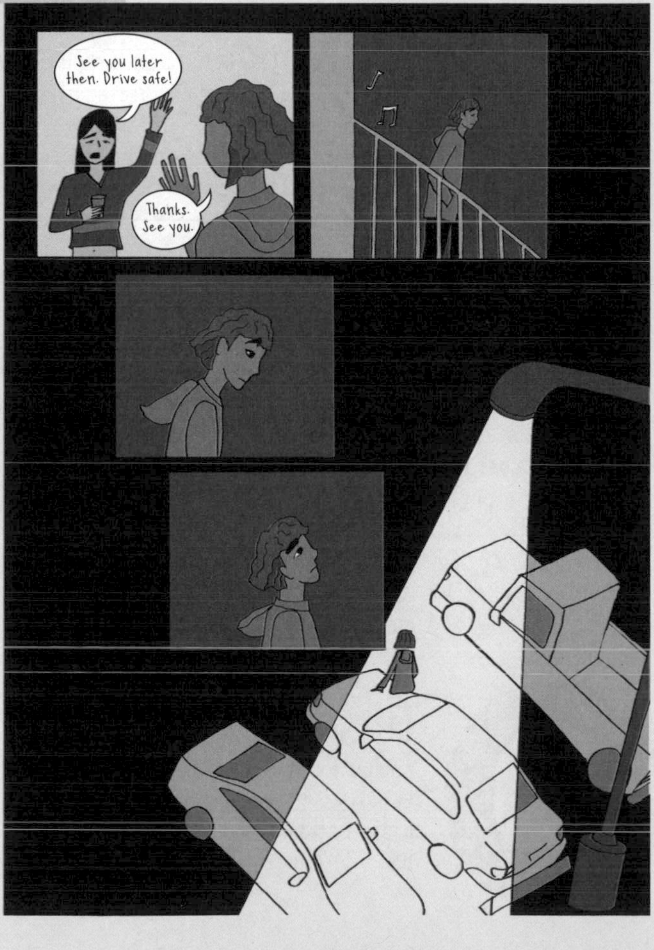
See you later then. Drive safe!
Thanks. See you.

Student Bios

Candice Kim is an MD student who's also pursuing a PhD in education. She didn't start dreaming of becoming a writer until two years ago. Since then, she's performed her work in New York City and San Francisco, led creative writing workshops in Portland and Napa Valley, and published articles about the value of the medical humanities for training future physicians. She dresses in all black and secretly wishes she could wear leather pants every day (but they're really bad in the summer).

Katherine Liu is a junior majoring in computer science. She spends a lot of time drawing, and in high school she wanted to start a webcomic but never got around to it. She used to wish that she took the Stanford Graphic Novel Project class in freshman year, but she is glad that she made this book with these wonderful people. Find her art at dysphania.tumblr.com or instagram.com/poxei.

Lily Nilipour is an English major and plastic lizard collector. She does many useless things with her free time, such as working on a book that currently has more than eight hundred uniquely drawn and named cats. Practicing the piano, playing tennis, and doing crosswords keep her sane. In her recent writing she's found herself to be vaguely obsessed with the sea.

Sarah Shourd is an award-winning freelance journalist and producer based in Oakland, California. Her work combines rigorous journalism with the tools of creative nonfiction. Shourd's three-year investigation into solitary confinement took her to over a dozen prisons across the US and resulted in a book (*Hell is a Very Small Place*) and a play (*The BOX*). She has written for dozens of publications and co-authored a memoir about her own imprisonment, *A Sliver of Light: Three Americans Imprisoned in Iran*. Currently a 2019 JSK Knight Fellow at Stanford, in her free time Shourd enjoys redwood trees, popcorn, and irreverence. sarahshourd.com.

Lucy Zhu likes to draw..... a lot, I guess. She is majoring in computer science, so you can find her sobbing over a program because it took her three hours to realize that she forgot to add a parenthesis. If you get her boba tea, she'll be your friend for life >:3. You can find her stuff at hexagonsgalore.tumblr.com!

Peter DiCampo is a JSK Journalism Fellow at Stanford and an award-winning photojournalist whose work has taken him to more than thirty countries. He is most known for cocreating the viral Everyday Africa project, through which he and a collective of photographers work to broaden perspective on the continent beyond the usual media stereotypes. Secretly though, he wishes he could just write comics and listen to metal all day. www.peterdicampo.com

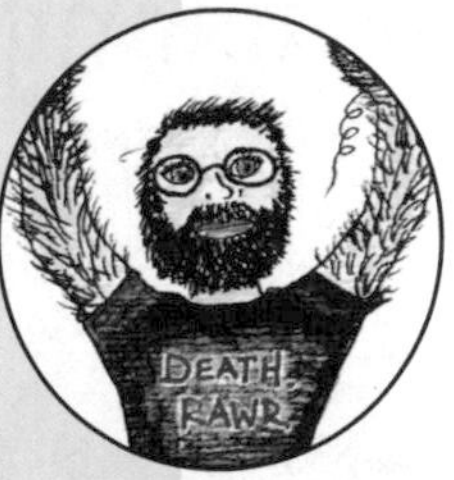
DEATH
RAWR

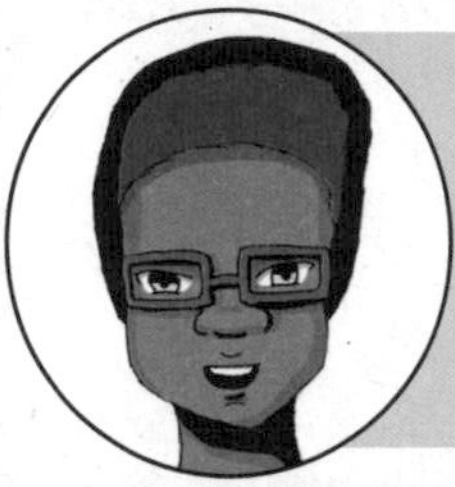

Nik Wesson is a current sophomore at Stanford University studying film and media studies and art practice. She enjoys drawing, reading, and watching television. However, the thing she enjoys most is sitting down to create a great story.

Elena Kamas is always having a party and knows that ducks wearing shoes transcend all other mediums of humor. She is studying mechanical engineering but would rather be playing Ultimate, drinking ginger beer, hanging out with totem poles, or hiding Easter eggs. She hopes to invent something impressive and useful one day, but for now she is content with sewing stuffed animals for her friends. @stitchesgetbitchez

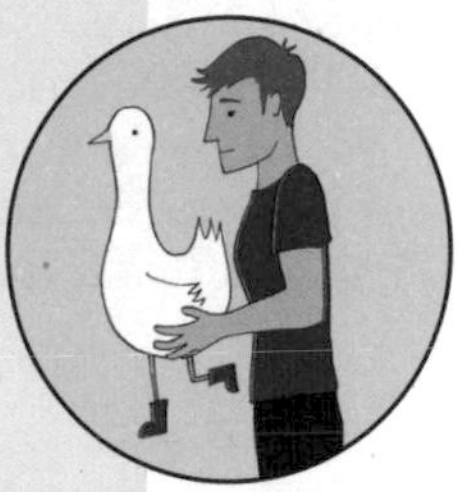

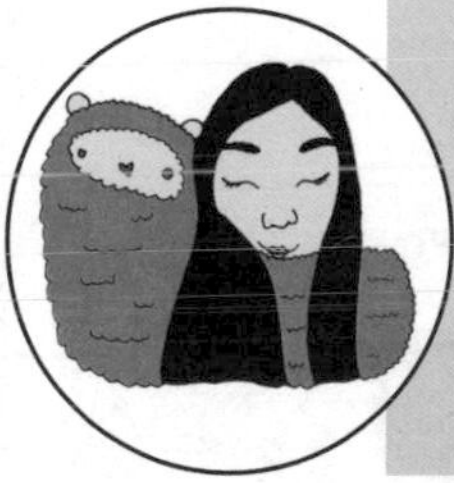

Serena Zhang is a sophomore majoring in film and media studies and minoring in creative writing. When she's not writing and dreaming of directing the next Oscar-winning film starring an all-Asian American cast, you can find her passed out in a coma-like slumber or injecting Sriracha sauce directly into her veins. Check out her work at xiaosez.weebly.com.

Sharon Tran is a sophomore majoring in English and minoring in human rights. When not thinking about writing, she can be found either acting onstage or working behind the scenes for an Asian American Theater Project production. Her hobbies include looking for chips and salsa, making lists, and wearing clothing with colors that match the graphic novel's color palette.

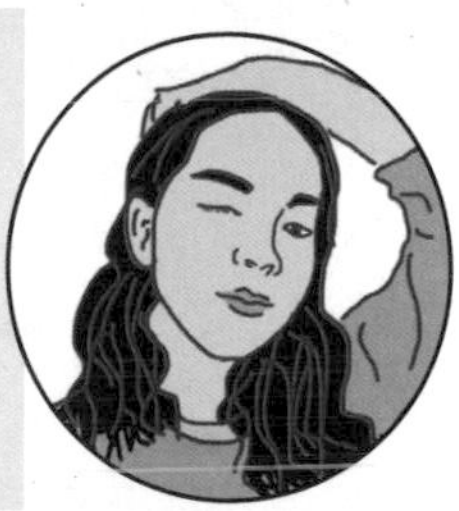

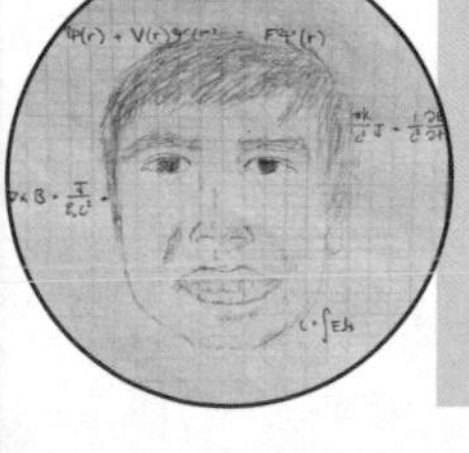

Danial Shadmany is a sophomore majoring in physics and minoring in creative writing. He consumes what most people would probably call an unhealthy amount of literature. When not banging his head against his fluid dynamics textbook, he's writing. He doesn't have a website to list here, because he's suspicious of the internet.

Teaching Assistants

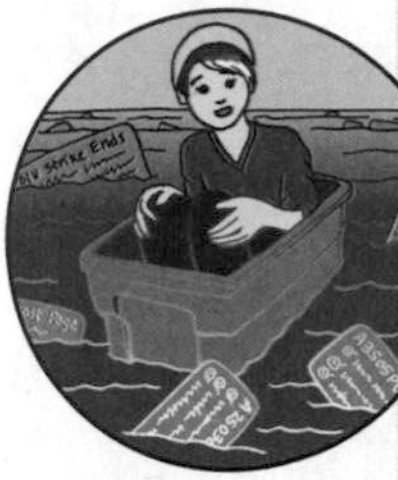

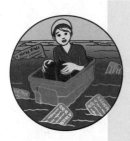

Bae is *still* a work in progress. Some fun facts: they can play music with their teeth, they have never been stung by a bee, they are lactose intolerant and allergic to cats (but that doesn't stop them from living life to the fullest). They were a student in SGNP's 2016-2017 cohort, which produced *Luisa*. This year, they were a TA for the class. Check out their portfolio, also very much a work in progress, at designed-by-bae.com

Luke Soon-Shiong was a TA for this project for a hot second, but then he had to leave to do a marketing job in Oakland. Outside of comics, Luke's an anthropologist who loves how buckwild and crazy the internet is. Luke was also part of the team that worked on *Luisa*, SGNP's previous book. You can visit their website lukemakes.art to find podcasts, paintings, prints, more comics, and an ongoing ethnography of the internet. Luke is a part of the Splorse artist collective and visual radio station at splorse.com. Thanks for reading this good good book.

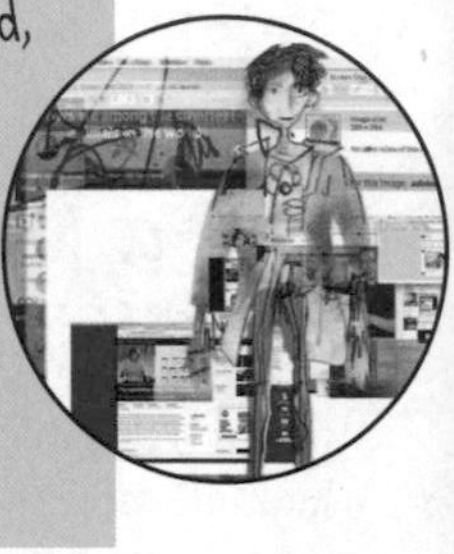

With additional work by Shay Yano

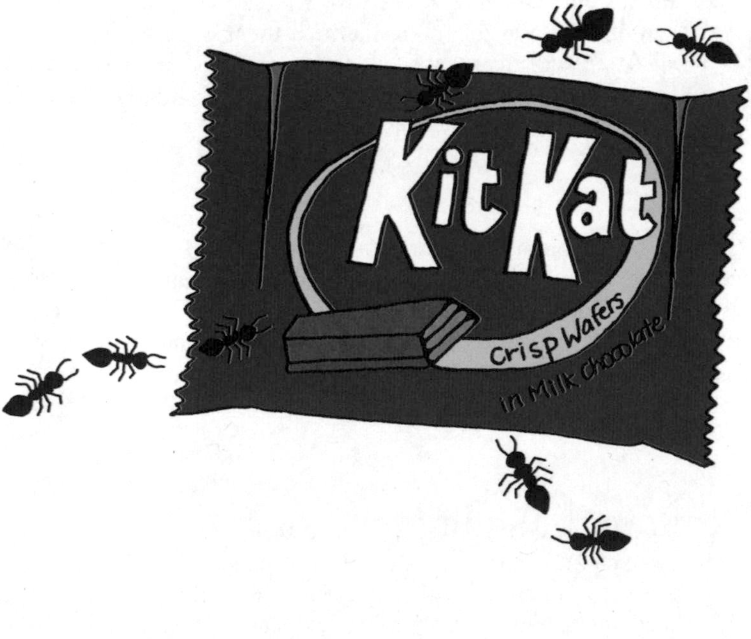

KitKat
Crisp Wafers
in Milk Chocolate

Instructors

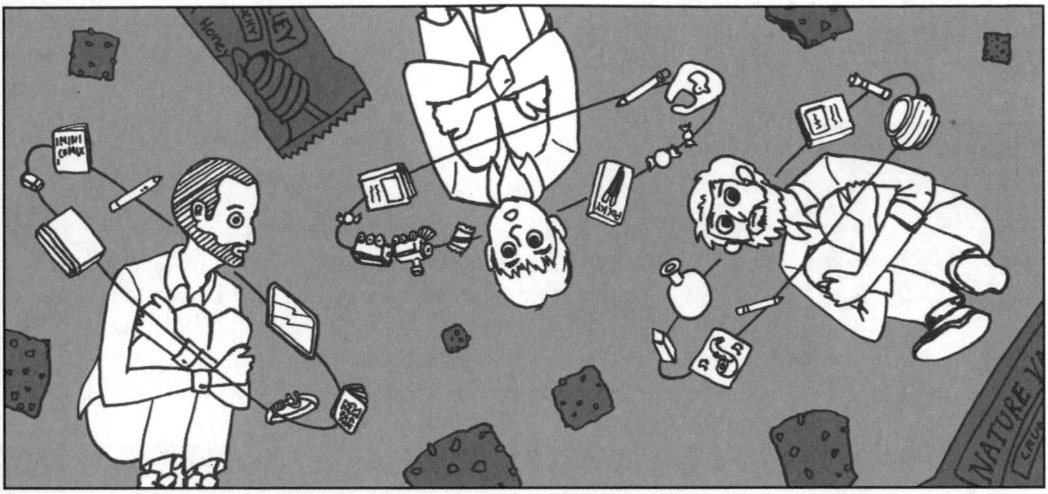
Honey

Scott Hutchins is the Jones-Draper Lecturer in Creative Writing at Stanford University. His work has appeared in *StoryQuarterly*, the *Arkansas International*, *The Rumpus*, the *New York Times*, *San Francisco*, *Catamaran*, and *Esquire*, and has been set to music. His novel *A Working Theory of Love* was a *San Francisco Chronicle* and *Salon* Best Book of 2012.

Shimon Tanaka is a lecturer in the Creative Writing Program at Stanford. He has received fellowships from the Stegner Program, the Fine Arts Work Center in Provincetown, and the Asian Cultural Council. His fiction has won prizes from and appeared in a number of literary magazines and the anthology *Best New American Voices*. He is at work on a novel and a short-story collection.

Andy Warner is a comics journalist and teacher. His book, *Brief Histories of Everyday Objects*, was a *New York Times* bestseller, and his comics have been published by *Slate*, the United Nations Human Rights Council, KQED, *The Nib*, American Public Media, the Showtime Network, the Center for Constitutional Rights and *Buzzfeed*. His new book, *This Land is My Land*, will be published in May 2019. He makes his comics in a garrett room in South Berkeley and comes from the sea.

Other Titles by the Stanford Graphic Novel Project

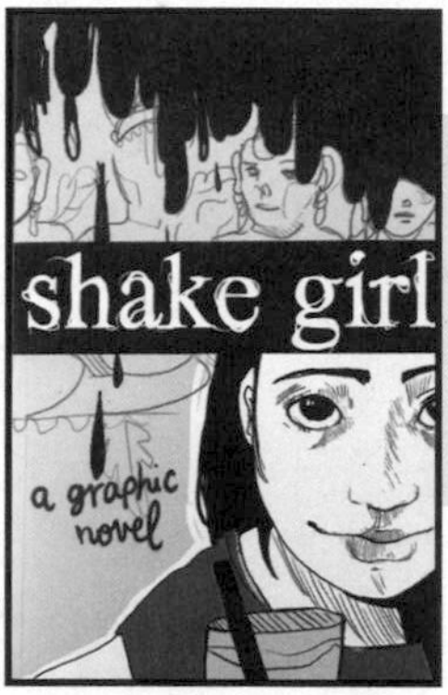
shake girl
a graphic novel

Shake Girl (2008) Inspired by the stories of similar victims, *Shake Girl* tells the story of a young woman in Phnom Penh who falls under the control of a powerful, corrupt Cambodian government offical and becomes the victim of an acid attack.

Virunga (2009) Virunga National Park's first female ranger struggles to prevent the slaughter of mountain gorillas in a story that reveals itself as a microcosm of the Democratic Republic of Congo's larger problems: civil war, displacement, loss of resources, and sexual violence.

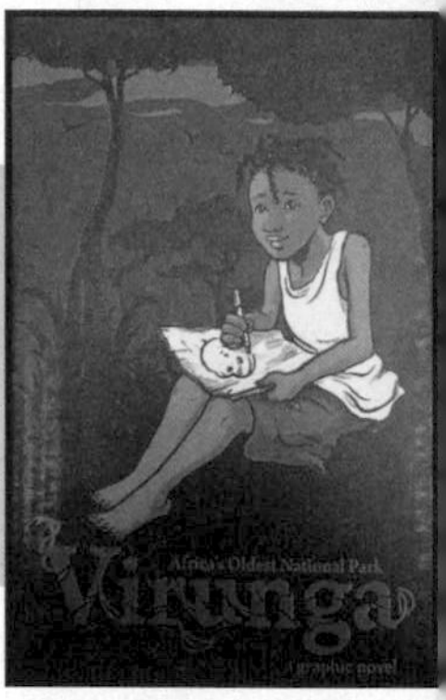
Africa's Oldest National Park
Virunga
a graphic novel

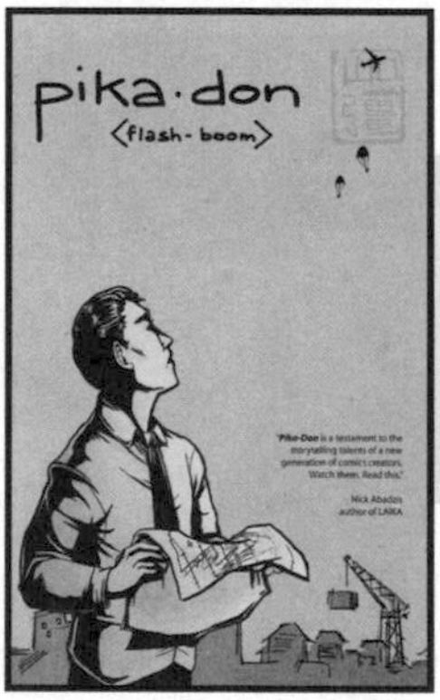
pika·don
<flash-boom>

Pika-don (2010) An average man--engineer, husband, new father, poet--Tsutomu Yamaguchi is swept up in an impossible war and placed in a circumstance that no other human has ever faced: surviving the ground-zero detonations of two atomic bombs.

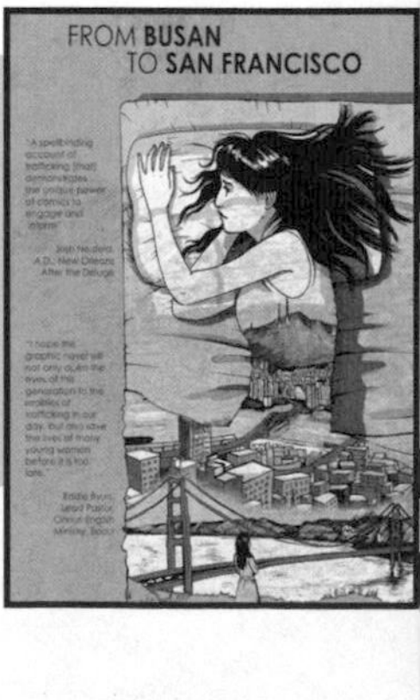
FROM BUSAN
TO SAN FRANCISCO

From Busan to San Francisco (2012). When her credit card debt endangers her parents' house, a young college student in Busan, South Korea, comes up with a desperate solution: give up her passport to work for "tea" houses in the United States. Caught in this system of sexual exploitation, she must convince everyone--herself the most--that she can find a way out.

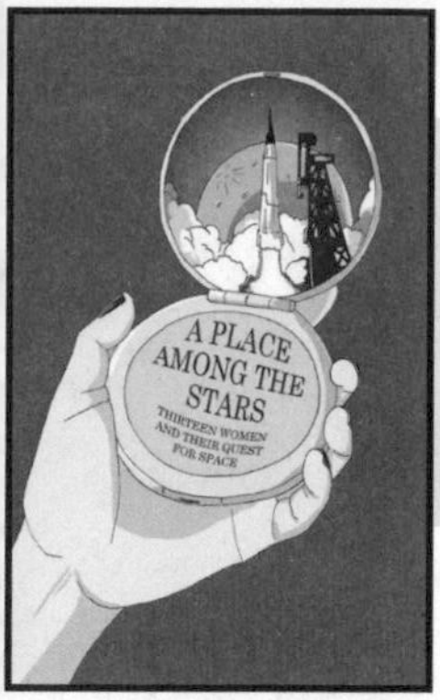
A PLACE AMONG THE STARS
THIRTEEN WOMEN AND THEIR QUEST FOR SPACE

A Place Among the Stars (2014) In their tenacious and inspired attempt to be astronauts, America's foremost female pilots must confront the rampant sexism of the Space Race era, taking their fight to Congress, NASA, and the court of public opinion.

American Heathen (2015) In the late 1800s, immigrant writer and activist Wong Chin Foo exposes corruption in his community, fights the racism of the Chinese Exclusion Act, and coins the term *Chinese American*. This newspaperman and professional gadfly advocates for anyone in his path who faces injustice.

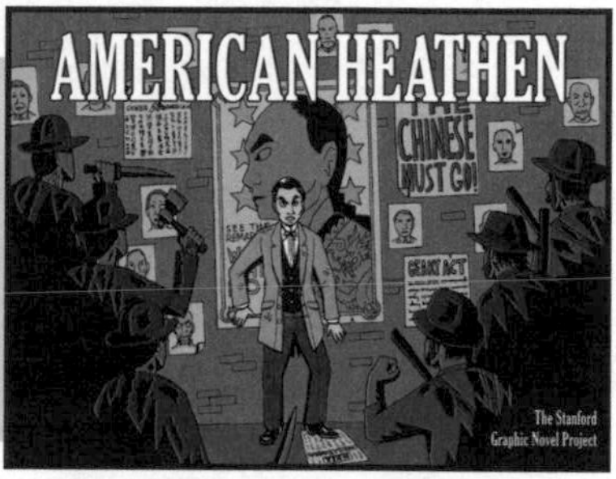
AMERICAN HEATHEN
THE CHINESE MUST GO!
The Stanford Graphic Novel Project

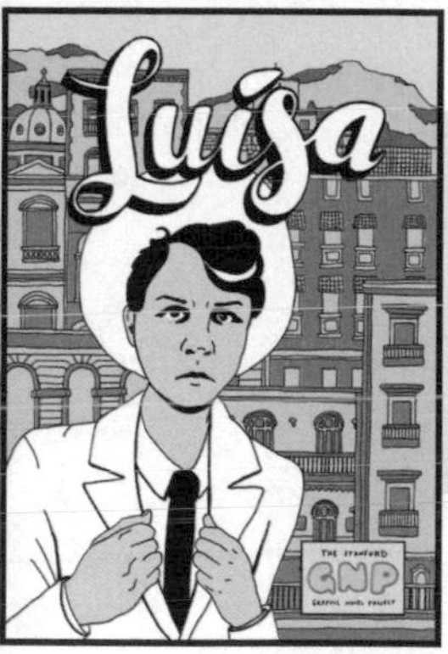
Luisa
GNP

Luisa (2017) Feminist, anarchist, and labor organizer Luisa Capetillo criss-crosses nineteenth-century Puerto Rico, organizing farm and factory workers. But when she's arrested for dressing "immodestly" (aka like a man) she must draw on her wits and her arguments to continue the fight.

For librarians, teachers, and other readers...

If you'd like more information on the Stanford Graphic Novel Project, please visit our website: graphicnovel.stanford.edu. Here you can download digital versions of our three most recent books, as well as find more information on some of the artists who have contributed to these stories. If you are interested in making your own comics in a collaborative, educational environment, you'll find a description of the course as well as a sample syllabus. Feel free to reach out with any questions!

Acknowledgments

The Stanford Graphic Novel Project is an enormous undertaking and would not be possible without the support of a great number of people. First and foremost is the Creative Writing Program. Our director, Eavan Boland, has been a great friend of this project from its inception. Thanks to Elizabeth Tallent, Ken Fields, Chang-rae Lee, and Patrick Phillips for their support, and to our administrators Christina Ablaza and Ose Jackson for helping us literally every week.

The entire concept of creating a project-based course around graphic storytelling is the brainchild of Adam Johnson and Tom Kealey. They fearlessly pioneered the path and were unfailingly generous with their teaching material, wisdom, and time.

Thanks to Casper and Io O'Clast of ABO Comix for sharing their groundbreaking activism in prison comics and for reading a draft. Thanks to Jean Casella from Solitary Watch, Amy Fettig from the ACLU, Jessica Sandoval from Unlock the Box, Alan Mills from Uptown People's Law Center, and the Pulitzer Center on Crisis Reporting, whose generosity allowed us to print more books.

Sarah Shourd, a 2018-2019 JSK journalism fellow and internationally recognized expert on solitary confinement who is herself a survivor of the practice, generously shared her extensive reporting on the California prison hunger strike. This project depended heavily on her. Our research also benefited greatly from a visit by Charles Carbone and the letters of Rafa Cacique.

The SGNP relies on the multimedia rooms run by Beth McCullough, and we cannot thank her enough. Thanks to Chris Young and his wonderful team at Prolific, who are a pleasure to work with.

Our TA this year, Bae, was essential to the project week in and week out--its brain and its bright spirit. Thanks, too, to our co-TA Luke Soon-Shiong for his artistic help.

Finally, thanks to the people, most of them unsung, who have struggled against the psychological torture of solitary confinement. You've knocked down a wall of indifference. The fight is far from over, but a battle has been won.

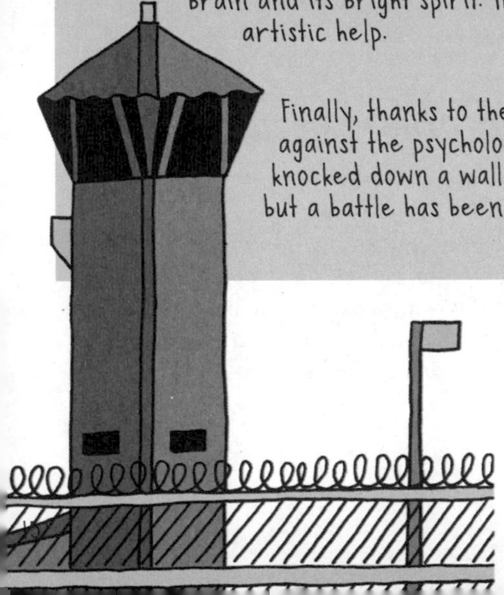

Pulitzer Center

UPLC
UPTOWN PEOPLE'S LAW CENTER

THE NATIONAL CAMPAIGN
UNLOCK THE BOX
TO END SOLITARY CONFINEMENT

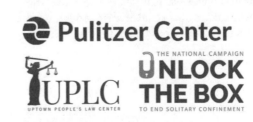